THE HEART OF A WARRIOR

BEFORE YOU CAN BECOME

THE WARRIOR...

YOU MUST BECOME THE

Beloved Son

MICHAEL THOMPSON

HEART & LIFE
PUBLISHERS

The Heart of the Warrior:
Before You Can Become the Warrior, You Must Become the Beloved Son

Published in Grand Rapids, Michigan by Heart & Life Publishers, a division of Miles Media, LLC. (www.heartandlife.com)

Editor: Bob Hartig
Cover Design: Emily Barahona
Cover Photos: Patrick Dunnagan
Interior Layout: Frank Gutbrod

Printed in the United States of America

Warriors are not what you think of as Warriors.
The Warrior is not someone who fights,
because no one has the right to take another life.
The Warrior, for us, is one who sacrifices
himself for the good of others.

His task is to take care of the elderly,
the defenseless,
those who cannot provide for themselves,
and above all, the children,
the future of humanity.

—Sitting Bull
Sioux Chief/Holy Man
(1831–1890)

TABLE OF CONTENTS

ACKNOWLEDGEMENTS

To Robin: What an honor it's been to learn to fight for you, and what a glorious adventure it is to fight alongside you. I love you.

To Ashley, Hannah and Abbey: God has partnered with you to teach me so much about love. You make me want to be better. I love you.

To my Friends, my Brothers: You know who you are. You are brave, strong, and valiant. Thank you for walking with me and allowing me to walk with you, discovering the truths of the Kingdom, the privilege of walking with the King, and the glory of taking up his noble cause. I love you.

To my fierce and tender God, the Mighty Trinity, the Father, Son and Spirit: What glorious days we have had in the growing up of me. Becoming more settled and more free is a journey that has encompassed the hardest moments and the best of days of my life. I look forward to more, for with you there is always more. I pray that every man will know the overwhelming love of you, Father; enjoy deep, deep friendship with you, Jesus; and hear your wonderful guiding voice, Holy Spirit. You are all I need, my God, and my heart finds its rest, courage and strength in you. I love you.

INTRODUCTION

When people find out I wrote a book, if they ask anything, it's usually, *What's it about?* Not a bad question, and not one that I have figured out how to answer in an elevator speech. Seldom am I asked, *Why did you write it?* This is a much better question. I still might not be able to deliver the answer in less than a minute, but here is *why* I wrote, *The Heart of a Warrior*. Two reasons:

Hope
and
Entrustment with Something Valuable

In the film *Braveheart*, there is a great exchange between the boy William Wallace and his father, Malcolm. I believe it is one of the many significant reasons most men love the film. It occurs early in the story, shortly after William's father and older brother go to a summit of Scotsmen at which most are brutally murdered by Longshanks, the evil and oppressing king of England. Upon the surviving men's return, the boy hears the tragic news of his father's death.

That night, young William has a vision. He is lying next to his father. Malcolm turns to young William and, with tenderness and a conviction, says to his son,

Your heart is free. Have the courage to follow it.

I have seen men get better and I have seen them go the other way. I have asked God, "What makes the difference?" God has shared much with me—personal, intimate, and critical insights. I believe he wants to reveal them to every man willing to ask questions. God wants to entrust to a man the things he must know to navigate this fallen place and see others, especially his wife and children, brought along with him. I resolutely hope for an uprising of men, oriented men who will make a kingdom difference in this world—simply by living loved. It is the hardest thing to attain in this world. But it is also the most transforming thing in the universe. So I dare hope for it. I dare believe for it in accordance with Hebrews 11:1: "Faith is confidence in what we hope for and assurance about what we do not see" (NIV).

A little more than a decade ago, I started a journey, the one I just attempted to describe. Though I had spent all my life in church and accepted Christ into my heart several dozen times (to make sure it took, you know), something was awry. I couldn't have described it as much as I could just feel it: a nagging sense that I wasn't enough. I was not doing enough, sharing enough, serving enough, giving enough, and so on.

Then one day, I'm sure by the grace of God, I saw it: the truth of grace and the Father's tremendous love for me. I wasn't particularly looking for it; it was more as if I was awakened from a coma I didn't even know I was in. You know: one moment you're asleep, then suddenly you're not, and just on the other side of not knowing is *knowing*. One second you don't see; the next, you do. That's how I began the masculine journey of becoming truly me.

For more than ten years (I'm now fifty), God has been Fathering me in a way that has fueled my hope and filled my heart. Over time, he has incrementally crafted and delivered experiences in my life that have changed me. Made me better. And over time, in the partnership and process of walking with my Father, there has been an *entrusting*, a bestowing, a giving of something valuable, which in this book I will do my best to share.

"Getting better," by the way, doesn't mean life has gotten easier, nor does it always go well. I don't know any men who live like that. Not when you get a little deep with them, into the landscape of their lives where the truth of their circumstances and relationships is unveiled. There I find men struggling, some well and most not so well. Very few are free. While in the coma, most men are outwardly active, but the drama that plays within them far outweighs the drama unfolding around them. Most men are asleep to their inner world, asleep to the inner voices to which they are constantly subject. Asleep to the judgments and accusations they live under and which, at times, they feel justified delivering to those close to them. That's how I was.

Was.

Like Saul on the road to Damascus, confident he was heading in the right direction and doing the right thing, I needed Jesus to intervene, remove the scales from my eyes, and set me free.

At a pivotal moment in *Braveheart*, Wallace rides forth with the many men he has inspired to face their enemy on the field of battle. In this moment, his army joins forces with their other fellow Scotsmen, those not yet a part of the rebellion, those not there to fight. Rather, they are there to negotiate, accepting the enemy's terms so they can retreat and live small. But just before they are bullied into compromising, William Wallace speaks:

> WALLACE: I am William Wallace! And I see a whole army of my countrymen, here in defiance of tyranny. You've come to fight as free men—and free men you are. What will you do with that freedom? Will you fight?
>
> VETERAN: Fight? Against that? No! We will run. And we will live.
>
> WALLACE: Aye, fight and you may die. Run, and you'll live—at least a while. And dying in your beds, many years

> from now, would you be willing to trade all the days, from this day to that, for one chance, just one chance, to come back here and tell our enemies that they may take our lives, but they'll never take . . . our freedom!

Being entrusted with something valuable is a wonderful thing. There is an honor to it, and the conviction that *I am enough. I'm enough to see it kept safe, and I'm enough to deliver it to where the owner wants it shared.*

This I desire to be and this I desire to do. The wild thing about it is, when what is entrusted is to be shared, it becomes open to both acceptance and rejection. Some will want it; some won't. It is my deepest hope that what has been entrusted to me will, in my attempt to share it with you in this book, find your acceptance and either begin or advance your God-journey. I hope you will be impacted in a way that lets you come to experience, through receiving love and fighting the good fight for love, just how valuable this Way is—and just how valuable *you* are.

I hope this book finds your heart ready. And by the time you reach the end, I hope you will be eager to join a great reformation: the reforming of men's hearts into those of oriented and settled Beloved Sons. Warriors ready both to live in the kingdom and *advance* the kingdom. Men partnering with Christ to take back lost ground and, in the process, set free all that Christ has intended to be truly free.

THE HEArt OF A WARRIOR

PART ONE

THE BELOVED SON

FROM BELOVED SONS TO WARRIORS

ALL THAT'S NECESSARY FOR THE FORCES OF EVIL TO WIN IN THE WORLD IS FOR ENOUGH GOOD MEN TO DO NOTHING.

—EDMUND BURKE

IN A BATTLE, ALL YOU NEED TO MAKE YOU FIGHT IS A LITTLE HOT BLOOD AND THE KNOWLEDGE THAT IT'S MORE DANGEROUS TO LOSE THAN TO WIN.

—GEORGE BERNARD SHAW

When Jake was ten years old, his uncle took him fishing. It was an experience Jake never forgot, though he often wished he could—because that afternoon, on the shore of a secluded lake, Jake's uncle molested him for the first time.

Confused and afraid, Jake never told anyone. To whom would he have gone? His mom, raising Jake and his little sister on her own, would never have believed such a thing about her brother. His alcoholic dad was never around, and anyway, he would have just called Jake a loser and knocked him around, same as he used to before the divorce.

So from then on into high school, similar incidents continued when Jake's uncle visited, up until the day when Jake finally got big enough and mean enough to put an end to the abuse. By then he had been in plenty of fights with other kids his own age. Compensating for his shame, anger, and insecurity with aggression, Jake was usually the initiator. Using his fists was the one thing he did well. His grades may have stunk, his home life may have been a disaster, but my goodness, the kid could fight.

Jake kept bad company, and drugs naturally entered the picture, and when Jake was twenty, so did his first break-in and then his second. His third landed him before a judge, and for a lot of young men, that would have been the end of such activity. But for Jake, it was just the beginning.

To shorten a long, violent, and tragic story, Jake finally found himself behind bars for a quite a long time. It wasn't his fault, of course. If that gas station attendant had just kept his mouth shut, everything would have turned out fine. Was the guy stupid? You don't argue at gunpoint.

Now here was Jake, twenty-nine years old and facing a lengthy stretch of his life in prison for assault and armed robbery.

Contemplating verse two of the Twenty-Third Psalm for his upcoming sermon, Nathan was surprised to feel his eyes moisten.

He makes me lie down in green pastures.

"Lord, I could use some of that," Nathan thought. A place of repose, a chance to relax. As the pastor of his small town's largest church, Nathan knew all about juggling the demands of his profession, but somehow he had lost track of the green pastures. His early passion for ministry had eroded and now he was on a treadmill. And the treadmill just seemed to keep spinning faster and faster. Now, at age forty-six, Nathan rarely felt passionate anymore. What he did feel, often, was stressed-out. That and just plain tired.

He leads me beside quiet waters.

"Not me," thought Nathan. No quiet waters. Success, yes. If success could be measured in attendance numbers, a beautiful new building, and state-of-the-art music and communication technology, then Nathan had attained. But where was the joy?

Nathan preached salvation by grace. But when it came to *living* by grace, it was hard for him to believe what he wasn't experiencing himself. Board meetings, fund drives, budget and staffing concerns, programs, leadership development, counseling sessions, visitations, disgruntled church members, his own relentless drive for church growth—all of these and more described Nathan's life. There were endless hoops to jump through, but there wasn't much grace. Just the voice of his dad echoing from his childhood: "Don't disappoint me, son. You can do better."

He was trying to do better, trying so hard. And to all appearances, Nathan was a glowing pastoral success story. But beneath the surface, his wife resented playing second fiddle to the ministry. His daughter and two sons wished like anything for a normal family life. And Nathan himself was unhappy. Was this really what serving God was all about? A one-man crusade to build the most dynamic church in town at the price of family dysfunction and personal burnout?

He restores my soul.

Restoration—yes, that was what he needed. Just reading the word made him long to experience its reality. For years he had preached to others about the love of God. Now, as he sat behind his cherry wood desk in the solitude of his office, it occurred to him how badly he needed to know that love for himself.

The tears came. Just a trickle, but there they were.

Jake and Nathan: two very different men with vastly different lives, but both have the same problem. Each of them desperately needs to experience what it means to be the Beloved Son of an everlasting Father. And each needs to become *oriented*, through training in the art and heart of being a Warrior who fights for a cause higher than his own and a King greater than himself.

Countless other men are like them in this respect. You may well be one of them. Your story is your own and your struggles are unique. But for you, as for Jake and Nathan and every man, there is good news. No matter how hopeless your circumstances may seem or how great they appear to be, God is up to something deep in your life.

There is a love for you to experience that can transform you.

There is a battle for you to engage in that is worth fighting.

And there is a Story for you to live in that is far bigger and better than you've known.

SOMETHING ANCIENT

Much has been written regarding the crisis in masculinity, and so it should be. It should continue until we make right all that is wrong. Possibly our greatest challenge is getting on the same page regarding the problem plaguing men. Men are casualties of an ancient and relentless masculine identity crisis. They suffer from a lostness that regenerates itself generation after generation.

Men have it in them to rise up, contribute, offer, provide, and protect, but countless of them are wounded and taken out by confusion, fear, and uncertainty. Too often they go limp when confronted with the trials and challenges necessary to make a man a man. Men have long suffered from being ill-equipped, ill-trained, and ill-prepared to play their part. The effect is cumulative; many factors contribute to the crisis of masculinity. But if we follow the tripwire to its source, the wounds and injuries we men carry are due to a lack of love—the kind of love received by a son from his father which makes him a man. If we can pinpoint what ails us and its source, then we can and should go for treatment.

Once treated, we can then enter into training. But not until then. If an athlete undergoes training before he gets treatment for an injury, the injury only gets worse. The first mission must be to go back and find the origins of our injuries and what is plaguing our hearts, stealing our glory, and diminishing our roles.

We live in a very Large Story, and neither you nor I are its author. Often, though, we seek to write our chapter on our own, because the story involves something we would rather avoid—something that, though glorious, is also unpleasant, frightening, and painful: battle.

My work with men these past twenty years has convinced me that men are either entering a battle, they are in a battle, or they are emerging from one. If not for their own lives, then men are battling for the lives of those they deeply desire to protect and provide for. There are many moments when the actual Author of the Larger Story, God, invites a man to be a man, called up and into important moments of conflict. If the New Testament is true, there is *never* a time you and I are not at war. There will always be a need for Warriors.

BELOVED SONS

I have a hope for men, a vision that fuels me as I write this book. It is this:

> *I hope to one day see the hearts of men so foundationally settled, so well-trained, so well-equipped, and so well-engaged that when evil dares raise its head, Beloved Sons/Warrior men will know what to do and will do it well.*

In order for this to happen, a man needs to recover his true heart—the good heart filled with the life of Christ and stamped with his character that the Father gives his sons at rebirth. And he needs to experience that he is indeed the Beloved Son of a good Father. Then that man can be shown his Warrior Heart. A Warrior is a Beloved Son trained and equipped to engage in the life-and-death battles that are continually going on in him and all around him.

What does it mean to be a Beloved Son? We need to be clear on this from the start, because everything that follows flows from it. A Beloved Son is one who experiences the unconditional love of his Father in a way that deeply impacts him and leaves him with:

> *Nothing to Hide,*
> *Nothing to Prove,*
> *Nothing to Fear.*

That kind of love leaves a mark; it has an encouraging and empowering effect on the son. Because of it, a man is completely free.

When you were born again, you became a son of God, deeply loved. That's your rock-solid identity. Circumstances shouldn't alter it, and the enemy's lies ought not to steal it. But knowing that truth in your head isn't the same thing as experiencing it in your heart as a daily reality—as the thing that frees you, gives you joy, transforms you, gives you hope, sustains you in the hard times, and motivates everything you do. That's what being a *Beloved Son* is about. It's both who you are and who you are becoming, the awakening of your heart to who you really are to the Father and who he is to you. Your true identity is now in place, and you will continue to grow into it. Experiencing the Father's love is to have a liberating and empowering impact on how you live.

The apostle John put it like this: "Behold, what manner of love the Father hath bestowed upon us, that we should be called the sons of God" (1 John 3:1 KJV). Can you sense the old disciple's wonderment, his utter amazement, as he penned those words? He was expressing a truth that resounded in his heart and permeated his being. And that's how it's supposed to be for you and me too: not just a Scripture memory verse but a living, breathing reality for us to walk in confidently, gratefully, joyously, and powerfully as God's love for us ignites like a flame within the hearts of Beloved Sons.

We were worth his dying for, and he is worth living for! Belovedness answers the core questions of our hearts as sons: Do you see me? Do you love what you see? Am I strong? Can I come through? To answer these questions, God must take us on a journey in which the *bestowing of* and the *calling out* of strength, courage, and love are God's holy and divine intent. These qualities are how men bear his image, and they are what he intends to see restored in us.

It's your heart's experience of the Father's love for you that will change your life, not just once but again and again, and make you dangerous to the enemy. Woe to him if you get a grip on who you really are! That's why Satan does everything he can to keep you from trusting and enjoying the truth. Because once you do, the training has begun for a Beloved Son to become a Warrior: a man who knows how to fight with love and for love.

THE WARRIOR'S WAY

Much of what God is up to in a man's life is training: training in the art and practice of being a loving Warrior. There is a relationship with God and a journey with him in which a man becomes more of whom God intends him to be. This comes as the man is trained and equipped to offer himself for the hearts of others. The Father brings missions, moments, and relationships to his Beloved Son that require a man with an oriented and settled heart to bring kingdom ways to the situation. More on those words *oriented* and *settled* in a bit; but first, let's look more deeply at what it means to be a Warrior.

Warrior is an ancient word which describes a role that, in its essence, is that of a skilled peacekeeper. The ancient Celts had a saying: "Never give a sword to a man who cannot dance." Being a Warrior involves more than force. It goes deeper: there is a deftness to it, an intuitiveness, and a gracefulness. Only when a man knows firsthand the joy and beauty of life and how to live it well—does he possess not merely the weapons but also the graceful movements of the heart in order to wage war over what is most precious.

Knights lived by a code that held them to protect the helpless. Jesus taught his band of brothers to be as cunning as snakes and as innocent as doves (Matt. 10:16). Nobility, wisdom, and purity of motive are as much components of a Warrior's life as fighting. Men who fit the description of a Warrior are desperately needed. But they are far too rare. The reason is a matter of orientation and a settled heart.

The term *Heart* is also ancient. In early Hebrew culture, it meant the center, the core, the deep well of a man or woman. The Hebrew people were taught to guard their hearts above all else (Prov. 4:23), to store up wisdom in the heart (Prov. 3:1–5), and to believe, trust, and love from a whole heart (Prov. 6:21; 22:11; 23:19; 27:19). They passed these truths down through the generations.

There is an *Art* to the Warrior's skills and abilities, a learning and practice of a craft that makes its presence felt. The way of a Warrior is something that brings relief to the oppressed and trouble to the oppressors. But mastering it takes time, patience, wisdom, understanding, and failure. Yes, failure. It takes that . . . and the faculty of teachers, some great and glorious, while others harsh and unkind, who are attempting to invite us to who we are *and* who we are not.

The fashioning of a masculine heart in a man is not the matter of a single moment but of cumulative "single moments" that equip the Warrior with his art. Elbert Hubbard, a turn-of-the-century artist and poet, wrote, "Art is not a thing—it is a way."

Warriors are dangerous characters in any story and they can be lured into roles and causes that run counter to what a Warrior is made and trained to be. We see it every day in the headlines and it is tragic: men taking shortcuts, making compromises, stepping across blurry lines, hiding or striving. It is killing us. Men today are ill-trained, ill-advised, naïve, angry, fearful, confused, hurting, tired—the list goes on describing the current condition of men's hearts. The confusion has resulted in what I call *disorientation* and a forecast of what will continue unless an ancient way is recovered—because disoriented men produce more disoriented men, and the legacy of failure will pass from one generation to the next.

In this book, I hope to persuade men to go with God back into their stories to remove whatever things block them from receiving the love God offers them: the love of a Father for his Beloved Sons. Then, with their ability to receive the Father's love recovered, I hope to instill in men an awareness of the ongoing training required to see disoriented men become *oriented.*

What does it mean to be oriented? An oriented man grounds his life and actions on three things: his identity, his environment, and his mission. He knows

1. *Who he is.* In Christ, he is a Beloved Son of the Father. An oriented man finds his security and strength in that deep identity alone.
2. *Where he is.* An oriented man has "eyes to see and ears to hear" what is going on around him. He is alert to the spiritual forces at work behind physical circumstances. He knows that he lives in a zone of ongoing conflict.
3. *The good that God is up to.* An oriented man seeks to partner with his Father's redemptive purposes. He looks for the good God is doing in his life and through his life, and he views his circumstances and relationships with an awakened and engaged heart.

Over time, the oriented way of life leads to a more *settled heart*—a deeper stability that comes from ongoing experience. A settled heart (a man who has nothing to hide, prove, or fear) doesn't come overnight. It is the result of discovering and rediscovering, time after time, the grace and effectiveness of walking with God and living an oriented life until that way of life becomes more than just an approach. Through deep renovation of the heart, you and I can become true men.

Make no mistake: training in the oriented life isn't easy and is always in progress. The questions are, who is doing the training, and what is the training all about?

A BETTER WAY?

The ancient Scots and Celts believed that a man's spiritual journey demanded both outward and inward wandering. The man was to seek God in a great adventure often not knowing where God would lead. Pilgrimages were a part and practice of a man's journey to manhood, and enlightening discoveries along the way greatly benefitted those who boldly set forth. Through experience, a man came to know three vital truths. One was, *the story I live in is much bigger than I am.* The second was, *I am in continual need of understanding and training. There is always more.* The third was, *I am needed.*

Not all pilgrimages went well, and not all men got what they desperately needed. That is still true for us. If the journey's three life lessons aren't internalized, then a man either has not traveled far enough or, more likely, he is walking in the wrong direction.

The vast majority of men are lost or, at a minimum, dazed and confused (disoriented). They are looking in the wrong direction for initiation and validation, turning to culture for answers to their core questions about life and who they are. But culture is clearly a mess, and it doesn't have the stuff required to grow men. A man is to bring who he is to the world around him, not get his identity from it.

I am privileged to have a front row seat in the lives of pastors and men who have attended church their whole lives. So I know full well that the stereotype of churchgoing men as "better" than men who do not attend church just doesn't hold water. The church today is as challenged as our culture when it comes to growing men who are settled, trained, and engaged.

Engaged? Engaged in what? In all that God has for men to receive from him and participate in with him. Men who are engaged continually come to God for anything and everything, from healing to training. Such men seek to stay intimately connected to him in order to understand and partner with God in bringing his kingdom ways into the circumstances around them.

Our churches' typical method for dealing with men doesn't produce engaged men, or trained men, or settled men. Instead, we arm men with a few Bible verses and a weekly speech. Then we send them off to a "life group" at someone's home, where it's assumed they will "connect" by talking about that week's speech. What so many men get out of all this is that they have to do better and do more. And that message is coming from what someone else is telling them about God, not from their own relationship with him. The training they're getting is for a domesticated life, not the adventure of personally walking with God. Is that the best we can do? Because it is not what men dream about or hope for, if they still dream and hope at all.

Men deserve a better way. Men *need* a better way. Men need to be equipped, guided and then deployed by God to remain in partnership with him, entering into battle for the hearts of others.

A KING TO FIGHT FOR

Every Warrior needs a cause and a king—something and someone much larger than himself, something he can fight for and someone he will fight with, because fight he must. The story we are living in is one of conflict, a war of epic proportions. The evidence of this is constant and painful. Today's news reminds us from page one to the last page, story after story, that something is wrong with our world. We all agree on this, but far too few of us know what the problem is. We want to be on the side of right and good, not caught in the middle or on the wrong side. But unless we become properly oriented, we will swing our swords at the air and even at each other while failing to recognize our true foe.

Because they are Beloved Sons, oriented men have nothing to hide, nothing to fear, and nothing to prove. How many men do you know who live like that? How many do you know who are strong and tender of heart? Good men, settled, free? What if *we* could be those men who live well, love well, and fight well as true peacekeepers? As

Beloved Sons with Warrior Hearts loved by a glorious King and living with a great cause?

Sadly, today there are too few worthy causes and even fewer good kings. Where are the good kings? Where are the noble men for us to follow, emulate, learn from, and align our hearts with? Kings who live in the context of the Larger Story, who love well and are looking for good men with whom they can trust and share life?

There is one such king: Jesus. To see him as anything less would be to aspire to less. Yet tragically, the Son of God and Son of Man has been misunderstood and misrepresented. He has been made out to be less than the fiercest yet tenderest, strongest yet most compassionate man among men. That is one of the great accomplishments of our enemy: to make men misunderstand and mistrust the heart of the King so they will compromise and eventually replace him with inadequate substitutes, convinced they can arrange a better life for themselves. Separate the men from their King, the sons from their Father, the apprentices from their Teacher. Divide and conquer: it's the oldest trick in the book, as old as the fall in the garden.

> A pupil is not superior to his teacher, but everyone [when he is] completely trained (readjusted, restored, set to rights, and perfected) will be like his teacher. (Luke 6:40)

If we are to become like Jesus but we don't really like him, that is a huge problem. What could be the cause? Misinformation? Misjudgment? Mishandling? Misconception? To all of these, I say yes.

HAVING A PLAN

The practice of a Warrior changes with the stages, responsibilities, and privileges of a man's journey. A thirty-year-old with a wife and young children needs the same foundation as a sixty-year-old man with grandchildren, but the two men's honed skills and time-crafted abilities are different. A well-trained veteran of the Life God intends for us—Life with a capital L, Life with God, from God, and by God—is able to step into a variety of moments and love well. Over the years, he should have experienced God's love guiding and empowering his life in the context of a love story set in the midst of a great battle. Here is where the training takes place. It happens through the tragedies and triumphs of the battlefield, especially on the man's home front. That is the primary place where he is to bring what he has learned about being loved and offering love.

Few things that are made quickly endure. Unfortunately, we live in a culture that wants everything now and rewards younger men who produce results fast. The cost down the road is tragic: the forfeiture of our kingdoms when we are older, with devastating collateral damage to our wives and families. That's not what God has in mind for us. We need a plan for living that can guide us into his plan for our lives:

> "I know the plans I have for you," declares the Lord, "plans to prosper you and not to harm you, plans to give you hope and a future. Then you will call on me and come and pray to me, and I will listen to you. You will seek me and find me when you seek me with all your heart. I will be found by you," declares the Lord, "and will bring you back from captivity." (Jer. 29:11–14 NIV)

God's intentions for us are clear, and they are wonderful. But they involve learning, and I am not the Teacher. I know him, though. He has been training me for a number of years, and he is always eager to take on new apprentices, Warriors to train and share his way with. It is not a journey for the faint of heart, but it is unique, noble, unpredictable, and good. As a man in training, I can tell you, both humbly and unashamedly, that I am becoming more like my Teacher. That is what he does, and it is what is supposed to happen. That is what his way is all about: helping a man become his true self—whole, shaped increasingly into the image of Jesus as the journey and training continues. I have had my moments of compromise and failures, but I am learning, and more and more I am becoming whom I was meant to be. It can be the same for you.

Author Norman Mailer once said, "Every moment of one's existence, one is growing into more or retreating into less. One is always living a little more or dying a little bit." Mailer described one of his own failures and great regrets as "another episode in my life in which I can find nothing to cheer about or nothing to take pride in."

Much of what we learn on this journey of heart is forged through the experiences of both the good and the bad, the victories and defeats, the times of hearing "Well done" and the times of "Not so well done." What we do with every moment makes and shapes our conclusions and perceptions, our beliefs about what is true. We hold these beliefs in our hearts, and not all that we believe is true. Who is there to teach, counsel, guide, and train you? Who is there to help you accurately interpret the moments of your life? Who is there to comfort, inspire, initiate, validate and deploy you as a man into the Great Story in which you live?

You and I were never meant to go it alone. And we never are truly alone. We never have been and never will be. God has a plan, and it has always been more than just to save us from judgment, glorious as that part of the plan is. It has always been to share Life with us by bestowing love on us and giving to our hearts, through intimacy, oneness with and connectedness to him, a role in the Larger Story greater than we can possibly imagine.

In the epic film *Braveheart*, set in the thirteenth century, Scotsman William Wallace finds himself caught up in a war for the freedom of his people. He hasn't gone out looking for a fight, but a fight has come to him. The Larger Story thrusts him into the role of Warrior, and he brings many along with him. One person swept into this brutal engagement is the heir to the throne of Scotland, Robert the Bruce, who has made some brutal mistakes.

After his greatest compromise betraying William Wallace, bitter shame and regret leads Robert to a heated altercation with his father, who has often led him astray. With anger and tears in his eyes, Robert the Bruce looks at his father and declares,

I will never be on the wrong side again!

This must become our declaration as well. It is not the mistakes or compromises we have made that define us, painful and costly though they may be. It is our next choice. Yet too many men have been robbed of their ability to make a real choice. Defaulting to a false self and heeding the lies of an enemy skilled at deceit, they fall into patterns cast for them rather than wisely and freely choosing what is best.

For the rest of his life, a man is going to be trained in something. The only question is what, and there are just two options. Either the man will learn how to live and love from the heart, or he will learn to base his life on something else. I invite you to take this journey to becoming wholehearted, settled and free, a true Beloved Son of the Most High God. I invite you to recover your Warrior Heart, choosing to show up and be trained up in the Art of a Warrior by a glorious King with a good cause. Many hopeful hearts are waiting. It is your turn. It is your time.

GETTING YOUR HEART BACK

But the seed on good soil stands for those with a noble and good heart, who hear the word, retain it, and by persevering produce a crop.

Luke 8:15 (NIV)

The most critical need of the Church at this moment is men, bold men, free men. The church must seek, in prayer and much humility, the coming again of men made of the stuff of which prophets and martyrs are made.

—A. W. Tozer

I was attending a large men's conference with several hundred men. The opening moments were . . . nice. The worship band picked up everybody's spirits and did a nice job. The emcee was funny and his welcome was nice. Nice, nice, nice.

After the morning's main speaker was introduced, I could see men shifting in their chairs, getting their pens and notepads ready, dialing in, hoping this might be *the* talk that would change things.

The speaker was seasoned and polished. This was obviously not his first rodeo. His energy and message complimented each other. The title of his talk was, "You Need a Mission!"

"Men with a mission are *men*," he said, "and missions need men, and if you don't have a mission, then . . ." Something along those lines, vague enough to include every man yet also pointed enough to make each man feel a personal twinge of guilt. I think the speaker even unpacked a word for every letter in the word m-i-s-s-i-o-n. It was very *nice.*

It was also yet another ticking package delivered to men's hearts on how to *do* better, *do* more, *sin less,* and achieve more. Men love stuff like that—at first. Then they hate it. The men in attendance gave the speaker a standing ovation, and I couldn't help but feel exasperated. "It won't work," I thought. Because well-intended though it was, the message had two serious flaws. First, it was another one-size-fits-all approach that men buy into, hoping it will somehow, some way, fit ... and eventually make a difference. Second, the speaker assumed too much. How did he know these men were ready for a mission? Lumping them all together—was that really wise?

The men in the room were inspired, ready to go somewhere, anywhere, yet it was like no one could locate a door. Being fired up in the locker room isn't the same as being well-trained and oriented on the field. Trying to turn mission into a program, like an inspiring locker room talk, or a bunch of facts that can be delivered and received in an hour-long package rarely has much staying power. Like a New Year's resolution, seldom does it stick.

So what *does* make the difference in a man's life?

MISSIONS FIND YOU

Men do want and need a mission. With the founding of parachurch ministries like Campus Crusade (1951), InterVarsity (1941), Navigators (1930), Fellowship of Christian Athletes (1954), and

Young Life (1941), most Christian men have been taught over the past seventy-plus years to connect "mission" with the Great Commission. "Go and make disciples"—that's the mission.

But perhaps we've understood mission too narrowly. A sampling of "men on mission in the Bible" reveals:

- a farmer told to build an ark
- a shepherd commissioned by a burning bush to free a nation
- a father, up in years, instructed to sacrifice his son
- a boy sent to bring his soldier brothers their lunch who, in the process, slays a giant
- a fisherman summoned to leave his nets and follow a teacher
- a tax collector invited to push away from his ledger and follow the same teacher
- a religious leader blinded in order to see

What are we to conclude? These men weren't trying to create a mission. Heck, it doesn't appear as if they were even looking for one!

Try this: *Missions find you.*

You don't have to find them. A man will have several missions in his lifetime. They are bigger than he knows and always have a purpose that includes both his heart and the hearts of others.

However, two dangers come with attempting to create your own mission. The first is this: If a mission is up to us to craft, then it will be one that we make manageable, small enough that we can accomplish it on our own. Yet we see just the opposite with men (and women) of the Bible. They don't "make up" their own missions; rather, they are caught up in missions that are multifaceted, larger, unmanageable, and more significant than anything they could ever have dreamed up. Missions in which the only means of success, and even survival, is to walk with God.

The second danger in crafting our own mission is the converse of the first: we, if left to our own, may manufacture a mission that is massive and grand beyond reason. Then we are forced to enlist the help of others by either paying them or manipulating them. The only safeguard against this danger, as with the first, is to walk with God. Neither extreme, aiming too high or too low, will be good for our hearts or the hearts of others, because with both, the pull to self-reliance is too great.

It is not a matter of *if* but rather *when* you will find yourself, like those Bible characters, called up or caught up into a mission. If you and I are not on a great mission in our lives, then we are in grave danger, because the scales remain over our eyes and we are blind to what we must see and overcome.

You've heard the old adage "Time is of the essence." In this case, *timing* is of the essence—not just when something must be done but also in what order. Too many men put the cart before the horse. So consider this: Jesus spent three years with his closest friends, three intimate years. Then he deployed them, gave them their mission—because only then were they ready. They had come to know who he truly was and how he felt toward them. And that knowledge settled their hearts.

Before you can become the Warrior, you must become the Beloved Son. And in order to truly become the Beloved Son, you will need to reclaim your heart. That is the first mission that will find you and every man: the dangerous and glorious mission of getting your heart back. Until you've accomplished that, anything else you attempt is moving out ahead of your training as a Warrior. Men who enter the battle too soon, unprepared, untrained, and unaware of what is out there . . . well, just look around. It's not a pretty picture.

THE HEART

From all that has happened to us in our lifetime, all we have encountered and experienced, we have drawn conclusions about life and how to make it work. We form our conclusions in order to protect and provide for ourselves. Like bricklayers constructing a house, we build our belief system brick by brick from our stockpile of conclusions. We consult our experiences to determine how the world operates, who we are in it, how to avoid pain, when to promote our self, and more. All of these moments, and all the conclusions we draw from them, are stored in a precious place called the *heart.* A man's heart is engaged with his belief system regardless of his condition. Whether alive in Christ or spiritually dead, the heart is in constant danger of being compromised and wounded.

The ancient Hebrew word for the heart is *leb.* The *leb* is a deep well in which all the experiences of one's personal history are stored, fully operational and in the deep interior of every image-bearer. *Vine's Dictionary of Biblical Words* defines the heart this way:

> The heart is regarded as the seat of emotions, of knowledge and wisdom, conscience and moral character.

According to *The New Unger's Bible Dictionary*,

> The ***heart*** is: (1) the *center* of the bodily life, the reservoir of the entire life-power . . . strengthening of the whole man; (2) the *center* of the rational-spiritual nature of man . . . of thought and conception; the heart *knows*, it *understands*, and it *reflects*. The heart is also *the center of the feelings and affections* . . . the seat of conscience; the field for the seed of the divine word. It is the dwelling place of Christ in us; of the Holy Spirit; of God's peace; **the receptacle of the love of God**; the closet of secret communion with God.
>
> It is the center of the entire man, the very heart of life's impulse.
>
> (My condensation, emphasis added. See appendix for the complete *The New Unger's Bible Dictionary* definition.)

No wonder two kingdoms, Light and Dark, are at war over such a beautiful and vital piece of real estate. Is it any wonder that men's hearts are in serious need of renovation? In our core, our center, are stored up the attitudes, beliefs, and conclusions shaped by our experiences. These need God's attention, because we don't get by without being hurt, missed, or wounded in this central core of places.

Scene after scene in our lives is experienced, interpreted, and recorded through a grid. And that grid is quite capable of recording inaccurately unless it undergoes God's restorative work. It is with good reason that the Scriptures tell us, "Guard your heart above all else, for it is the source of life" (Prov. 4:23 HCSB).

What every man has left unguarded for much of his life needs his and God's attention. There are things growing there and wandering about that have gone unattended far too long.

AN INVITATION

> Are you tired? Worn out? Burned out on religion? Come to me. Get away with me and you'll recover your life. I'll show you how to take a real rest. Walk with me and work with me—watch how I do it. Learn the unforced rhythms of grace. I won't lay anything heavy or ill-fitting on you. Keep company with me and you'll learn to live freely and lightly. (Matt. 11:28–30 MSG)

Is it just me, or does this sound too good to be true? Healing, rest . . . *relief?* You mean I don't have to continue living a life of control? A life of religious or false systems? Of self-promotion, self-protection, self-provision? Or as Thoreau put it, one of "quiet desperation"?

There is a remedy to the false-self life from which we all suffer. There is another kind of life, another way of life, and it is almost too good to be true. Almost. It is the life of a son of God, a Beloved Son, one who knows how to fight and knows how to rest, knows how to be loved and, in time, learns how to love.

The old Scottish poet George McDonald once wrote,

> God is tender—just like the prodigal's father—only with this difference, that God has millions of prodigals, and never gets tired of going out to meet them and welcome them back, every one as if he were the only prodigal son He had ever had. There's a Father indeed!

Oh, how my heart longs for that! And if it does, then there must be something in it that only the Father's love can touch. Like the prodigal who came home, I tend to also try to write into the script of my life something like, "Maybe I can be a servant in my Father's household." But the Father has a better idea.

His idea is to restore what has been lost. As that begins to take place, a man starts to see challenges in his inner life that can and must be overcome. He also begins to see who he can become and the role that is his and his alone to play. These things happen simultaneously and yet distinctively.

SEEING WHAT MUST BE OVERCOME

The enemy of our hearts knows that we are never alone. But if you're not ready, then you're not ready. And most of the men I meet aren't. A man can be so fooled, so tricked into believing his false self is his real self, that he isn't ever ready to fight against it. Like an old shirt, it becomes comfortable and even indispensable.

God wants to change all that if a man is ready. But again, most men aren't. One dead giveaway is, they don't ask questions and they don't listen. Not just to God, mind you, but to anyone. They are closed off; their lines of communication are deeply infiltrated, and the enemy wants to keep it that way. Most men don't know the effect their life has on those around them. Either they've never had the courage to ask, or no one in their life has had the courage to tell to them. Deep within them, a lie is firmly entrenched: *Whatever you do, don't let them know you don't know anything.* Or worse: *Whatever you do, make sure they know that you know everything.* Where did we men learn this along the way, and how has it served us?

The invitation for a man to see the things within himself that need caring for, and then bring those things to God for treatment and healing, is just another great day of training in the kingdom. It was Francis of Assisi who said, "Above all the grace and the gifts that Christ gives to his beloved is that of overcoming self."

Overcoming the *false* self, to be exact—the outer layers of a man, both the good and the messed-up and sinful, that he mistakes for his deepest identity. Things began to change in my life when I began to observe my false self. They continued to change when I let my true self, my core identity in Christ, take over my false self. Things needed to change. Seeing what had to be overcome was a huge step toward actually overcoming it!

Some things need to be unlearned. One of the first steps in training is to circle back to what has already taken place in our story. What we learned along the way and why we have become the way we are requires a lot of our attention if we are to become truly free. Early in training, regular visits with God to explore one's personal history are standard practice for men to shed the false self and to become true men.

Think of your life as a great construction site. The foundation should consist of being loved well; a strong base of love makes for a strong structure. For a boy, being seen, wanted, invited, and encouraged provides tremendous foundational materials. Having his young heart handled lovingly and intentionally during his formative years furnishes sound building blocks for fashioning a man of quality. A good father makes sure his son gets plenty of such materials; he oversees his son's development, thus leaving his mark for the strong, well-designed reconstruction to come, and the building that he will be.

But what if our father (or mother) had unfinished foundations of their own? What if our parents' parents delivered substandard materials, so that our mom or dad experienced a poor building environment during their own formative years? What if, during childhood, our fathers' and mothers' hearts were belittled or painfully neglected? What if one or both of our parents experienced a great absence of love while growing up? Maybe their own mother and father, your grandparents, fought all the time but never enjoyed simple conversation with each other or showed mutual affection. Feuds, affairs, or divorce rather than harmony, faithfulness, and security may have characterized the home your dad or mom were subject to as a child. What would the foundation look like for the child he or she once was, growing up in such an unprotected and unsafe environment? What would that foundation later produce when it was their turn to go to work building yours?

A young heart constructed with inferior, even dangerous materials, like fear, anxiety, uncertainty, guilt, and shame makes for a very unstable foundation. An inspection of the materials passed down from one generation to the next could explain a lot of why we are where we are today.

Awareness of what damaged us and who was responsible doesn't in itself stop the damage or pain. Healing does. But in order for healing to happen, our ill-constructed legacies must first be seen. Seeing what happened to us is the crucial first step to the even greater work of healing and the renovation of a man's heart that will bring orientation and the glorious presence of having a settled heart.

SEEING WHOM YOU MAY BECOME

It is critical that we fight the battles of our past. Most of us don't know how to fight today because when we were younger, no one showed us. When we were boys, no one was there to intervene, to defend our hearts by stepping in to fight for us. No one was present to teach us the reasons behind the battle or coach us in the art and practice of warfare. One man told me, "I know what I should be doing with my son, but I just don't have time." Which of the two needs counseling first, the father or his young son? Neither knows how to fight, or why.

A man's first moments of training are to recover from his past, from the losses and wounds accumulated in the course of his life journey. We don't go back to the past to stay in it; we go back as men to honor our moments of loss, to grieve them, to acknowledge that they happened, they hurt, they mattered, and they need to be treated. We go back with God for our healing. When we do, God extends his love and compassion to our hearts. One at a time, one wounding moment of our past and then another, he addresses them, or this can happen whenever we sense our enemy tempting us to live in the power and authority of our wounds. Thus begins one of the greatest comebacks of all time: the restoration of a man's heart as he removes all blockages to his experience of being the Beloved Son of his heavenly Father.

You can start right now. Take a pause and set down this book, grab some paper or sit behind a computer, and then ask the Father these questions:

> Who delivered the messages and materials that formed the beliefs of my heart?
> What happened to me that brought on loss of heart?
> In my life journey, who inflicted hurt, guilt, fear, or shame? When? Where?

This is just a first step, so be gracious to yourself and patient. You're not on a schedule; every man is different. Answers, understanding, and healing often come in installments over weeks, months, and even years. Sometimes I bring a particular matter to God; at other times he brings it to me. Why doesn't he bring it all at once? Probably because of his mercy and grace. There is far too much to do in one grand sweep, and altering experiences would be forfeited with no wisdom gained.

Exploration is usually best accomplished in a quiet setting where one can have a good heart to heart conversation with God. I think he likes it that way. Take a few minutes, as a first installment, to reflect on your story and pray David's prayer from Psalm 139: "Search me, O God. . . ." Then actively listen by writing down what comes to mind. Grab the Father's hand and see where he wants to take you in your story, your history. I believe God wants a man to know his own story before God rewrites it. I've seen it done. It has happened to me, and I know it can happen to you.

When taking inventory of your losses and wounds of the heart, bear in mind that some men have more than others. The amount matters, as does the treatment; the first were customized attacks on your heart, and both will be personalized in your healing. Be encouraged! True masculinity, becoming the Beloved Son, is just one courageous step away, followed by another, and another, until you're experiencing your true self and a new normal.

YOU ARE NEEDED

In order to become Beloved Sons/Warriors, we men must first get our hearts back. In the fight for life and love, we are going to need them. Being the Beloved Son is part of the orientation that leads to our becoming wholehearted, full, settled, and at rest. Such a man knows that he is first and foremost truly a son, who is then further trained up in the art of warfare.

So we must go with God to dislodge the lies our enemy has embedded in our heart—in the core of whom we are, where our true identity dwells. The enemy's attack in our formative years is like a virus in a hard drive, infiltrating, sabotaging, and compromising who we are and what we might truly become. As John Eldredge wrote in his bestselling book *Waking the Dead*:

> To find God, you must look with all your heart. To remain present to God, you must remain present to your heart. To hear his voice, you must listen with all your heart. To love him, you must love with all your heart. You cannot be the person God meant you to be, and you cannot live the life he meant you to live, unless you live from the heart.
>
> [The enemy's] plan from the beginning was to assault the heart. . . . Make [men] so busy, they ignore the heart. Wound them so deeply, they don't want a heart. Twist their theology, so they despise the heart. Take away their courage. Destroy their creativity. Make intimacy with God impossible for them.

Why? "Because," says Eldredge, "the enemy fears you and what you might become." He therefore wants to separate you from intimacy with God, from belovedness, from the very thing for which you were created. Separate a man from the Father and that man is *lost*. Saved? Sure, but lost . . . unable both to receive what God has for him and to provide for and protect the hearts of others.

Recovering your heart will take time. Just as the wounds it received came over time, so will its healing and restoration. It typically takes two to three years for a man to truly get his heart back *if* that man walks with God and stays the course. The question often is, how earnestly do you want what you seek? How badly do you want your heart back? How *free* do you want to be?

It is in the healing of a man's heart that the greatest training takes place. Much is at stake, more than you know. Seeking to reclaim your heart is your first step in fighting for many other hearts as well. Remember, your story is part of a Larger Story—and you are needed.

IT'S WORSE THAN WE THINK

DON'T BE NAIVE. THERE ARE DIFFICULT TIMES AHEAD. AS THE END APPROACHES, PEOPLE ARE GOING TO BE SELF-ABSORBED, MONEY-HUNGRY, SELF-PROMOTING, STUCK-UP, PROFANE, CONTEMPTUOUS OF PARENTS, CRUDE, COARSE, DOG-EAT-DOG, UNBENDING, SLANDERERS, IMPULSIVELY WILD, SAVAGE, CYNICAL, TREACHEROUS, RUTHLESS, BLOATED WINDBAGS, ADDICTED TO LUST, AND ALLERGIC TO GOD.

—II Timothy 3:1-5 (MSG)

THE WORLD IS A DANGEROUS PLACE TO LIVE, NOT BECAUSE OF THE PEOPLE WHO ARE EVIL, BUT BECAUSE OF THE PEOPLE WHO DON'T DO ANYTHING ABOUT IT.

—Albert Einstein

It happens to men often: moments of clarity but not transformation. Great starts that fall shy of the finish line, resolutions that eventually fade, and a growing collection of wouldas, shouldas, and couldas.

Paul the apostle talked about running so as to win (1 Cor. 9:24; Phil. 3:14), yet men tire and then get stuck at various mile markers along life's marathon course. It is a dangerous course where every decision matters, and if that in itself isn't hard enough, someone or something seems set against men as they run. Many are aware of this, but they can't put their fingers on the nature of the resistance: "Yep, we feel the opposition. But what is it and what can we do?"

Something *is* set against us, and often the course we're on is littered with minefields, poorly marked signage, taunters, hecklers, and downright nasty conditions. There are also other imperfect men running with us—casualties of the blind leading the blind, the disoriented leading the disoriented, the wounded wounding those around them. This dangerous course we men travel is aptly depicted in the story *Pilgrim's Progress*, written by John Bunyan in 1678. The journey of the main character, Christian, is every man's journey of life and faith. Here is one of my favorite parts:

> The hill, though high, I covet to ascend;
> The difficulty will not me offend;
> For I perceive the way to life lies here:
> Come, pluck up heart, let's neither faint nor fear.
> Better, though difficult, the right way to go,
> Than wrong, though easy, where the end is woe.

The critical mile markers a masculine heart must encounter in becoming a true man lie along an ancient path. But it is a road less traveled, and such a road is often lost as one generation gives way to the next. Today we need voices from the past to tell us about that ancient way—voices of the pioneers, explorers, and teachers who lived the journey and shared about it. They left warnings and instructions for other sojourners looking for help. The generations coming up can see true masculinity when they look to those forerunners who walked in intimacy with God and in deep friendship with one another. They were transformed men who hoped to see more transformed men.

WE'VE LOST GROUND

It is about 2:30 in the afternoon, and on this particular day I have been meeting back-to-back-to-back with a consecutive run of men. That's largely what I do. I had started at 7:00 a.m., moving about town, connecting with my different appointments, and now in mid-afternoon a familiar theme was becoming apparent—again.

Faces change and so do a few of the variables: a husband struggling to love his wife, a man hamstrung by lack of finances, a dad in pain over a teenager whose heart is in the far country. The men come from many walks of life. Some are just starting their careers while others are several years into their third one. Some wear suits; others, blue jeans. Dads, grandfathers, sons, husbands—a common thread weaves through all their stories: they are wounded. Like a medic moving across a battlefield, on my left and then on my right I hear their desperate cries, sometimes no more than a whisper: medic—*medic.*

Sitting across from men at Barnes & Noble or Panera Bread, in their office or mine, I see the victims and casualties every day and hear their collective outcry. Sometimes with anger or frustration, sometimes with deep sadness from all the pain, the chorus cries out again and again: *Help! We are losing ground.*

Not every day is as I've just described. Thank you, God! There are many days when I get to hang out with oriented men, men who are not bulletproof in the battle but who get hit far less than they used to, men with struggles but who struggle well. They may not be experiencing good in all their circumstances, but as oriented men they know God is at work for a deeper good in their lives. They are taking back lost ground in their own hearts and partnering with God for the hearts of others.

In the spring of 2000, I was one of those men yelling "Medic!" I was thirty-seven years young and a husband of eleven years to a woman who was and is a great partner in life. I was the father of three beautiful, ponytailed girls who at the time were eight, six, and three years old. And I can honestly say, I didn't know what I didn't know. Not realizing that something was very wrong, I kept living in the delusion that someday things would get better; I just needed to hang on until they did. It wasn't a very good plan. No one ever wants to hear the physician's words, "If we had just caught this a little earlier . . ." I was suffering and wasn't sure from what. My "man symptoms"—anger, frustration, sadness, boredom, low-grade guilt and shame—all seemed unfortunately normal, not like chronic abnormalities. After all, the men I knew and with whom I compared my life, had similar tales to tell. For all of us, the cause of our collective condition was a disoriented heart caused by years of untreated wounds.

I did not have an unbelieving heart, mind you. I, and most of my friends, were all followers of Christ. Back then, with my disoriented heart and misplaced sense of nobility, I would have said with a quiet arrogance that I was a committed Christian. (You know, "committed"—a word that describes someone so disoriented he's been checked into a facility.) Yet what I had been taught, and what I believed deep down about God and myself, was far worse than I knew. I was disoriented.

NAIVETÉ

In his book *Fathered by God*, John Eldredge observes that "most men and most boys have no real father able to guide them through the jungles of the masculine journey, and they are—most of us are—unfinished and unfathered men."

"Unfinished" and "unfathered" are two core ingredients of disorientation. One reason I can often recognize another disoriented heart is because I lived in that condition for so many years. It doesn't necessarily mean we had *bad* fathers. But, like I said earlier, it may very well mean that our fathers were themselves unfinished and unfathered.

One sign of disorientation is a man who settles for being a servant of the kingdom rather than a Warrior for it. Service that originates from the wrong source, as it so often does, is in itself enough to anesthetize your soul. Duty-bound serving will take its toll until life is either boring or irrelevant. You can be a servant and not a Warrior, and if you do, then you're missing the boat. However, it is impossible to be a Warrior and not a servant.

For years I was haunted by the thought that there was far more available to me than what I had become. I knew there had to be more than the constant, low-grade frustration, fear, anger, and sadness that regularly bubbled up. Things were not well with me, and naively, I believed the reason had to be one of three things: either I wasn't *serving* God well enough, or everyone else was the problem, or God wasn't running my life right. No matter which one I picked, the result was the same: I felt cheated and inadequate.

Somewhere in my masculine journey, I crossed a bridge into some significant responsibilities: wife, kids, mortgage, credit cards, and so on. The few skills and scant equipping I had obtained up to that time weren't serving me well. Occasionally, with a sharp pang, the recognition hit me that I wasn't ready for what lay ahead on the path. My household was on the brink, and if I went down—and worse, didn't rise up—then others would suffer.

As more weeks and months clipped off, it became increasingly evident that I was ill-prepared, ill-equipped, and ill-advised. The worst part was the deeply felt conviction and often audible whisper I heard from within, "I am alone."

My wife and children needed me to step into my greater role in the Larger Story, the role God created me to play. But how? Serve more, give more, do more? Sin less? That was the good old religious program I had been working at for several years. But it was doing far more harm than good. As with smoking cigarettes or living in a home with asbestos insulation, what you take in over time can kill you.

The American Heritage Dictionary of the English Language defines *naiveté* as "having or showing a lack of experience, judgment, or information; credulous . . . having or marked by a simple, unaffectedly direct style reflecting little or no formal training or technique." That was me, and it's many a man whose wounded heart leads to naiveté. This is what most often keeps a man from moving forward into the role that is his and his alone to play in the Larger Story.

I was "retreating into less," and because of my naiveté, it felt normal. Like a man trying to climb up a down escalator, I was active and moving but getting tired and losing ground and approaching a dangerous bottom, dying a little bit each day and not knowing it. *Settling* often goes undetected for years, until one day a man reflects on all the damage he's collected *and* caused, the opportunities he's let slip, or worse, has never seen and entered into.

You and I were made for more. Not to *do* more. Made *for* more.

In the recovery community there is a saying: "You don't know what you don't know". (That's naiveté!). In the recover*ing* community we add, "until you finally know what you needed to know."

COMPROMISE

Back to the story of *Braveheart*. For those who have seen the film, who can forget the father of Robert the Bruce? His counsel to his son is true to his way of thinking and what he believes is the mission in this life. But his words are neither noble nor good: "You admire this man, this William Wallace. Uncompromising men are easy to admire. He has courage. So does a dog. But it is exactly the ability to compromise that makes a man noble." These are poisonous words to the son, that eventually led to the son's compromise, to say nothing of the rest of Scotland's men and the future of its people.

Every man hears voices telling him who he is, what he is, and why he is the way he is. Few have taken the time to research their origins. Because the sources of the voices have not been searched out, perilous compromises are always at the door, inviting a man to fear, prove, or hide. If a man never awakens to these inner voices, telling him his interpretive and concluding abilities are not tainted, then the problem starts there. If a man believes that the only "voices" he hears are his own, then *waking up* is the first order of business. There is an enemy with a vested interest in building a man's identity and life based on false assumptions and hand-me-down falsehoods.

Forces are at work both for us and against us. It's time we wake up, see, hear, and engage in training, and enter the Larger Story to reclaim our hearts and our true voice then our noble roles as men. In order to be uncompromising men, we must journey with God and explore what is noble and good within us—and what is not. There *is* something *very good* God is after, someone he wants to see recovered. And when it is, a different Life emerges, a restored and free Life. It's the one a man was meant to have, meant to live, and meant to share.

There is nothing greater in a man's life than when the deepest part of him, his heart, becomes whole. But few take the journey toward wholeness because compromise has taken its toll. At the moment of salvation, when a man is born again, he is given a new heart. That heart is now standard equipment, and he's going to need it. For the rest of his life, he will be trained up in how to live and love from his new heart.

> I'll give you a new heart, put a new spirit in you. I'll remove the stone heart from your body and replace it with a heart that's God-willed, not self-willed. I'll put my Spirit in you and make it possible for you to do what I tell you and live by my commands. You'll once again live in the land I gave your ancestors. You'll be my people! I'll be your God! (Ezek. 36:26–28 MSG)

This is a forecast for many moments in a man's life. God will arrange them in order to invite, grow, and develop the true man. In these moments, the man will recover what has been lost, restore what has been compromised, and initiate and validate what is needed.

THE LOWER LIFE

The mistakes made and the wounds taken early in a man's journey will later stunt his growth. When something is stunted, its normal growth is hindered or its progress ceases, and this is true of the heart. It can get stuck and pinned down many different ways. A significant loss. An attack on one's innocence. Shame and embarrassment at the hands of critics or scoffers. Simply not knowing how to do something can turn into a major assault on a young heart. No wonder most men are stuck somewhere in their past.

As my pastor friend Scott says, "We have an epidemic of *boys* who shave, wear suits, and drive." It's because young hearts are often forced to defend themselves too early, to learn to hide in order to protect themselves, or to grow up too soon, forced to take on responsibilities beyond their years. These things have kept many a man a boy.

Few are the men who can tell wonderful stories of provision and protection as a boy. Fewer still can boast of being trained up in love at the hands of a good man and in the company of good men. Without these things, the results later in life are catastrophic. Some men become violent men, men who could be described as "mercenaries," fighting to benefit themselves, not others. Boardrooms and living rooms have become their OK Corrals. Their motto: "If it's to be, it's up to me." Their strategy: "If they get in the way, mow 'em down. Do unto others before they do unto you."

Passive men are the other extreme. These men learned early to not even try. Rather, they hide behind "mediocre" and under a message of "you're just good enough." Their motto is "Do whatever it takes to get by" and their strategy is "Just freeze and let the moment pass you by."

Because unfinished, stunted men look at the world through a disoriented lens, it stands to reason that the conclusions they draw about themselves and their world will be distorted. Their views and attitudes will in turn lead to behaviors that are harmful rather than helpful on a daily basis. Such men live as consumers of others, using and taking life rather than offering it. Or they are checked out, disengaged; they play it safe by avoiding, obsessing over, and controlling their own and other people's surroundings. Both the violent and the passive men, the consumers and the hiders, make life about themselves, as boys will tend to do.

Most men practice life in one or a combination of all these ways. But there are those among them who desperately long to change—to move from being disoriented to oriented men. What they need is a new interpretation of their lives and an understanding of what needs to happen. And that's exactly what Jesus calls us to. In Matthew 10:39, he says, "Whoever finds his [lower] life will lose it [the higher life], and whoever loses his [lower] life on My account will find it [the higher life]".

The journey and hope is to find the capital-L Life. A man who seeks to provide for and protect others knows the difference. Finding Life is a dangerous pursuit, but you don't make it alone. Jesus promises, "I am with you" (Matt. 28:20). A change of heart is in the making. The journey will demand much, which is why so few men even take the first step. And when the going becomes too hard, a man may stop taking risks and settle for where he is. He stops because there is a force, a bully at work making attempts on his Life. But as Oliver Wendell Holmes wrote, "When a resolute young fellow steps up to the great bully, the world, and takes him boldly by the beard, he is often surprised to find it comes off in his hand, and that it was only tied on to scare away the timid adventurers."

The masculine journey is a journey worth taking, an exploration worth making, and a fight worth entering. It will alter the life courses of many. Breaking free from the effects of *fallenness* is high on Christ's agenda for each and every man. Turning in our lower life for the higher Life comes with promises. It also comes with warnings about the pitfalls. But "Follow me" remains the invitation, and what you lose can't possibly be compared to what you'll find.

CALLED UP

I was fifteen and going about my daily ritual. Basketball had become very important to me and was the way I wanted to make a name for myself. Whether in the driveway or a gym, shot after shot, I was determined. One day I was at a basket at the other end of a gym where a bunch of men were gathering to play. They had nine and needed one more. All the shots, all the dribbling drills, all the moves I'd practiced, all the collective hours logged, were now being invited into this moment.

Early in the game, the older men didn't pay much attention to me, but by the end of the third game, the better players were trying to guard me, and my new teammates were trying to get the ball in my hands. From this one incident, I came to believe that *if anything matters, then everything matters.*

We can all look back on particular days that shaped our lives and carried us into a new day. Indeed, we have no idea how pivotal certain moments were *unless* we look back. I walked into that gym a scrawny, unsure fifteen-year-old, but I left with a new ingredient: confidence. Not cockiness but a budding trust in my own abilities.

One of my favorite scenes in all the "guy movies" ever made is near the end of the film *The Kingdom of Heaven*. It is the time of the Crusades, and the main character, Balian, has advanced to a position of influence. Many are looking to him for what will happen next. He is a long way from the blacksmith shop where his story started; what he had in him to become, he is now being. His father, just before his death, made Balian a knight, and now a time of testing lies in front of him.

On the brink of the climactic battle against Saladin's hordes, Jerusalem's massively outnumbered defenders possess the slight advantage of defending the city wall. A disheartened bishop declares, "We have no knights!" In response, turning to the hundreds of men, Balian tells them to take a knee. Then he recites the oath his father pronounced over him:

> "Be without fear in the face of your enemies. Be brave and upright, that God may love thee. Speak the truth always, even if it leads to your death. Safeguard the helpless and do no wrong. That is your oath. Arise a knight!"
>
> "Who do you think you are?" the bishop exclaims. "Will you alter the world? Does making a man a knight make him a better fighter?"
>
> Balian fixes his eyes on the bishop.
>
> "Yes."

I have yet to meet a man who is not inspired by this scene. Why? Because it calls up something deep in our hearts. Every man wants to matter, wants to contribute, to be called up and make a difference. Balian's words speak to that special place in each of us where dwells our deep desire to be a man and to have someone declare it so.

Just after telling them to be brave and just before letting them know he was leaving, Jesus made a similar life-altering declaration to a bunch of men on the brink of entering battle:

> I'm no longer calling you servants because servants don't understand what their master is thinking and planning. No, I've named you friends because I've let you in on everything I've heard from the Father. You didn't choose me, remember; I chose you. (John 15:15–16 MSG)

He is calling them up, again. They are a long way from their fishing nets and ledger tables. They have seen things and done things that have altered them as men. They had come to know who he was, and at that moment they felt the weight of being called up because of who was calling them. Most men have never been called up and therefore have never been told,

> *You can do this!*
> *You can become more. You are more!*
> *You have it in you, and I will help you!*
> *Come with me. Follow me—I'll show you the way.*
> *Let's go!*

FIRST THINGS FIRST

All men have suffered loss, and we will again. But we can recover from life's most terrible losses, including the most terrible of all, the loss of heart. We can reclaim our hearts from bondage. Jesus has made the way, and we must step through it. We *can* become wholehearted—not just for our own sake, but also for the sake of others.

In order to love others well—truly love them in a way that alters their lives, leaving an impression and initiating change—we need to have first received and known love for ourselves. Caring for our heart is not selfish; it is both noble and necessary. What help can we be to the injured around us when our own wounds continue to cripple us?

God loves *first* and loves *most* (1 John 4:19). Jesus says it is in receiving from him that we are redeemed, reborn, and refashioned into Beloved Sons. Those Beloved Sons can then be made into Warriors, taking up the King's mission and cause through intimate friendship with the King. If a man is not settled, if he does not know he is the Beloved Son, he will get his butt kicked on a regular basis through discouragement, despair, anger, resentment, and depression. But when a man does drink deeply and often from this well of living water, everything changes. Oh, this lineup of characters will still come calling, *but* they will have no place to land. No place to infect, and later, incredulously impact.

We don't have to try to matter, because we know that somehow we were worth dying for. We are more than just washed clean: we are drowned *in* love. I'm not talking about a theory or a theology. I am talking about being loved on extravagantly and excessively, and about being passionately *in love.* We were originally made to experience and encounter God's love. We were made to experience and encounter a great romance, a long-established love affair between two hearts that have journeyed together for years in a passionate and intimate marriage, like a bridegroom and bride.

But until we actually experience this love firsthand, all we men have is a brochure or a theory. Looking at a recipe is not the same as enjoying a bite. Reading about or hearing about God's love is helpful, but it's not the same as tasting and seeing that he is good. Love is the point. Love is the first step in becoming a man . . . then receiving love again and again and again.

TAKING A STEP

At odd times in his masculine journey, a man will be invited to step up, step in, or just courageously take another step, period. Doing so often won't be convenient, and it never seems to be easy. There are times when a man will have to fix his gaze, lower his shoulder, brace himself and take a step. The results aren't guaranteed, yet step he must, and in the right direction. The step will be personal, an original for each image-bearer. I can't script it for you, just as you can't for me. We can't even script it for ourselves; if we could, we would demand far less of ourselves. But God is the One authoring our stories, and he is at work making oriented men out of disoriented men. God is designing a man's steps of recovery, customizing each man into what he would truly want to be: fierce, tender, filled with strength and compassion.

> In his heart a man plans his course, but the Lord determines his steps (Prov. 16:9 NIV).

It's not just a single step. A man will have to take multiple steps because the gravitational pull of fallenness on him is toward the center of a smaller story. In that fallacy, the narrative revolves around the man, and he believes life is up to him. Few men pull away from the center of that smaller story; pushing against the pull takes a courage most aren't aware they have within them. But it is in that struggle where a man finds what he is made of and what within him still needs training. It is easier to settle and take the path of least resistance (the road more traveled) to compromise and be pulled back into the center of the smaller story, to buy again the lie—hook, line, and sinker—that we can author a greater role for ourselves than God can.

If courageous steps were easy, then many more men would show more courage and less compromise. Advancing from the center of the smaller story and stepping into a more prominent place in the Larger Story is no easy task. Doing so will take something greater than what a man can muster on his own. It is a collaboration in which God must be in charge of his healing, restoration, and training.

To recover from boyhood wounds and journey into becoming a true man is a transition that is as significant as stepping from the part of a naïve civilian into the role of a skilled Warrior, trained and true. The first courageous step a man must take is to head back to what shaped him in his youth. The boyhood years, from birth to about age fourteen, can be a wonderful time—or a brutal one. In a fallen world with fallen people all around you, what are the chances of getting to even your first birthday unscathed?

Imagine moldable clay waiting for hands to gently shape it. That's your vulnerable young heart, dependent upon, and at the mercy of, those who will make their impression. In different ways, all boys' hearts fall victim to wounded and broken parents, family members, teachers, coaches, and others. Many are the shaping forces of a disoriented heart. But the good news is, you can become healed, oriented, and rise above their effects.

BETTER THAN WE CAN POSSIBLY IMAGINE

Early in the *Braveheart* film, when William Wallace is just a boy of nine or ten, he is faced with the tragic loss of his father, a good man killed by a bad king. Moments after the funeral, a man rides in on a white horse. William has no idea who the man is, but the man knows William. Later that night, with bagpipes playing, they stand side by side at the freshly mounded grave. William's uncle, Argyle, catches the lad admiring the great claymore sword of his father. In the thirteenth century, these swords were owned by Scottish knights involved in the resistance against English tyranny. When William touches the sword, tries to lift it, Argyle gently pulls it back. William looks up; Argyle looks down. Then he says,

> "First, learn to use this" (pointing to William's forehead).
> "Then I will teach you to use this" (holding up the sword).

This is a better offer than young Wallace can possibly imagine. His rescue is accomplished and his training has already begun. And so is the offer of our heavenly Father to us.

A man must learn the way of Life, which is the narrow road, and he must know the voice of the only One who can truly teach him. There is a language, an understanding, a path, and an experience that leads to a practice. That practice is a way of Life that every man must learn if he is going to be an oriented man. A big question is, *Will a man trust the heart of his Teacher . . . is his Teacher good?*

No matter how young or old you are, how inexperienced or experienced, there is One who wants to intervene in your life and take you on this quest. There is One who wants the significant role of teaching, loving, initiating, validating, and turning you loose into the world to be dangerous for good. There aren't many men in training, collaborating with God, partnering in a glorious alliance of hearts. Look around you. Loss of heart is everywhere. Loss of Life is extensive. The situation is far worse than we thought.

But the Life that is available to you—Life hidden in Christ—is far better than you can possibly imagine. And it's available to all who seek it out.

WHERE IT HURTS

We who live in this nervous age would be wise to meditate on our lives and our days long and often before the face of God and on the edge of eternity.

—*A. W. Tozer*

The most important thing about a man is not what he does. It is who he becomes.

—*Dallas Willard*

In my work with men for more than a decade, I have seen a recurring theme. It's an understated but felt assumption that men are underachieving, whether in the media, the culture, or, most alarmingly, the church. I've seen the "new" churches that proclaim, "We aren't your Grandma's church," but still they keep the two-by-four in the corner to coax a man into submission. Grandma may have some new clothes, make her music loud and upbeat, and allow you to check the ties and dress shoes at the door, but it's still her church when the core message delivered to men's hearts doesn't change. Week after week, the subtle lie gets reinforced: "Men you're the problem. You're a mess. Try harder! Do more, give more, and sin less. Men, you have to get serious, get out of the way, get going, and get more committed."

This negative chest-poking message isn't nearly enough to sustain men on their journey to becoming whom they are meant to be, and it's certainly not producing the effect those who spread it want it to have. They're right about one thing: we men *are* made for more. But the message they're selling puts pressure on a man to use his own resources instead of the resources of the One whose life can be lived through us. They unfortunately are attempting to start with training instead of healing and it won't work.

Men are exhausted from being told, "If you would just apply yourself, you would be better. But you really won't get better because you are what you are—a *sinner.*" This paradox, delivered so often to men in the church, tells them they can't be trusted but need to try harder anyway. Religious leaders who tell born-again men they are simply "sinners and a mess" and who then get mad at those men when they sin and make a mess—hmmm. How is that helpful? Men rise to the level of the message, but the message is far too unhelpful, and it plays right into the hands of our enemy.

Until the healing and training of men becomes the central mission of the church and not just one of the many ministries it offers, men aren't going to find what they need within its walls. Programs and service often land on a man like chores: he's glad to do them (and needs to do them), but he won't get Life from them. When sin plays on a man's heart with guilt and shame, he will serve in the church out of a sense of obligation rather than freedom.

The gospel is about way more than just being forgiven for sin. Wonderful though that is, if we stop there, then we're vastly short-selling the hugeness, the surpassing glory, of what God has accomplished through Jesus. The gospel is about *restoration*, a future, and a hope. For all you bottom-line guys, here is what the gospel in its fullness is about:

God calls us up to something much larger than we can imagine. He invites us to take a journey, a journey with him that will transform us as men. On it, we will discover that our mistakes were taken care of even before we made them. It is a journey in which our King, God himself, is continually guiding us, training us, equipping us, initiating us, validating us, and turning over the family business of his kingdom to us. Such a King calls. Such a mission exists, and we are on it!

We must recover our awareness and understanding that we live in a Large Story, and the Author of that story both invites us and warns us. He invites us to live courageously, to walk with him in a far greater role than so many of us have settled for. He also warns us of the evil that is dead set against our becoming more whole—because if we become more whole, then we become freer; if we become freer, then we become more *alive* and a bunch of men who are more alive is bad for evil.

Journeying with God is all about discovering who he is and who he made us to be. It's about discovering who we are, and just as important, who we *aren't.* Walking with God is an invitation to training. The masculine heart will be summoned and tested, tried and proven, counseled and trained. That is how a man is entrusted with more. When passing the test, handling the obstacle, dealing with the enemy, God sees fit to entrust a man with more opportunity, more privilege, more impact, and more power and authority. "You have been faithful with a few things; I will put you in charge of many things. Come and share your master's happiness!" (Matt. 25:23 NIV). More responsibility often comes through living with risk, faith, perseverance, trust, and enduring hardship. How did we ever come to believe it was going to be easy or comfortable? That's not what God promises nor is it what the records of the first disciples' (Jesus' friends) lives revealed.

We, like those first disciples, desperately need to experience who Jesus is and that we are like him *and are in the process* of becoming, like him, Beloved Sons. We also need to understand whom he was up against, the enemy of Life and love, because that also is whom we are up against.

Jesus lived kindly, lovingly, and fiercely during his mission here on earth. His teaching was about showing us how the kingdom works, how love works, and how to have Life in the kingdom of God. He taught that Life is connected to him. And if we are going to sign on for that Life, then we are going to need some deep healing. We will need everything taken out of the way—the lies, the shame, our false self—that hinders our friendship with him and our enjoyment of the One for whom we were made. Any hurtful way that opposes God's intentions for us as men, needs to be identified, treated and healed.

EVERY MOMENT MATTERS

The Larger Story reveals two kingdoms that are at war over the vital piece of real estate the Scriptures call the heart. Both kingdoms know its value and its worth. One kingdom offers lies, the other the truth. One offers death, the other, Life. Both kingdoms know that *if you get the heart of a person, you get the whole person.* The respective rulers of those kingdoms don't underestimate the magnitude of the conflict nor take it lightly and neither should we. Every heart matters. Every choice matters. Every moment matters.

I was a sophomore in high school, trying to find my place in the world, playing basketball and hoping to matter, hoping to belong, to be somebody. One fall Friday night after our football team won an away game, we students returned to our high school to welcome the buses and celebrate the victory. My friend and I were waiting in the pack of other sophomores, laughing and watching all the activity, when a senior, a star on the basketball team, wheeled up in his Camaro not ten feet from us. He rolled down his window and hollered my name. Imagine my excitement! *Whoa, summoned by a senior!* With many people watching, I did my coolest walk over to the car.

When I got close, the senior reached up, grabbed me by the jacket, pulled me almost inside the car, and started yelling at me. Shock went through my system, paving the way for the shame and embarrassment that immediately followed. I could smell the guy's previous activities on his breath. He finally discarded me with a shove and called me a piece of something, which is exactly how I felt. He and his friends in the car broke into a chorus of derisive laughter, and many standing around nervously joined in. Bewildered and hurt by his seeming hatred toward me, I left and endured the next few days until another high school drama replaced me in the headlines.

This moment mattered greatly in my life and affected me for months, even years. But it wasn't my first run-in with shame, nor would it be my last. Shame always makes me wonder, *What is wrong with me?* It whispers, "Be anywhere but here. Be anybody but me. Hide!"

The critical work of returning with Christ to our past and fighting today what we didn't know how to fight back then is a work of redemption into which every man must step. Our stories can be redeemed. What's more, our future can be rewritten. Just because no one showed us how to fight for our hearts in the past doesn't mean we have to be haunted by those moments the rest of our days.

Early twentieth-century author Napoleon Hill wrote, "Every adversity, every failure, and every heartache, carries with it the Seed of an equivalent or greater benefit." Regardless of how long ago a particular wounding moment occupied ground in your heart, you can reclaim that place—and you must. It's not just "the moment,"; it is the shame or other foul spirit that accompanies the moment that needs attention and great care.

COME OUT OF THE SHADOWS

In the film *The Legend of Bagger Vance*, Captain Rannulph Junuh, a once-great golfer before World War I, returns to Savannah, Georgia, a hero. He feels like anything but a hero, though, because none of the boys from Savannah who were under his command survived. He was the only one to return. The guilt, shame, and regret he carries inside are so overwhelming that the only way he knows how to cope is to hide and drink.

In order for Junuh to recover and move freely forward into the glorious life for which he was created, he must take some significant steps back.

A mission and a missionary come after him in the form of a golf match and a caddie. In a brilliant scene, Junuh faces the most difficult shot of his life. Late in the match, he has hit his drive deep into the woods. (Life for so many of us has been lived too long in the shadows of the woods.) There among the trees, the familiar smells, terrain, and conditions transport him to another moment: the battlefield of WWI where he lost all his friends.

Junuh hunches over the ball, sweating, overwhelmed, his knees buckling. On the verge of collapse, he is about to reach down, pick up the ball, and then do what he has learned to do so well: hide. Flee back to the shadows of life. But in that moment, his caddy's voice intervenes:

> BAGGER (interrupting) You gonna be wantin' a different club there, Mr. Junuh?
>
> JUNUH: I can't do this.
>
> BAGGER: You might just loose your grip up a smidge. A man's grip on his club is like a man's grip on his world.
>
> JUNUH: (interrupting) That's not what I'm talking about.
>
> BAGGER: I know.
>
> JUNUH: No, you don't.
>
> BAGGER: What I'm talking about is a game—a game that can't be won, only played.

JUNUH: You don't understand.

BAGGER: I don't need to understand. Ain't a soul on the entire earth who ain't got a burden to carry he don't understand.You ain't alone in that. But you've been carrying this one long enough. Time to go on, lay it down.

JUNUH: I don't know how.

BAGGER: You got a choice. You can stop or you can start.

JUNUH: Start?

BAGGER: Walkin'.

JUNUH: Where?

BAGGER: Right back to where you always been. And then stand there—still, real still, and . . . remember.

JUNUH: It's too long ago.

BAGGER: Oh, no sir, it was just a moment ago. Time for you to come on out of the shadows, Junuh.

Time is a different thing in the eternal world. It's kind of funny to even put those two concepts in the same sentence, but this is something a man must come to know: how to tell time. To restore something is to turn back time—to bring something back to its glorious condition before all the scratches, dents, and dings, the abuse and neglect. Restoring the heart means returning it to a condition before guilt or shame were inflicted on it. To see God restore the mishandling and mistreatment of a heart, to see him redeem the wounding moments and their wounding messages, is one of the most glorious moments you can witness—and it's even greater to experience for yourself!

And it's like that. Several moments lead up to the one moment, the moment when *healing* happens.

Much of whom a man becomes and what he settles for has been learned over time and through the shaping experiences and conclusions he makes during his life. Can you imagine the sum of all our conclusions, all the beliefs we hold in our hearts, being accurate? Some of them, yes. But all? No way. We all harbor inaccuracies, lies about ourselves, others, or God, in which we have learned to hold and live. These lies arise from wounds, they become *ways* in themselves, and our wounded ways in turn affect others. It is therefore of paramount importance that we experience healing and treatment so something glorious and good can replace the pain, guilt, and shame. Just as wounded hearts wound other hearts, so a whole heart can help other hearts become whole as well. The damage is reversed and the wound is redeemed. What was intended for bad, God makes good, so now what is passed down comes from the good stored up in the heart. It is part of what Jesus was talking about in Luke 6:45 (NIV),

> A good man brings good things out of the good stored up in his heart.

We need to receive from God the good things we didn't get and give to him the bad things we did get. We need to experience the reality of being Beloved Sons; then we'll be able to take our rightful place in the story God is telling and the part he has created for each man to play.

JUST A MOMENT AGO

Most days I spend time with men tending to the wounds they have accumulated and exploring with them the hope of better days and a healed heart.

My friend Kelly was an only child, and when I met him in his mid-fifties, he was living with a lie that had affected him most of his adult life. During a college summer, Kelly was home working and doing what most college kids do, hanging out and surviving being back at home. One particular July evening, his dad came home from work and abruptly reminded his son that he hadn't cut the grass. Kelly looked up from the TV and replied, as curtly as he was addressed, "I'll get it tomorrow." Next thing he heard was the mower cranking up and his dad taking care of the lawn himself.

Then came the wounding moment, a lost battle of epic proportions. There was a scream from the kitchen window and Kelly found himself racing his mother out the back door to the idling mower and his dad laid out across the line of cut and uncut grass. As Kelly told me his story, tears welled up, he hung his head, and out came his confession of longstanding shame: "I killed my father."

Many of us have experienced a friend sharing a painful moment from the past. The emotion he exhibits is as intense as if the incident had happened only minutes ago. He speaks and you see it, feel it: he is *in* his past, transported back into that moment. Its effect on his heart is current and on display.

Jim is a close friend of mine with a tender heart. You can tell because whether he is listening to you tell a painful story from your past or sharing one of his own, behind his glasses his eyes swell with tears.

Dozens of times he has recounted a moment when he was four years old and was terrified during a thunderstorm. "I remember my dad putting on a big raincoat, picking me up, and zipping me up inside next to his chest," says Jim. "Then, holding me close, he walked with me out into the rain."

My dad softly told me, "I got you Jimmy. It's okay; there's nothing to be afraid of."

"It was still thundering and the rain was coming down, but I believed him." Jim smiles warmly but his tears still reflect pain. "It is the only memory I have of being with my dad and being loved."

Jim used to tell this story with regret mostly because he lacked other good memories. During too many other storms in his life, no one came for his heart or protected him or comforted him. But this story is now one of many that have been re-filed in Jim's heart. Now he tells it to encourage other men to step back into a moment with Christ for healing and freedom—because considering how scenes from our story affect the way we see and do life is vital to moving forward.

RE-SEARCH

What are the odds of our hearts getting through this great battle unscathed? Zero. In order to enjoy the *more* we were created for—to become Warriors who know freedom and are trustworthy, faithful, and good for the hearts of others—we must first recover from the wounds of our story and be restored as Beloved Sons. But I find most men don't know their own story. They were there, but they have never taken the time to recall their heart's journey nor to explore what happened to them and its effects.

Again, I invite you to research your story with God—to know it, uncover the wounds it holds, and take them to God for treatment. With his help, you can get answers to your heart's deepest question: *Who am I really—to you, God?* As he replaces the lies you've believed about yourself with the truth, then the tide of the battle will turn. As Jesus promised, you will lose one life and find another. In the words of A. W. Tozer, "We who live in this nervous age would be wise to meditate on our lives and our days long and often before the face of God and on the edge of eternity. For we are made for eternity as certainly as we are made for time, and as responsible moral beings we must deal with both."

A step toward becoming the Beloved Son is to rewrite your story. Ask God, "What happened to me?" Don't make it a one-time, quick-answer question; walk with God in it, and consider the travels of your heart. Please ask these questions, similar to the ones before, *When and where were the defining moments of my life? What do I love? What do I hate? What am I most hopeful for, most afraid of?* If you've ever wondered why you feel the way you feel and believe what you believe, the answers are in your story.

Wounds that have formed over time take time to heal. But remember, Christ wants to heal you even more than you want to be healed. So, patiently he waits. He waits for you to come to him with your burdens, hurts and hopes. He waits for you to want him so he can help you with yourself.

THE CRASH

During my senior year in college basketball, I crashed.

I had been working my tail off for three years trying to earn a starting role. Now, at last, all the sweat and even a few tears seemed about to pay off. The preseason went well, and we were forecasted to be a good team heading into the season. During daily practice, our head coach would have guys flip their reversible jerseys to play in different combinations and scenarios. We always knew who was getting a look.

Then it happened. It was early in the season on the night of a game. We gathered at the chalkboard in the locker room, and there, among the starting five . . . my name wasn't listed.

Deep sadness with side orders of anger and mistrust filled my heart. I played that night, but it felt like a consolation prize, not even close to filling the hole in my chest. So I hid. With great intention I retreated to what I knew best, the way I had learned to treat rejection: "I'll show them." That meant extra shots, extra running, extra weights, all in an extra, self-imposed regimen to remedy a loss of heart.

We all have our remedies, internal attempts to avoid or stop the pain. And so mine began—again. Late nights looking at the ceiling. Daytime distractions of the if-onlies: *If only I had . . . if only I could . . . if only they would . . .* the inner voices that I naively assumed were all mine.

Several nights into this saga with classes, practice, and dinner long over and midnight nearly at hand, I was back in the gym shooting on my own. One successful shot after another, twenty in a row, twenty-five—it just added to the pain and frustration. Finally I walked over to the wall and sat down. Tears started to mix with the sweat dripping down my face, mingling and hitting the hardwood floor. And at last, I crashed. My heart cried out in frustration and pain, "I love this game."

There and then God showed up. Interrupting my thoughts, he whispered, "It doesn't love you back. I do."

He came after me. The spell was broken and as the first light of freedom began to flicker, so did the questions: "God, what else? How else? Help me! I don't know how to do this."

His response: "I can work with that." It was manna for my heart.

I invite you to ask even more questions: *What are you loving that isn't loving you back? What have you given your heart to that isn't giving back? When did you learn to turn to them for Life?* The answers are in your story.

BREAKING FREE

Wounds and their messages have a subtle and remarkable way of pinning us down, caging us in. Cages come in all shapes and sizes. Nowadays, our enemy's traps, snares, and nets are so subtle that few caged men realize the prison in which they are being held. But prisons they are whether a performance system or a religious system (the two are just about the same). Either way, a system created for control ensuring that a man settles for less and lives less, is the mission of our enemy.

If we are to become Warriors, we must see these traps and the eventual cages that are meant to hold us. We must see exactly what it is that has bound us, kept us confined and under control. A. W. Tozer wrote,

> It becomes the devil's business to keep the Christian's spirit imprisoned. He knows that the believing and justified Christian has been raised up out of the grave of his sins and trespasses. From that point on, Satan works that much harder to keep us bound and gagged, actually imprisoned in our own grave clothes. He knows that if we continue in this kind of bondage . . . we are not much better off than when we were spiritually dead.

With the help of Christ, we *can* break free and recover the lost and precious ground of our hearts. And we must! The battles we must fight, the missions in which God wants to deploy us as men will require us to be wholehearted. It was twenty years from the time I walked an aisle to "receive" Christ to the time when I finally began to walk a path of healing, restoration and strength. Recovering that lost ground in my heart was my first significant mission and it is the first mission of every man.

Twentieth-century poet and WW II veteran E.E. Cummings wrote, "To be nobody but yourself in a world which is doing its best, night and day, to make you everybody else means to fight the hardest battle which any human being can fight; and never stop fighting."

My three children need different things from me at different times. Fathering them all the same way would be unwise. They are each so different; therefore, I have different ways of loving them individually. That's how God deals with us. We each matter to him far too much for him to lump us all together and love us generically. And each of us will ultimately need a custom map to break free and a personal guide to show us the way out of bondage and into glorious freedom.

Every man must step into a union, a collaborative effort between his heart and the Father's. And as with Junuh in *The Legend of Bagger Vance*, each man's first steps forward on his journey will involve his stepping *back* into his story.

MAY I HELP YOU?

The Bible has a way of always expanding and becoming more to those who frequent its pages. Like the Grand Canyon or any beautiful landscape, the stories of the scriptures all offer far more than what a first glance can possibly take in. That is an amazing reality about the Scriptures: every time you take them in they have the potential to *evolve* in your life as a Christ apprentice. Here is one passage that recently moved from black-and-white to color in my journey:

> Later when Jesus was eating supper at Matthew's house with his close followers, a lot of disreputable characters came and joined them. When the Pharisees saw him keeping this kind of company, they had a fit, and lit into Jesus' followers. "What kind of example is this from your Teacher, acting cozy with crooks and riffraff?" Jesus, overhearing, shot back, "Who needs a doctor: the healthy or the sick? Go figure out what this Scripture means: 'I'm after mercy, not religion.' I'm here to invite outsiders, not coddle insiders." (Matthew 9:10–13 MSG)

It is Jesus giving people a clue as to what he is about. Remember Luke 4?

> He has anointed Me [the Anointed One, the Messiah] to preach the good news (the Gospel) to the poor; He has sent Me to announce release to the captives and recovery of sight to the blind, to send forth as delivered those who are oppressed [who are downtrodden, bruised, crushed, and broken down by calamity]. (Luke 4:18)

If that is what he has come to do—heal the sick, set captives free, give sight to the blind, and heal the brokenhearted—then the implication is, we must need that!

Over and over again in the Gospels, we see Jesus interacting with people . . . broken, hurting people. And time and time again he asks them, "How can I help you? What is it you want?"

Why would the Messiah ask such questions? Can't you just picture the disciples rolling their eyes as they come across the next lame man, blind man, or leper who finds himself the object of Jesus' inviting questions? *Yes, what can I do for you?* It's like he is provoking a response, forcing the hurting and broken to spill it out. . . .

I want to get well!
I want to be healed!
I want to see!
There, I said it.

I can imagine Jesus' response. He smiles, nods "okay then," and lifts up the person's head to meet him eye-to-eye. And looking into the eyes of Love and Life dispels shame and invites hope that something extraordinary is about to happen. Imagine Jesus saying, just above a whisper, "Oh dear one, let's take care of that right now. Your faith has made you well. (Pause for effect.) And by the way, your sins are forgiven too."

The broken and hurting of Jesus' day always got far more than they requested. So why does he ask, "May I help you?" (In other words, "What do you want?")

Jesus seems to want us to be aware of our pain in order to bring it to the surface, whatever *it* is. He makes us aware of what we truly want, and what we don't want, so he can show us his extraordinary care and attention in what comes next. Jesus is an expert at stirring up desire, hope and faith. All these are items that easily get buried deeply beneath the layers of life's disappointments and the unrelenting onslaught of a ruthless and ever-so-subtle enemy.

In order to know what we hope for, we must admit what the longings of our *hearts* are—the things we do not yet possess—and acknowledge that we are tired of reaching for it ourselves. Isn't it interesting that the hurting and broken don't come to Jesus for forgiveness? They come to him for a better life! Jesus takes care of what they want, but he always gives them what they *need* as well. It's his way. He's generous and abundant. Jesus lays out for us the first step in becoming the Beloved Son: healing. And it starts with our admitting, "Not all is well. I need help."

Acknowledging that "I am wounded and in need" expresses just enough hope, a smidge of faith, and a little bit of desire that things could be different. And with that, I arrive at *if only*.

If only my life were different.

My desire is aroused. I confess to God, "I want more." And now Jesus can go to work to give me the desire of my heart.

It is hope, faith, and desire that move Jesus' heart and invite him to work on ours. If we are going to get our hearts back, experience deep healing from the wounds of our past, and actually be the Beloved Sons, a lot of patience and healing work will be required. How whole do you want to become? How well do you need to be in order to take your rightful place in the grand story God is authoring?

IF YOU TURN TO ME . . .

Each of my girls has spent some time being mad at me. It comes with the territory and the title "Dad." Just the other day, my middle daughter, Hannah, had me arrested (in her mind) for not allowing her to do something I knew wouldn't be good for her.

Three days into the cold-shoulder treatment, she called me in tears, upset about a moment that had just happened at school. *Hurting* so often trumps angry, and just that quickly I was invited back into the game, back into a role I love and an important place in her life. When she called, it was not the time for a lecture on how she had treated me the past three days; it was a time to care for her and enter into her pain. I was so glad she turned to me.

Jesus got a little angry from time to time, upset with the disciples and often at odds with the religious leaders of his day. I believe what upset him most and caused him the most pain was that they wouldn't turn to him. They wouldn't let him love them. John's gospel quotes a prophecy from Isaiah regarding the people Jesus loved, people he came to heal yet who were keeping him at arm's length:

> Their eyes are blinded, their hearts are hardened, so that they wouldn't see with their eyes and perceive with their hearts, and turn to me, God, so I could heal them. (John 12:40 MSG)

This comes just before an unbelieving audience gets to see and hear "upset Jesus" give an invitation from the Son of God on the Son of God:

> I am Light that has come into the world so that all who believe in me won't have to stay any longer in the dark. (John 12:46 MSG)

Do you hear the pinch of anxiousness in Jesus' voice? *Please, please listen to me. Whoever believes in me—real life awaits you. You won't have to continue to stumble around in the dark. Let me be your light, please!*

Bringing broken things to God is a necessity and a glorious provision of our relationship with him. He knows where it hurts, but he wants *us* to know, and sometimes where it came from, and he wants us to bring those hurts and our stories to him. God says he will never leave nor forsake. He says he identifies with our every pain. He says, "I love you. You can trust me with your heart, your story, and the remodeling of *you*."

HEALING IS REQUIRED

As I have mentioned, don't be fooled into thinking we're all on the same narrow road or at the same place on that road. Every man is on his own journey with God to recover and become, and the details are between each man and the Father. The whiteboard of my life is as unique to me as yours is to you. As men, we have much in common, but we're never identical.

In the above mentioned John 12 passage, it seems clear what Jesus wants to do. It also seems pretty clear that the people won't let him do it. Much of our understanding of the gospel comes down to how we hear Jesus, how we perceive him as he delivers his words. Is Jesus mad and threatening or is he yearning and inviting? His ministry years weren't the only time he felt the sting of being taken advantage of and they weren't the last. His offer still stands today with a wild hope that we will take full advantage of his invitation. Yet far too many still refuse to let him love them—and I am not talking about the unsaved, the unchurched, or the unaware.

I cannot stress this enough. *Healing is required in order to become a Beloved Son.* It is the foundation on which the Father will rebuild a man. God desires to rebuild a man into something every man longs to be: something strong, courageous, fierce, and loving. Deep down, every man longs to come through, to make a difference, to give his life to something larger than himself and a cause worth fighting for. Every man has it in him to be a Beloved Son and then a Warrior.

> God knew what he was doing from the very beginning . . . And then, after getting [his children] established, he stayed with them to the end, gloriously completing what he had begun. (Romans 8:29–30 MSG)

We bear the image of *the* Beloved Son. God wants his image-bearers back so he can heal them, train them, equip them, and then turn them loose into a battle where many are waiting for the sons of God to enter the fight for freedom. If we truly understood what the Father was up to, we would sign on to partner and collaborate with him for the healing and restoration of ourselves! Will we take up the Father's offer? Will we take Jesus by the hand? Will we let the Holy Spirit have his way? It is a surrender that has great and glorious benefits!

BELOVEDNESS

AND THE HOLY SPIRIT DESCENDED UPON HIM IN BODILY FORM LIKE A DOVE, AND A VOICE CAME FROM HEAVEN, *SAYING*, "YOU ARE MY SON, MY BELOVED! IN YOU I AM WELL PLEASED *AND* FIND DELIGHT!"

—*LUKE 3:22*

ALONG WITH THE SPIRIT, A VOICE: "YOU ARE MY SON, CHOSEN AND MARKED BY MY LOVE, PRIDE OF MY LIFE."

—*LUKE 3:22 MSG*

FOR IN CHRIST JESUS YOU ARE ALL SONS OF GOD THROUGH FAITH.

—*GALATIANS 3:26*

Every man lives in a battle over which kingdom we will give our hearts to, and every man has taken hits at varying points along his masculine journey. The wounds of accusation, guilt, shame, and fear are too often left untreated. This prevents a man from receiving and offering love, possibly for the rest of his life. That's what our adversary hopes for: to entangle a man in a web of wounds and lies. The wounding experiences are so well placed and well crafted that a man feels certain their lies are true, and as a result, he becomes entrenched in a false self. Oh, he may get by, but a getting-by life is a far cry from an abundant one.

Understanding is a precious thing. If someone comes up to me and shoves me down, my initial reaction might be to get up and give him a left hook. But if he then explains that there was a snake behind the log I was about to step over, a quick shift takes place. That person turns from bully to hero in a nanosecond. Wounding moments won't be healed or relieved simply by understanding alone, but it is a huge start.

Getting a better understanding of our past sets us up for redemption and our next great step forward: moving into the critical healing and training we need as Beloved Sons. Once we see the lies we have lived under, we can invite Jesus to treat them. These wounded places foster false guilt, shame, and hatred toward ourselves, others, and ultimately, God. Again, these moments had lessons, we learned something from them. Ask yourself, what wounding moments, and the false declarations that rise from them, stand in the way of your freedom? Of your becoming a Beloved Son? What heavy burdens might you be carrying in your heart that it's high time you stopped toting around?

Speaking for myself, the fear of "not being enough" led me to the statement "I'll show you." Sometimes my false self expressed it in anger. At other times, it was more of a desperate plea: "I'll show you I can. Please let me try. Choose me—give me another chance." Either way, I would do anything to not ever feel or be rejected, whether it meant proving myself or pleading. Neither approach displayed my true self and it did not come from a settled heart.

By walking with God, we go back and retrace our steps to find where it hurts. We invite God into our story to show us how to collect and then connect the dots. John Eldredge wrote, "The true story of every person in this world is not the story you see, the external story. The true story of each person is the journey of his or her heart."

RETRACING STEPS

Soren Kierkegaard said, "Philosophy is perfectly right in saying that life must be understood backward. But then one forgets the other clause—that it must be lived forward." Today we say, "Hindsight is twenty-twenty." The path every masculine heart takes in becoming a man includes significant mile markers posted during boyhood.

Early in our story, the enemy of our Life gets a jump on the fight for our hearts. Before we even know we are in a fight, darkness is inflicting injury, wounding us at our core as a boy. The enemy takes ground in our young heart and uses it against us, both in the moment and also in the future. Growing up, some of us had it far worse than others.

As a boy, my friend Tom was scolded time and time again by his father: "I would have never even thought about doing what you did." Another friend, Jay, heard "If you would just apply yourself." Remember Jim? Well, Jim never truly knew what his dad felt toward him. Jim was the oldest of six kids, and there simply wasn't time enough for Dad to get around to all of them. Maybe you are familiar with the concept that "in the absence of information, we go to the negative." Just as kind and loving words bring Life, harsh words or the absence of words bring pain. Doubt, uncertainty, negative judgments, shaming or degrading pronouncements, and even sheer silence all weigh a heart down and make us susceptible to negative interpretations. "Negative" is putting it nicely, some are downright evil. Some are like a pebble in a man's shoe; others are like a backpack full of rocks, while others haunt us. Any and all will hinder and encumber a man on his journey to becoming a man.

With our hearts weighted down, enduring and making the best of things often becomes our plan. Even worse than carrying the pack of lies is getting our strength from its contents. Being fueled by our wounds and their messages is a recipe for disaster in a man's life, one our enemy loves to cook up again and again.

The pack of lies produces the kind of man I call *disoriented*, badly motivating a man to hide, prove, or fear. No man escapes this condition, but every man can be freed from the presence and pain of the lies. The weight of men's packs may differ, but every man has an incredible amount of say as to whether he stays loaded up and weighed down or finds freedom.

Pausing to take off your shoe or unloading your personal pack is an act of the will. Standing firm against evil starts by asking God, *Father, what is this held up in my heart? What am I carrying in me that is set against me?* God has been waiting for you to ask, seek, and knock for quite some time. In response, he may take you into a memory, or he may take you into a current moment to bring the pain of the past to the surface again. Whichever way he chooses, he is inviting you to do some good and important redemptive work by retracing your steps. Unpacking the lies of your past and giving them over to God opens you up to the new packages *he* has for you: gifts of redemption and restoration that make up your Belovedness.

A FATHER'S LOVE

Belovedness is being dearly loved—and we are! (See Rom. 5:8; 1 John 4:10; I John 3:1–2.) But experiencing our belovedness is a choice. Letting, allowing, turning, engaging, reaching up to take our Father's hand, crawling up into his lap . . . all of these expressions describe what we need to do again and again to receive God's love, our part in the collaboration. Doing so both fills and fulfills our relationship with the Father. His pursuit of us with love is met with our wanting to be caught.

Oh, how a man needs this kind of relationship if he is ever going to truly be a man! And it is not a once-and-done proposition. God is continually offering it because we will continually need it. This connecting with God brings both his heart and ours into alignment, God the giver and us the receiver. Repeatedly receiving his love produces what this world and its imitations never can—a settled heart. We experience the lightness and goodness of being loved! But like a cup with a lid on it, we must uncover our heart and open up to being loved; otherwise, God can't pour his love into us.

Paul wrote to the Ephesians,

> Mostly what God does is love you. Keep company with him and learn a life of love. Observe how Christ loved us. His love was not cautious but extravagant. He didn't love in order to get something from us but to give everything of himself to us. Love like that. (Eph. 5:1–2 MSG)

The Father invites a man, his image-bearer, to partner with him, walk with him, trust him, depend on him, and align with him for more. First on the agenda is redeeming the man's past, which is also where the early days of training begin. God is guiding each man toward a great comeback. God directs the steps. Christ has set the table and much of the work has already been accomplished. But we are to play our part. We have a contribution to make, a corresponding choice, an exercise of our will. What God desires to do first in a man's life is to initiate and validate him by pouring his love into him. Doing so settles the man's heart and, in the process, invites him to partner with God in deconstructing the explosive work of the enemy and our false self impostor.

A LESSON FROM EBAY

My dad and I talk each week. Sometimes we catch up on things, maybe a weather report or a medical report. At other times, we hit something deep and important and talk about Life. One of my favorite parts of each call is the end, when I get to see if he will say it: "Love you, bud." He doesn't always go there, but when he does, it lands in a deep and good place inside me.

What if our heavenly Father is *always* saying that, whispering at the end of every call, "I just want you to know that I see you. You are amazing to me. I love you, bud."

This level of intimacy between Father and Son got Jesus crossways with the religious leaders. When Jesus called Yahweh "Abba"—*Daddy*—the Pharisees pulled a muscle: "Who do you think you are—someone special?"

Can't you just see Jesus smile and nod, "Yep." Up until that point in history, no one had ever addressed God so affectionately. It wasn't kosher. I like what Linda Boone writes in her book, *Intimate Life Lessons; Developing the Intimacy with God You Already Have*: "God's desire is to not only have you experience His love, but to totally overwhelm you with His love. To have you experience it to overflowing. To have you sense, feel, taste, and touch His love for you. He really wants you to experience Him!"

Jesus knew he was his Father's Beloved Son, "the firstborn of many" (Rom. 8:29). Jesus wants us to align with the Father—to connect with him and know what Jesus knew (John 17). I believe this is what he meant when he promised us "abundant life" or *Life to the full.*

Just as our hearts, well into manhood, long to hear our earthly fathers deliver the packages of worth and value, "I see you and am proud of you," so our deep masculine hearts also need this from our heavenly Father time and time again. As his image-bearers (Gen. 1:27), we are the object of his fierce and passionate, tender and overtaking love. You are worth the price paid.

If eBay has taught us anything, it has taught us this: the value of a thing is what someone is willing to pay for it. Unlike eBay, the Father wasn't bidding, hoping to get a bargain or steal us away in the last moment. No, the Father made a grand and glorious declaration through the Son: "I love them and I want them. They belong to me!" Through Christ we have been ransomed. The ultimate price is paid—his life in exchange for our freedom, that we might have a Life. That theme is in all the epic stories that move our hearts, because it is in *our* story.

TYPES OF CHRIST

In the story *The Lion, the Witch, and the Wardrobe*, C.S. Lewis offers us a glorious picture of our value. Aslan, the Great Lion, has come to partner with Peter, Susan, Edmund and Lucy and restore all of Narnia, which is under the curse of a perpetual winter without Christmas. A type of Christ, Aslan goes to the Stone Table (symbolizing the cross) to redeem Edmund, Son of Adam (the image-bearer).

Having paid the terrible price of death for Edmund's ransom, the resurrected Aslan tells Lucy and Susan how the "deep magic" of his redemptive work was accomplished: "It means," said Aslan, "that though the witch knew the Deep Magic, there is a magic deeper still which she did not know . . . she would have known that when a willing victim who had committed no treachery was killed in a traitors stead, the (Stone) Table would crack and Death itself would start working backward."

We see this theme repeatedly in all the epic stories. In the movie *Gladiator*, Maximus, slain in the arena for the freedom of his men and of Rome, whispers as he dies, "Now Lucius is safe." In *Braveheart*, William Wallace will not compromise himself nor the mission that found him, so he fights for freedom and inspires a nation to neither settle nor compromise. At the end of the film, the narrator says of Wallace's death by torture, "It did not have the effect Longshanks thought it would. Instead, in the year of our Lord 1314, patriots of Scotland, starving and outnumbered, charged the fields of Bannockburn. They fought like Warrior Poets. They fought like Scotsmen. And won their freedom."

Mr. Darcy comes for Lizzy (*Pride and Prejudice*); Nathaniel rescues Cora (*Last of the Mohicans*); Jack dies so Rose can live (*Titanic*); Noah reads to Ally and she remembers (*The Notebook*); because Ray builds it, his father comes and there is restoration (*Field of Dreams*). All the things that move our hearts in these great stories are but shadows of the Larger Story.

All of these characters, these *types of Christ* personified in the epic tales, borrow their strength and heroic storylines from the one true Hero. Everything we love about these heroes we find true of our Savior-King who traded places with us so we might be free (Gal. 5:1). He comes, he rescues, he heals, he defends, he sacrifices, and he dies inviting us to live. He restores all for love and in love he moves our hearts to freedom.

The freedom Christ purchased was a freedom from the penalty and presence of sin in our lives—freedom *from* so we can be free to *become.* Free to become *more,* to become who we truly have in us to be. This isn't just a good deal for us. God also benefits greatly. He gets what he wants. He gets back the desire of his heart, what he is most fiercely after: his image-bearers, his beloved children, and the chance to love them.

Over and over we tell tales of love and sacrifice, rescue and redemption, good versus evil, all with the hope of the great line, "And they lived happily ever after." We don't just watch these stories. We *feel* them. Yet too often, this response of the heart is lost in translation. We men are unable or unwilling to see and hear these stories, which are reflections of our stories in the context of the Larger Story. The heroes in the stories that inspire us invite us to see what our hearts are made for. When we fail to connect the themes in these stories with the themes in our own stories, then we miss the larger life for which we are being called. Often we miss our moment to step up and in to play the hero's part because we don't see and hear these moments of invitation. Opportunities to love well, fight well, and offer a true masculine presence, compassion, and strength.

THE JOY SET BEFORE HIM

The writer of the book of Hebrews states that "for the joy set before him [Christ] endured the cross (Heb. 12:2 NIV). Guess who *the joy* was that was set before him? You and me! We are that joy! This is to be another part our foundation, a reality we must feel, know, and enjoy. Brent Curtis, coauthor with John Eldredge of *The Sacred Romance*, wrote, "We are the ones to be called Fought Over, Captured and Rescued, and Pursued. It seems remarkable, incredible, and too good to be true. There really is something desirable within me, something the King of the universe has moved heaven and earth to get."

We are his Beloved, the joy set before him. Every man must experience this in a position of knowing who he is as a Beloved Son, and return here again and again.

As a father of three children, I often get to see this truth in action. My kids have no idea how much I love them, nor do they know the depth and weight of what I am doing on their behalf or how I am working behind the scenes to provide for and protect them. Just as I lived for a long time having no idea of all that my father was doing for me, so my children go unaware. I don't see it as my "job" to love my kids (although there are those days when it seems like a task!). Rather, I see it as a challenging and wonderful opportunity to look out for them, to love and delight in them.

Does our heavenly Father *have* to do the same for us—or does he *long* to?

It was Jesus who said, "How much more will your Father in heaven give good gifts to those who ask him!" (Matt. 7:11 NIV).

For the record, Christ's followers *are* Beloved Sons. Our freedom is won. We are adopted into the Father's family, and our name is written in the Lamb's Book of Life. Through Christ we are sons—sons who have been pulled from dead end streets and orphanages and given Life: acceptance, worth, and a place to belong. We have literally and transactionally been brought into the glorious family of God with all its privileges and responsibilities. This has always been the Father's intention (Rom. 8, John 3:16, Luke 19:10, Matt. 20:28): Life through Jesus and Life with him. Through the work of Christ in his cross, resurrection, and ascension, we have been ransomed, rescued, and redeemed. Much of the heavy lifting has already been done. Now, most of what the Father is up to in our lives is *restoring* us through healing, initiation, validation, and training. We turn in what isn't us (the false self) for what is … our true self. And in the process we move from disoriented to oriented, from unsettled to settled.

SETTLING OUR HEARTS

I was twenty years old, a junior in college, and had just returned from a two-month summer mission trip. Having received financial support from friends at church and a couple of the Sunday school classes, I was now reporting in. I hit the first adult class and shared some important stories and a few of the crazy things my team encountered. I thanked the members of the class for their generous support and moved down the hall to the donors in the next class.

My hand was on the door to open it when I heard my dad's voice. Peering through the little window on the side, I saw him standing in front of the class. He started to speak of how proud he was of me, how the trip had impacted my life, and surprisingly to me, his life. Then he paused and brought his hand to his face. I thought for a minute that he was laughing. Then I realized he was crying. I waited a moment, then jostled the door and entered the room. He turned, smiled, and announced, "Here he is. He can tell you all about it."

That was one of the best days of my life, because I could *feel* my dad's love for me.

Twice in the Gospels, the Father in heaven made a validating statement to the Son on earth and to all who were within earshot. The first time was at the baptism of Jesus:

> And the Holy Spirit descended upon Him in bodily form like a dove, and a voice came from heaven, *saying,* "You are My Son, My Beloved! In You I am well pleased *and* find delight!" (Luke 3:22; cf. Matt. 3:17)

The second time was at Jesus' transfiguration:

> While he was still speaking, behold, a shining cloud [composed of light] overshadowed them, and a voice from the cloud said, "This

> is My Son, My Beloved, with Whom I am [and have always been] delighted. Listen to Him!" (Matt. 17:5; cf. Luke 9:34–35; Mark 9:7)

In these scenes, I imagine a deep and loving James Earl Jones-type voice definitively broadcasting the profound love a father wants to express about his son: "This is my son." How affirming, how validating, how loving! "Proud" might be the best word we could use today; "well-pleased" was how it came across in the first century. What son doesn't long for such words? And what good father would ever withhold them?

It isn't hard for me to imagine that Jesus had more of these moments, receiving more validation and more instruction from his Father. Quiet and private moments spent together, Father and Son. Maybe that is why Jesus snuck off so often to spend some good time with Abba-Dad. Some of my friends whose fathers have passed away tell me, "What I wouldn't do to have one more day with him." I suspect Jesus knew this feeling as well and he connected with his Father as often as he could.

ENGAGING OUR HEARTS

If Jesus got to hear this from the Father, perhaps even *needed* to hear it, then the effect must have been gloriously settling. Why settling? Because both times, what happened next in Jesus' life was *un*settling. On both occasions Jesus went from validation into battle.

The first time, the Father validates the Son as he emerges, dripping wet, from his baptism. The Scriptures record what happens next:

> Jesus, full of the Holy Spirit, returned from the Jordan and was led by the Spirit into the desert, where for forty days he was tempted by the devil. (Luke 4:1–2 NIV).

The second time after his transfiguration Jesus comes down from the mountain and proceeds by instruction from the Father to go to Jerusalem, where at first he is greeted with palm branches but then is led to a garden, then to a crown of thorns and finally to a cross.

These validating moments are more than pep talks; they are ceremonies, occasions where one heart acknowledges and validates another. Jesus seems to have needed these moments, because the moments to come would question him at his core and battle for his heart.

In the desert, Satan challenged his identity: "*If* you are the Son of God . . ."

During his trial, the crowds in the streets declared, in effect, "You can't be the Son of God!"

Experiencing that his Father's heart toward him was good enabled the Son to endure whatever might come his way. Jesus' heart was full and settled, and therefore his mission remained clear to the end:

> For even the Son of Man did not come to be served, but to serve, and to give his life as a ransom for many. (Mark 10:45 NIV)
>
> For the Son of Man has come to seek and to save that which was lost. (Luke 19:10 NASB)
>
> I have come that they may have life, and have it to the full. (John 10:10 NIV)

BEING LOVED

One of my earliest memories goes back to when I was about four years old, and my younger brother, three. At the end of every day, he and I would go on alert, listening for Dad's fan-tailed Chevy to pull into the driveway. Dad usually prompted us with a couple of pops on the horn. My brother and I would gasp, jump up, and run around yelling, "He's home, he's home!" My mom would jump in and add to the drama with "Hurry, hurry!" as she went to the hall closet, grabbed a big blanket, and brought it into the family room. That was our cue to crouch on our knees and tuck in our arms, legs, and heads; then Mom flapped the blanket out like she was spreading it for a picnic and covered the two of us, hiding us from Dad just in time.

Into the house Dad would step, hollering, "Hi, Mom! Where are the boys?" Then he'd say, "Are they in the closet?" as he loudly turned the knob and swung the closet door open.

"Nooo, not in the closet. Are they in the kitchen?" We could hear chairs in the kitchen getting resituated.

By now, my brother and I were about to burst. Dad would tromp back into the family room, whereupon we would spring up and yell, "SURPRISE!" What happened next was Belovedness: two boys and their father, tangled up in a blanket, laughing, tickling, and hugging.

This is what it is to be loved, to be fiercely pursued with affection. I'm not sure who enjoyed it more, Dad or us boys.

When we release God from the lie that he is either an angry dictator, has better things to do, or is simply a distant casual observer, and embrace him as the Father of all fathers, then we might begin to know we truly are the Beloved Sons. The cross lavishly accomplished more than forgiveness. It afforded us the privilege to be reunited, to feel our value and worth to a Father who paid everything he had to set us free (Rom. 5:8; Gal. 5:1; Luke 19:10; John 3:16; 1 Cor. 6:20). If you didn't get that kind of love from your earthly father (and far too many men didn't), then you need to circle back with your Father God. He will provide it for your heart.

EXPERIENCING THE TRUTH

The role and mission of an earthly father is to walk with God in such a way as to show his sons (and daughters) what the heavenly Father is like and, at some point, invite his son to turn to the Father for continued fathering. Author and counselor John Eldredge says in *Fathered by God*, "We aren't meant to figure out life on our own. God wants to father us. The truth is, He has been fathering us for a long time—we just haven't had the eyes to see it. He wants to father us much more intimately, but we have to be in a posture to receive."

But count on this: the lines of intimacy and communication, of receiving love from our Father God, have been *infiltrated*. Sabotaged. Compromised. And so the first captive I need to set free is *me*.

Partnering with God, a man can hunt down that which has previously hunted him: the agents of darkness that taunt, assault, and labor to build and use a man's false self to entangle, enslave, and encumber (2 Peter 2:20, Gal. 4:9, Heb. 12:1). Remember, John 10:10 (NIV) has a Part A: "The thief comes only to steal and kill and destroy." Thank goodness for Part B: "I have come . . ."

With each reclaiming of what was lost, stolen, or put to death in a man's heart, a man becomes more and more free. Freedom to receive love results in a man becoming more whole, and wholeness increases the man's freedom to offer and bestow love. And that is what the battle is *all* about: LOVE—a man's ability to be loved and his increasing skill and ability to love others. The creator of our hearts knows how to treat our wounds and bring about their healing by removing the old and replacing it with the new. The truth replaces the lies. And just as each wounding moment is an experience, so it is also an experience when the truth comes and replaces the lie on our journey with God. Jesus said,

> You will know the truth, and the truth will set you free. (John 8:32 NIV)

With our acceptance of his invitation to heal, and with our participation, Jesus removes the lies and heals the broken places of our hearts with his presence and his words. He deconstructs the time bombs inside us. He sets us up to move forward freely without further injury to ourselves and, more significantly, the others in our life who are there in order for us to love. If wounded hearts wound, then free hearts can free hearts.

WHAT HAPPENED TO YOU?

What if the intended role of the Beloved Sons is this:

> *To receive life and love in order to fight for life and love.*

What if it's about having a settled heart where rejection and insult have no place to land? A heart on which guilt, shame, and fear have no effect because we *know* better? When we hear the Father tell us who we truly are, then the matter isn't up for debate and our hearts are settled. Yet our wills figure into the process of settling; they need to come in alignment with his will.

John Eldredge wrote in his book *Epic*, "We live in a Love Story set in the midst of a great and fierce battle." No man goes through this journey without taking wounds to the heart.

Moments in the stories of our lives—that can pinpoint for a man why he is so angry, confused, hesitant, determined, loud, passive, hiding, afraid, lonely, embarrassed, striving, self-critical, demanding, demeaning, vengeful, hurtful, sarcastic, aggressive, silent—become opportunities for freedom.

However young we were or if it were just the other day when we agreed to the judgments and accusations of the enemy, and when we accepted and signed for the package from the kingdom of darkness, we gave away something: access to our hearts. Now our adversaries wield an authority within us to bind and oppress us, and the wild thing is we gave them permission. Trust me, you want this stuff out of you. Whatever darkness we subscribed to, it's time to unsubscribe.

God will show you what and where the lies are, what they have come to mean in your life, what power they hold over you, and what they have produced. He will reveal how they have come between you and your capital-L Life.

Healing *starts* with understanding. In *It's Your Call*, Gary Barkalow writes,

> If you go back into a person's story, you can usually find their deepest desires and the assault against those desires—the words and actions that made those desires seem foolish, or dangerous . . . Look, the enemy doesn't have to kill us to prevent us from becoming a display of God's splendor. He just has to distance us from our hearts and desires so that we become disoriented, disabled, deactivated and disconnected. This distancing happens slowly, incrementally over time until we are so far from our heart that we don't even know it exists.

Healing the heart is our Father's imperative work and our introduction to training. Training? Yes, *training*, learning to experience being a Beloved Son. In the midst of battle, the enemy counts on a man never experiencing that he is a Beloved Son. Lack of this aspect of training makes for a far easier fight for our enemy and a continued small-story existence for us, dominated by the false-self creature.

It is time to turn this around, to engage by taking up the Father on his offer to heal our hearts. Time to begin the great comeback and watch "all hell break loose" because it *will* break loose so we can break free!

Far more is opposed to your Life than you know—because you are far more significant and valuable to God than you can possibly imagine. You are more crucial to the kingdom than you ever dared to hope and there are things in it for you to do:

> I assure you, most solemnly I tell you, if anyone steadfastly believes in Me, he will himself be able to do the things that I do; and he will do even greater things than these, because I go to the Father. (John 14:12)

Really? Even greater things? Is that your experience? Looking back on my own life and what happened to me, I can tell you that I experienced something different. Before we can move forward, there is one critical place we must explore for deep, subtle, and powerful lies. There was a blockage in me to healing and freedom. It was in places I never would have guessed, and it damaged me in ways I didn't realize: deep down, at the heart level, where it matters most, I didn't trust God. And it is impossible to let someone you don't trust love you.

Way down inside myself, I believed some lies about my Father.

But like many of my wounds and their messages . . . when he touched these places, everything changed.

BEING FATHERED

TRAIN UP A CHILD IN THE WAY HE SHOULD GO [AND IN KEEPING WITH HIS INDIVIDUAL GIFT OR BENT], AND WHEN HE IS OLD HE WILL NOT DEPART FROM IT.

—*PROVERBS 22:6*

"ABBA (DADDY), FATHER."

—*JESUS*

Every man has had authority figures in his life, and much of what a man perceives about God and projects onto God was shaped by those authority figures. At the top of every man's authority list is his earthly father. How your dad handled your heart has shaped you and contributed significantly to how you perceive God.

The odds of an unsettled heart falling then arriving at a disoriented man's view of God and life is 100 percent. You can have all the theology right and still have the Father wrong. Like memorizing facts for a history exam, you can pass the test but still not love the characters, enjoy the story, and engage in the drama. It is the difference between the head versus the heart. Starting from varying degrees of inaccuracy, men must journey individually with God to discover both who they are and who they aren't—and just as importantly, a man must discover both who the Father is and who he isn't.

For one thing, he isn't our earthly father. Like us, our fathers were wounded men with wounded hearts. They lived in the same story we live in. Our fathers and their fathers before them also had it rough, far worse than most of us sons and grandsons will ever know.

I often hear men say, "Dad did the best he could." That can be either an excuse or compassion. It all depends on how well the son knows his father's story. Most thirty to fifty-year-old men don't know it and haven't earned the right to say their dad did his best. What a man discovers from learning his father's story will change his heart toward his father. Misinterpretation and excuses are replaced with understanding and compassion.

Besides our dads many other authority figures have had access to our hearts along the journey. Some had a positive impact, but there were others who should have provided for us and protected us—but didn't. Tough coaches who punished us with extra wind sprints, challenging teachers who enjoyed pointing out when we answered wrong, preachers yelling at us, older siblings embarrassing us, mothers "surviving" us, so-called friends lost in their own small stories betraying us: all of these reflect a reality I continually stress with a maxim I hope you'll memorize: *wounded hearts wound hearts.*

THE WAY WE SEE HIM

When my oldest daughter was about eight, she asked me if I thought she looked pretty. "Absolutely," I said. "Beautiful. Gorgeous. *Sooo* pretty." With a hint of dissatisfaction, she replied, "Dad, you're supposed to say that."

My daughter's statement expressed the way that I frequently felt about my heavenly Father when I was growing up—that He sent his Son to die for me, but that was his duty—that it was a large inconvenience to him—that He loves me—but then, he has to.

In other words, my Father didn't love me just because he loved me. He loved me because he was *supposed to* love me. It was a matter of obligation, not delight.

And on my part, I needed to be thankful and obedient and not rock the boat. Let a sleeping God lie. Try not to do anything stupid. But if I did, if I *sinned*, I was to wake God up to the fact, ask him for forgiveness, and then check myself into the penalty box to suffer for a time until he calmed down. Some days, the suffering started even before I hit the penalty box. That was usually my cue: *You have done something wrong; now go to your room!*

Most Sunday mornings at church reinforced this underachieving and grim life cycle: "Thank you for coming; you don't deserve his love; come back next week for more reminders of the abundant life." If I could just pull it together, maybe he would bless me or at least not punish me. Probably that wouldn't happen but I had to at least keep trying.

That is how I saw God for much of my life. And I'm not the only one. Many believe God is mostly mad at us, on the verge of getting even, and setting some record straight. Others see God as distant and disinterested, unconcerned about our daily affairs. Then again, maybe he's behind the inconveniences and hardships of our lives. I wish I had a nickel for every time I've heard a man talk about God "whacking" him upside the head with a two-by-four.

Which of that is true of God?

Is any of it true?

If there is more to God than that, then how does it all work? Who is he really? What is he truly like?

IS HE GOOD?

If a man lives with an undercurrent of mistrust in the Father in his deep masculine heart, then becoming the Beloved Son will be unattainable. Walking with the Father will be impossible, and fighting for the kingdom will not go well.

This is where many men's ministries fall woefully short of their mark. Their default is to start with training men what to do (or not to do) and how to live. In other words, they focus on men's behavior rather than on reworking the foundation of *who men are and who God is.* If they do address the "who we are," it is usually with a list of biblical truths to memorize or paragraphs of character traits to which we should aspire. Not all of this is wrong, but it is ill-timed. It puts the proverbial cart before the horse.

We've got to set the horse back out in front, beginning with what the *heart* of God is really like. Our greatest obstacle to becoming Beloved Sons may well be the lies we've bought about our heavenly Father and the belief that he is anything other than good.

As I've shared, for much of my life, I believed that God was mostly just a little ticked off. Not so mad that another flood was coming (he did promise not to do that again), but mad enough that I didn't want to cross him or draw more attention to myself than necessary. Opening my heart to examine how I really saw the Father, and why, and inviting him to show me, was both a challenge and a milestone in upgrading my beliefs. My "after" is still in the making, but I can tell you, it is far better than my before—and my Father is far better than I used to believe.

It is impossible for us to love what we don't trust. The nineteenth-century Scottish pastor and author George MacDonald once wrote, "To be trusted is a greater compliment than to be loved." We are loved to the degree that we are known and in human relationships we are known to the degree that we trust. God, of course, knows us completely and loves us unconditionally whether we trust him or not. The question then becomes, will we let him love us? Choosing to trust him is the key. In the words of Jesus, "Trust in me . . . let me love you." (John 14:1; 15:9). The Father is trustworthy! He knows what each and every man can become and he is all in.

Satan also knows what a man might become—and fears it! There are more forces at work in our story than just God and us. There is an evil that is out to steal, kill, and destroy. Evil is lurking, working far deeper behind a man's front lines than most men realize. More on this in pages to come, but suffice it to say, we live in a perilous fight, a dangerous environment, a place of high stakes. That is why I have written five chapters on why a man must first secure his heart. He must discern the propaganda he has been fed about God and himself and find his way to the true heart of the Father, trusting that the Father can show him who he truly isn't, who he truly is, and then set him free!

THE ONE FROM WHOM LOVE IS COMING

Is God good? All the other significant moments of redemption, recovery, training, and initiating a man in becoming a Beloved Son depend on the answer to this foundational question. The answer is always *yes*—but the enemy of our heart will always attempt to tell us no. It makes sense: how can a man be the Beloved if he doesn't trust the One from whom the love is coming and the form and fashion in which it comes?

If the source of love is believed to be imperfect, then the message of love from the Father of love will fall on deaf ears and a hard heart. A distrustful man will believe God isn't there or that God doesn't really care, or worse, that his life is a great disappointment to God. Most men deal with at least one, if not all, of these haunting messages daily and their responses vary. One man will try to hide so the messages won't come true. Another man will attempt some form of effort or control in order to dispel the messages. Neither man is living from a settled heart. The opinions and criticisms of others rule both of their lives. Neither man is ready to love; each is living afraid.

The fourth chapter of 1 John, verse 18 tells us that "perfect love casts out fear." If you could experience perfect love—complete, lavish, unconditional, sacrificial, intimate, deep, consistent, and continuing—would you allow it? Would you accept it? Would you enjoy it and its effect on your heart? Such love settles the issue of hiding and controlling. In the face of it, there is no need to hide, strive, or manipulate. *You and I are loved in just that way. We have nothing to prove, hide, or fear.*

Tragically, the enemy of our hearts planted the first seeds of doubt in Eden with the message, *You cannot trust the heart of God; he is holding out on you. Surely you won't die.* That lie continues to this day, perpetuating Satan's scheme to make our hearts distrust God's heart. Today, as on that day, the image-bearers take the bait and suffer the consequences. We have been unsettled and unsure of the heart of the Father. And today the Father asks the same question that he asked of Adam in the garden, *Son, where are you? Do you know where you are?*

THE PRODIGAL FATHER

A huge part of Christ's mission was to set the record straight about the Father's heart. Most of the teachings and parables of Jesus included significant "intel" about the Father. After all, you can't talk about the kingdom and not talk about the heart of God. Almost every parable Jesus tells is an invitation to see the Father.

For example, take the parable known as "The Prodigal Son." Maybe it should be retitled. The word *prodigal* means "spending resources freely and recklessly; being wasteful . . . extravagant . . . having or giving something in a lavish way." Who's the one being prodigal here?

> When [the son] was still a long way off, his father saw him. His heart pounding, he ran out, embraced him, and kissed him. The son started his speech: "Father, I've sinned against God, I've sinned before you; I don't deserve to be called your son ever again." But the father wasn't listening. He was calling to the servants, "Quick. Bring a clean set of clothes and dress him. Put the family ring on his finger and sandals on his feet. . . . We're going to feast! We're going to have a wonderful time! My son is here—given up for

> dead and now alive! Given up for lost and now found!" And they began to have a wonderful time! (Luke 15:20–24 MSG)

Is this story really about the son who ran away? What if Jesus was sharing the story to spotlight the Father? And what if, in telling it, Jesus was forecasting what he himself would one day do for Peter, reinstating the one who denied him three times (John 21:15-19)?

The Father's extravagant, lavish—dare we say reckless—and redeeming love is ready to cure our greatest ache. The Father's reaction was so over the top that the older son, who had never gone astray, responded, "Really? Really, Dad? You are going to do *that* for this wasteful, betraying, dishonoring son of yours?"

Simply put, the Father answered, "Yes, yes, and *yes*!"

And the Father doesn't stop with just his sons. No. All creation gets in on the deal of his love and care.

> Look at the birds of the air; they neither sow nor reap nor gather into barns, and yet your heavenly Father keeps feeding them. Are you not worth much more than they? (Matt. 6:26)

It is more than comforting. It is *necessary* to know that Someone is watching out for us, caring for us, making the wrongs in our life right, and giving good and meaningful gifts.

> If your little boy asks for a serving of fish, do you scare him with a live snake on his plate? If your little girl asks for an egg, do you trick her with a spider? As bad as you are, you wouldn't think of such a thing—you're at least decent to your own children. And don't you think the Father who conceived you in love will give the Holy Spirit when you ask him? (Luke 11:11–13 MSG)

What kind of gifts from the Father are you getting? Can't you just hear Jesus telling how great his Dad is? In the passage above, it is still the preseason before the gift of the Holy Spirit was fully delivered on the day of Pentecost. Now that we have the Holy Spirit, the gifts are to continue way beyond a single moment. They are to flow and be continually dropped off on the doorsteps of our heart. Beloved Sons with eyes to see and ears to hear know of what I write. The Father deeply wants his gifts to get through to us so we can *see* and *hear* and *experience* that he is good and has good in store for us as he grows us into men.

IT'S A SETUP

Because we are meant for such a glorious and weighty love, we are all set up for a fall: disappointment, heartache, and rejection. It's a setup because there is an adversary, a great villain in our story, who is hell-bent on making sure we do not know and experience *unconditional love.*

Our stories are full of people, other image-bearers who love imperfectly. There are dark forces in every man's story that make sure he feels, hears, and experiences . . .

You are alone.
Trust no one.
Arrange for life and love (validation, acceptance, worth) for yourself.

The conditional-love moments in a man's life result in his believing, *If I could do more of this or less of that, be this or be that, then people would love me.* Strategies form and harden in our inmost being and become the "system" a man both runs and is subject to. Repeatedly, that system attempts to create or manipulate ways in which a man can provide love for himself. The ol' "If it is to be, it is up to me" way of life lodges deep in the heart and clouds over every opportunity to arrange for love, tipping the vote of acceptance and worth his way. As a boy I learned to perform in order to obtain love, validation, acceptance, and worth and to create distance in order to protect myself from the pain of not experiencing the love I craved. This elaborate and pervasive system grows with the boy and takes its full, wretched effect years later when the boy becomes a man. Dark forces use this internal, conditional system, along with the opinions and words of others to reinforce their lies. Conditional love and the enemy align, setting the man up for a fall. It is not *if* we are disappointed or become a disappointment but *when*. Someone doesn't make us happy or we find it impossible to keep another happy—what then?

Taking matters of love and life into his own hands is guaranteed to promote and perpetuate a man's false self, which is self-reliant, self-sufficient, self-protecting, and self-promoting. The false-self life will always obstruct the true man and real Life: Life that is abundant and full is *uninhibited* by expectations, opinions, and circumstances. Our Father promises another Life to us. He guarantees another Love. When we seek him, he finds us. Then, and only then does the fall become a setup of a different kind: the setup for redemption … a man's great and glorious comeback. I am not talking about salvation which is the first move, or the installation of the equipment—the new heart—which is what a man needs to start learning how to Live. I am talking about *sanctification*. The healing from the inside out. The ability to now see what was in the way of truly seeing Life.

When a man turns away from the old false-self construct (of wounds, coping mechanisms, and conditions) and moves intentionally toward the Author of Life for the new Life Jesus has custom-made for him, everything changes again. And again and again. It takes time, a lifetime, but it happens choice by choice. The man makes his comeback and becomes who he truly is, the Beloved Son.

Love changes us. When we experience our true Father loving us, it heals us, restores us, and then sets us loose. But only if we come to him. And the primary reason we don't is that we don't trust him. Loving is trusting and trusting is loving. Each time I turn to the Father in trust, he responds with more training in the new ways of Love and Life, and I am another step closer to becoming the real me and another step further from who I am not.

IF YOU HAVE SEEN ME

After all they had been through together, all the miracles, teachings, campfires, long walks, times amid the multitudes, and quiet, private moments, the disciples still didn't quite get it. Right up until the end of Jesus' life, there were more than a few misunderstandings flying around among his closest friends about just exactly who he was and how it all was going to work. Three years they had accompanied Jesus. His great expedition became theirs. They were *there*; they witnessed the lion's share of the work of Jesus, more moments of healing and teaching than could possibly be recorded (John 21:25).

Yet in the late hours of Jesus' life, one of his closest friends requested of him, "Show us the Father." Jesus basically replied, "I did," likely with one of those classic Jesus smiles. "He who has seen Me has seen the Father" (John 14:8–14 NKJV).

If *they* can miss him, what chance do we have of seeing him for who he truly is? "The Father and I are one," Jesus said in John 10:30.

We have all misjudged Jesus. In discovering that I *also* had him wrong, I have found out that he cares a lot more about setting the record straight than I do about getting it straight. Setting me straight is high on his list, and doing it with love, kindness, mercy, and grace seems to be his favorite method. John Eldredge wrote in *The Way of the Wild Heart*:

> Wherever you are in your ability to believe it at this moment in your life, at least you can see what Jesus is driving at. You have a good Father. He is better than you thought. He cares. He really does. He's kind and generous. He's out for your best. This is absolutely central to the teaching of Jesus, though I have to admit, it never really struck a chord in me until I began to think through the need for masculine initiation, and came straight up against the question, "But who will do the initiating?"

NOTORIOUS LOVE

If there was one thing for which Jesus was notorious, it was love. Everywhere he went he loved on people, providing more and more and more evidence of what love really *looks* like. Jesus is love personified. Jesus initiates me over and over. It starts with his moving toward me. And in return, he wants me to move toward him.

The more he heals me, the more he wants me to walk with him. At a few stops along Jesus' ministry, he declared, in effect, "No more healing. You don't want me—you want the miracle. But there is no miracle without me" (Matt. 12:38–42). When we get him, we get the healing. Remember the story of the ten lepers in Luke 17? After they were healed, one came back. Only one. Just one wanted the One who did the healing, not just the healing.

At a critical point in Jesus' ministry, the disciples were faced with the choice to follow the rest of the crowds who were turning their backs on Jesus. Peter piped up on behalf of the twelve: "Where would we go? You have the life" (John 6:67–68). The fisher of men had the right idea. Years later, an aged and matured Peter wrote to the churches of the first century:

> May grace (God's favor) and peace (which is perfect well-being, all necessary good, all spiritual prosperity, and freedom from fears and agitating passions and moral conflicts) be multiplied to you in [the full, personal, precise, and correct] knowledge of God and of Jesus our Lord. For His divine power has bestowed upon us all things that [are requisite and suited] to life and godliness, through the [full, personal] knowledge of Him Who called us by *and* to His own glory and excellence (virtue). By means of these He has bestowed on us His precious and exceedingly great promises, so that through them you may escape [by flight] from the moral decay (rottenness and corruption) that is in the world because of covetousness (lust and greed), and become sharers (partakers) of the divine nature. (2 Peter 1:2-4)

How right Peter was the first time. "Where would we go? You are life." Sounds to me like the Peter of many years later is offering a taste of something he has stocked up on over his time as Jesus' friend. Peter feels compelled to share. (Don't we all when we find something glorious and good?) The old apostle *knows*, not just in theory but through life-altering encounters and Life-giving experiences, that the Father is *good*. Jesus made sure of it and makes sure of it still.

ABBA, FATHER

It all gets a bit messy when our life experiences tell us, *That kind of love—perfect love—it doesn't exist.* It does exist, and it's not just words on a page or theology in a book. It's far more and far greater than that. Those who experienced it wrote about it to provide a scriptural reference point so we could know that when God's love overtakes us, it is true. Our hearts are thus reassured that such love exists.

Paul says in Romans 15:13,

> May the God of your hope so fill you with all joy and peace in believing [through the experience of your faith] that by the power of the Holy Spirit you may abound *and* be overflowing (bubbling over) with hope.

Oh, to hope again! It is very far from "irrelevant" or "uneventful." The Father's love has a tangible effect. If you haven't been hit by it lately, overrun with his love, then it's time. If you haven't felt the goosebumps, been warm all over, experienced a cool chill, or felt a flood of joy filling you up, warming you, taking you to a place—if you haven't felt *giddy*—then it's time!

The question is, do you see it? In Romans 8, Paul says we can be certain that "every detail in our lives of love for God is worked into something good" (v. 28 MSG). A few verses later Paul concludes the chapter with,

> I am persuaded beyond doubt (am sure) that neither death nor life, nor angels nor principalities, nor things impending *and* threatening nor things to come, nor powers, nor height nor depth, nor anything else in all creation will be able to separate us from the love of God which is in Christ Jesus our Lord. (vv. 38–39)

My friend Scott experiences the love of the Father when God speaks to him in music, license plates, and ads in the newspaper (to mention just a few of the ways). Scott and I have a couple of worship songs we really like, and you wouldn't believe how often Pandora or Sirius or XM radio play them when we are together. Call it coincidence, but Scott and I know better. These are love notes from our Father right to our hearts.

Ashley believes God made butterflies for her. Kelly sees God in baseball. Travis encounters God's love in every hunt he goes on. David sees the Father in the houses he restores. My wife, Robin, feels his love when the clock turns to 11:11. She will say to me, "Look, Jesus loves me"; it's something special just between him and her. Shouldn't every love affair have something that's just between two hearts?

It starts and ends with the Father's love. He loved us first and he loves us most; he is the author and perfecter of our faith, and that faith is based on love.

Walking along the beach a few weeks ago, Robin and I strolled past hundreds of thousands of seashells, most of them broken. One shell among the masses caught my eye. There it was, looking up at me, the size of a quarter and the perfect shape of a heart! What are the odds? You can't tell me the Father wasn't saying to the Son, "Watch this, watch our boy Michael! Wait for it, wait for it . . . there! I *knew* he would find it."

There *is* a life the Father is imparting and bestowing to all his sons and daughters. It is a life *of* love and of training *in* love. Through ceremonies of validation and initiation, trials and errors, redoes and redeems, playgrounds and battlefields that invite us to engage, the

Father's love delivers Life to our hearts and then gives us the packages we can deliver to the hearts of others. Nothing can separate us from the Father's love. *Nothing.* And yet, there are things that can and do get in the way.

THE SWORD OF ARAGORN

The air is chilly, but the sun is warming me as I sit nervously, hopeful yet also bracing for disappointment.

I've never done this before. What if God doesn't answer? What if I'm not ready or I'm not good enough? What if he does speak and it isn't good?

Sitting there on the side of a mountain overlooking miles of valley below, I am experiencing uncertainty, apprehension, and the feeling that I am not qualified. Yet here I am anyway, optimistic that if this works it will change everything.

What do you think of me, Father? Who am I to you?

I sit, still and listening, waiting for a reply. I have never done this before. It is my first time asking the Creator of all that is good such a personal question.

All my previous conversations with God over the past thirty-some years of my life haven't really been conversations. They've been more monologues than dialogues. I did all the talking and he did all the listening. I would give him my list and hope we would have time to get to it.

Not this time. This time I have asked a question and I await an answer.

It doesn't take long—the distractions, I mean. *Oh, look at that bird! I wonder what kind of rock this is. Wow, the clouds sure are fluffy.*

Re-engaging, I close my eyes and drop back to my question, *God, what do you think of me? Who am I to you?*

My thoughts go to the epic story *The Lord of the Rings* and the character Aragorn. *I love that story, and I love who Aragorn is in his journey of becoming. He is brave, courageous, strong, and cunning. . . .*

Again drifting. *I suck at this!*

God, what do you think of me and who am I to you?

The character of Aragorn invades my thoughts and my time with God again. *I love how he fights for a cause larger than himself, all the while wrestling with a deep secret. I love his friends and the fellowship he is a part of.*

Dang it! Come on, Thompson. Back to prayer. This is serious! Stop messing around!

Too late. Time is up. I have to rejoin the ranks of the men at the retreat. Pushing up from the ground I conclude, "either God must be busy or I'm not doing it right." Neither answer feels good.

Fast-forward eight weeks. It is my fortieth birthday. Family is in town and we have had a great day. Cake, cards and presents!

There among the little pile of gifts and cards is a long box—a *really* long box and thin. I have been dropping hints for a shotgun, and by the looks of things today might be the day. Then again, it also could be golf clubs. My dad and brother are pretty good golfers and they are always trying to buy me a better game. It hasn't worked yet, but I always appreciate their efforts.

All the gifts are unwrapped except for this one. Obviously, it's the BIG ONE!

I truly feel a bit giddy unwrapping it. I remove the lid . . . my eyes take in what's inside . . .

And I am stunned.

Suddenly I'm both in the family room of my house and back on the side of the mountain at the men's retreat. Because gleaming up at me from the box is the Sword of Aragorn.

Tears begin to swell. Warmth pours into my body. Seconds pass. No one says a word.

Then my wife, Robin, breaks in. "Do you like it? I wasn't sure which sword to get you. There were dozens to pick from. I just knew God wanted me to get you a sword. Several weeks ago he laid it on my heart. I had another one picked out but it didn't feel right—then this one came to me on the website as an option. Is it all right? Do you like it? It's the sword of . . ."

I already know. God has partnered with my wife to give me a sword and not just any sword. This particular sword.

The Sword of Aragorn.

My wife and my Father have done this: affirmed me, validated me, and invited me to see who I am.

This—*this*—is Belovedness.

The Father has given me many, many other good gifts since he gave me the sword. But I know I'm not the only one for whom he does this. What have *you* gotten? How is the Father showing you who you are?

The Father is at work authoring, perfecting, and *rebuilding* something. That something is actually a someone—you and me. The Father is building his sons into men, strong and good men who bear his image. It starts with a foundation of receiving love and advances through healing our hearts through all the means necessary for our becoming his Beloved Sons.

For you see, it is Beloved Sons to whom he desires to entrust his power and authority. Some of the lessons are hard. But that is what makes the "ceremony" of becoming so good. It is the process we, his image-bearers, must go through in order for Life to be redeemed and restored to us. And as I have shared . . . it doesn't end there. We are then called to be his intimate allies, the peacekeepers, the courageous and compassionate, the fearless and caring—the Warriors of his kingdom, the men who know how to fight and know how to dance.

MADE FOR LOVE

What do I, the oldest of three boys, know about raising three girls? Answer: Nothing! Nada, zilch. But I am learning! They make sure of that. It has been on-the-job training from the first moment they were placed in my arms.

I vowed early in the game, "These little girls will know my arms in hope of preventing them from running to the arms of another."

All three have had their boyfriends. I don't like writing about it and even less talking about it, but my ignoring the subject doesn't stop them from having hopes and dreams of one day meeting their knight in shining armor. My hope is that in each case he will be a young Warrior who pursues my daughter's deep heart and invites her on an adventure rather than trying to make her the adventure.

Teenage girls aren't the only ones who've gotten in trouble through their longing to be part of a larger story. Boys, too, long desperately to matter to someone—to be significant. For better or worse, it's a condition we will not outgrow. To understand this longing and how it lures men to things other than the Father's love, we must return to the baseline of our story, the environment into which we were born: war.

We live in a fallen world where war is the reality. And in war, people get wounded. The enemy's ruthless and constant assault on our hearts is accomplished solely because of what we were created for, what our hearts are meant for, what little girls and boys never stop hoping and longing for as they become grown women and men. It is summed up in the phrase "I want someone to see me, want me, and love me." Our hearts were meant to experience and enjoy love.

Love is the greatest thing in the whole universe and love *is* capital-L Life. It is the conditional kind that is the source of our greatest woundings and the unconditional kind that is the source of our greatest healings. We are most alive when we are receiving or offering love. That explains why we so often try to make love and life happen on our own rather than let our Creator fill and sustain us. But our own efforts to fill our love tank don't work. It's as C.S. Lewis wrote in *Mere Christianity*:

> God made us: invented us as a man invents an engine. A car is made to run on petrol, and it would not run properly on anything else. Now God designed the human machine to run on Himself. He Himself is the fuel our spirits were designed to burn, or the

> food our spirits were designed to feed on. There is no other. That is why it is just no good asking God to make us happy in our own way without bothering about religion (faith). God cannot give us a happiness and peace apart from Himself, because it is not there.

"God is love," wrote the apostle John. So I propose that love is the fuel our hearts are meant to run on, because love is what we so desperately long for and need. But there is no love without God and without God there is no love. Anywhere, anytime, anyway in which love is expressed or experienced, God is there. Whether or not the Father is acknowledged or credited or honored in that moment, if it is loving, he is there in the middle of it. It doesn't have to be between Christians; God is much bigger than that. His fondness for us from afar often makes God the great Secret Admirer. He would rather be seen, acknowledged, and known, yet patiently he waits. God fondly looks on, waiting and wanting to be noticed, looking forward to the day when introductions are made and a romance for the ages begins.

He watches over many of us as we take our hearts to sources other than himself, including other image-bearers, in a vain attempt to fuel ourselves and meet our deepest need. Much relational bankruptcy boils down to the manner in which we make withdrawals from one another rather than deposits into one another.

The Father's love is continually, lavishly, and even fiercely in play. It waits, and will continue to wait, for us to grasp its reality and experience its joy more and more fully. God waits, all the while loving us, wooing us, wanting us—all of us who bear his image.

SHOW AND TELL

If God is in all the moments of our lives, and if he is good and up to good in all those moments, then it more than stands to reason that each man should be able to show and tell what good gifts the Father has been giving. Trusting that the heart of the Father is good is foundational to seeing and experiencing his ways, because not all the gifts he gives are shiny or pretty or opened at a party. Most of them come to us on our climb and along our journey of seeking after him. In the midst of the battle for Life and love, he leaves good gifts all along the way. But if a man misinterprets the Father's heart and the Father's ways, then, guaranteed, he will misinterpret the Father's gifts and training.

When I was thirteen, we moved from the West Coast back to Oklahoma. Eighth grade is a tough time to move. That spring I was one of about forty boys who tried out for a select baseball team needing a couple of kids to fill their roster. Every kid got to bat once, take a few grounders, and try to catch whatever ball got hit to him in the outfield.

I never knew if I made that team, because a few days later my dad announced that another team was being formed and he was coaching. The first day we got together, most of the boys looked familiar. They had been at the tryout the weekend before!

I remember playing the other team and wishing I was on it. Not until twenty years later, when I was in my thirties, did I learn the truth: we all had been cut, and my dad had gone to the league organizers and talked them into letting him start a new team. Someone was watching over me and that someone was better than I thought.

How do you see the Father at work in your life, counseling you, guiding your steps, and teaching you how to do and not to do things? When was the last time you made a major discovery about who you are and who he is, about how to love others and how to let him love you? What do you have to show and tell? What good gifts has your Father given you? Or are they piled up, sitting there and just waiting to be seen and unwrapped?

THE MAN I AM BECOMING

The new man we are becoming is expertly formed one surgery at a time through the removal (via confession and repentance) of lies and the installation of truth. Truth gets internalized as we experience it and understand that it is indeed true.

In my own life, I exchanged the message that "the Father isn't good" for the heart-renewing truth that "he is in charge of my life, and I get to participate." This has come to me one surgery at a time—one training, one validation ceremony, one initiating moment after another.

How radically can the Father's surgeries refashion a man? Let's go back to Peter. Compare the Peter of the Gospels with the Peter who wrote these words:

> Be content with who you are, and don't put on airs. God's strong hand is on you; he'll promote you at the right time. Live carefree before God; he is most careful with you. Keep a cool head. Stay alert. The Devil is poised to pounce, and would like nothing better than to catch you napping. Keep your guard up. You're not the only ones plunged into these hard times. It's the same with Christians all over the world. So keep a firm grip on the faith. The suffering won't last forever. It won't be long before this generous God who has great plans for us in Christ—eternal and glorious plans they are!—will have you put together and on your feet for good. (1 Peter 5:6–10 MSG)

That doesn't sound like the Peter who was quick to spout off whatever was on his mind. The Peter who, if he didn't have a sword, would grab someone else's. The Peter who, instead of simply listening, always felt compelled to tell the Son of God, "Jesus, I have a better idea." What happened to that Peter as he moved from his late twenties to his late fifties?

He encountered Jesus. He followed him. And after Jesus left he continued to walk with God and got Fathered, and he lived to tell about it in his two letters to the churches. What does it look like for a man to come out of his woundedness, turn, and be healed? Look at Peter.

Peter's healing and growth came at a price. It was surgery on top of surgery, healing after healing, training and more training. It was the old man giving way to more and more of the new man.

We are becoming. But exactly what is it we are becoming? Increasingly we are growing into more and more . . . we are becoming the Beloved Sons of a true Father. He loves us unconditionally. If we'll be open to it, we can experience his love. And when we experience it, everything changes.

BUILDING A SON

General Douglas MacArthur was an outstanding man both during World War II and in the times that followed. The leader of the United States forces in the Philippines regularly prayed this prayer for his son, Arthur, during his morning devotions:

> Build me a son, O Lord, who will be strong enough to know when he is weak, and brave enough to face himself when he is afraid; one who will be proud and unbending in honest defeat, and humble and gentle in victory.
>
> Build me a son whose wishbone will not be where his backbone should be; a son who will know Thee and that to know himself is the foundation stone of knowledge. Lead him, I pray, not in the path of ease and comfort, but under the stress and spur of difficulties and challenge. Here let him learn to stand up in the storm; here let him learn compassion for those who fail.
>
> Build me a son whose heart will be clean, whose goal will be high; a son who will master himself before he seeks to master other men; one who will learn to laugh, yet never forget how to weep; one who will reach into the future, yet never forget the past.
>
> And after all these things are his, add, I pray, enough of a sense of humor, so that he may always be serious, yet never take himself too seriously. Give him humility, so that he may always remember the simplicity of greatness, the open mind of true wisdom, the meekness of true strength.

INTENSIVE CARE

If broken lives and souls are to be healed, I must begin with teaching the practice of the Presence. . . . To abide in the presence of the Lord is to begin to hear Him. To follow through on that hearing is to find healing, self-acceptance, and growth into psychological and spiritual balance and maturity.

—*Leanne Payne*

There is a purpose to suffering, and if faced rightly, it can drive us like a nail deep into the love of God and into more stability and spiritual power than you can imagine.

—*Tim Keller*

Because there were battles in our past that we didn't know how to fight, and no one was there to step in and fight for us, the losses both small and great have had a cumulative effect. But we don't go back in our stories to stay there stuck in some moment of our personal history. We go back in order to see it, understand what happened, exchange it, and receive healing for brokenness and then move forward. It's critical to find out because most men *are* stuck; they carry the past into the present as pieces of a wounded and unsettled heart.

Paul Young wrote in his book *The Shack*, "Pain has a way of clipping our wings and keeping us from being able to fly . . . and if [it is] left unresolved for very long, you can almost forget that you were ever created to fly in the first place."

What is it that a man reaches for to cope and find comfort? Maybe the better question is, what reaches for a man when he is hurting, angry, or overwhelmed? In order to be free, a man must take inventory of the "packages" that have accumulated in the secrecy of his heart. What are they? How do the lies they contain shape so much of how a man thinks and what he does? The question is never whether there are such packages; the question is only, how many are there and what are their results? Wounding has left broken pieces in every life story, and those pieces get carried forward by a boy who is trying his best to become a man.

Take some time to grab a journal and walk with Jesus back into your own pain. Hold his hand as you search out the wounding packages. When did you receive them? What are the messages they contain? Here and now you can exchange them for healing.

David wrote, "Is anyone crying for help? God is listening, ready to rescue you. If your heart is broken, you'll find God right there; if you're kicked in the gut, he'll help you catch your breath" (Ps. 34:17–18 MSG). A heart healed and restored knows that being loved by God is the only way to freedom. And freedom is what allows a man to enter into the fight for others who aren't yet healed.

Show me a man who knows that he is deeply loved by the Father and I will show you a man fully alive. He is on his way to a restored and settled heart and to experiencing all the fullness of what it means to be a Beloved Son. He is *alive*.

EXCHANGING BROKEN FOR WHOLE

Taking the broken old answers a man has picked up along his journey and exchanging them for the one definitive opinion, the one majestic voice that truly matters is life-altering! It marks the glorious and painful beginning of a series of events that can take time to accomplish. *Painful*, because I am entering into surgeries in which Christ removes old beliefs and old ways that have fed my false self. *Glorious*, because now I am going to God rather than to other false-self, disoriented people to learn who I truly am and how to Live. Often I feel as if God is prying my hands from the only way I have known how to live in order to graciously teach me the only way I *need* to know. What a painful, glorious exchange!

Trading sorrow, fear, guilt, and shame for healing, restoration, freedom, and Life is an expedition of the heart. St. Augustine said, "God gives where He finds empty hands." A man whose heart and hands are full of old packages can't receive the gift of new ones. But when a man is willing, he will find far more than just forgiveness—he will find Life. He will not only see the old life he had settled for, but he will also begin to experience the new Life for which he was intended.

The man who steps out in faith to meet God, the man who calls out to the Father with the core questions of his heart, is not only ready to see who he really is but also to see his true Father. I cannot stress enough . . . this is a personal renovation—a customized journey back to God, different for every man. While there are similarities among all experiences, even more importantly there is uniqueness. God has a particular and intensive healing expedition laid out for each man and his deep, deep heart. Remember, since the wounds inflicted by the enemy of our heart are customized and personal, so are all the steps to healing.

I have been to the emergency room a few times both as a boy and as a man. I've been carried in, and I have also done the carrying. It is a rough scene for a father bringing in his daughter for badly needed medical attention. ER's specialize in x-rays, stitches, bandages, and casts. The medics are there to stop the bleeding and treat the wound. If you're fortunate, you are in and out in a few hours.

But even the best ER can't provide *all* the care and treatment required for the physical heart. Many ER heart patients are sent to intensive care for an extended stay. More observation, more tests, more diagnoses—these are good things when our physical wellness is in jeopardy. They are even more critical when it is a man's *spiritual* heart and identity that needs treatment. I have found that it is better to check in than to be carried in.

When Jesus talked about healing (Matt. 13:15), he was speaking of something far more significant and weighty than mere physical conditions. He was offering a standing invitation: "Check in for as many visits as you need to get well and as many as you need to stay well. The bill is paid. My insurance covers it. The care and attention are glorious, I promise! It is beyond anything in this world. And oh, what a difference it will make!"

If we will just take the courageous step of checking in to give our hearts over to Jesus' intensive care unit and let him heal us, we can experience how good he truly is. Will it hurt? Probably. But it's like the boy Eustace who declares in the film version of C.S. Lewis's *Voyage of the Dawn Treader*, just after Aslan transformed him from a dragon back to a boy, "No matter how hard I tried I just couldn't do it myself. Then He came towards me. It sort of hurt, but . . . it was a good pain. You know, like when you pull a thorn from your foot."

MORE ABOUT WOUNDS

There are many types of wounds and many kinds of wounders. A wounder is *someone who has power and influence over you through what they say or do, or by what they don't say or don't do.*

The package an image-bearer receives from a wounding person in a wounding moment is typically laced with guilt, shame, fear, or control. Something happens that shouldn't happen, or something that shouldn't happen does, and in that moment a package is delivered to the doorstep of our heart. Inside it is a message condemning us, assaulting us, belittling us, or dismissing us. And since we don't know any better, especially when we are young, we sign for it and accept it into our heart to our detriment.

Because the most prolific wounders in our stories are wounded hearts themselves, packages get passed along from one wounded heart—a mom, dad, sibling, teacher, coach, or friend—to another.

You look funny.
You aren't talented.
You're stupid.
You can't come.
You aren't enough.
You're too much.

And on and on—packages get delivered and messages signed for in a millisecond. It can be as simple as seeing someone roll their eyes after we say something. Or seeing one friend put his hand over his mouth to whisper to another. Our subconscious goes to work: *They are talking about me.* No force on this earth could convince us otherwise. And those are just the subtler packages. Abusive moments deliver their packages like wrecking balls smashing through concrete. No subtleties about it: these packages devastate!

My family recently went to Disney World. What a wonderful place! And what an incredibly wounding one. When you stroll Main Street USA, you can watch and hear the wrecking balls at work just an arm's length away:

Get in that stroller! If you get out of that stroller one more time . . .
No! And if you ask me again . . .
Shut up and eat it! You said you had to have it. If you don't eat it . . .

I don't want to hear that your feet hurt one more time! You say that again and . . .

What a "magical" place. But vacations are just for starters. Change the environment or change the characters and all kinds of war zones emerge. Homes, schools, stores . . . all these and more can be used by the kingdom of darkness to deliver awful packages in its network of wounding. UPS and FedEx have nothing on this dark heart-battering enterprise.

You can see how the packages accumulate. Their messages become like building blocks for constructing a life that self-protects, self -proclaims, self-provides, and self-promotes. It is a guarantee. We learn how to defend, deflect, hide, and retaliate, and thus secure the day when the wounded will become the wounder. Because, remember, wounded hearts wound hearts. They can't help it.

The wounding messages we collect during our formative years become definitive. Later in our lives, they falsely define us and then they recklessly drive us, and the false self becomes dominant—until we see it and bring it to God for the great exchange.

CARRYING THE PACKAGES

What packages do you carry? What messages run you and your life? When someone or something gets close to the wounded places in your heart, what do you do to ensure you won't get hurt, again? What strategy do you use to arrange for life or at least minimize the pain? What inner vows have you made, what declarations of control?

I'll make sure I never get overlooked again. These clothes will do it.
I will always have the answer from now on. Study, study, study.
I am never going to look a fool. Practice, practice, practice.
I will never let my dad embarrass me again. Keep him out.
I will always make sure my mom is protected. Nobody will hurt us.
My kids will do what I say or I'll . . .

I am not proposing that our enemy crafts and delivers every bad or inconvenient moment in life. But the kingdom of darkness, being opportunistic (Luke 4:13), takes advantage of such moments to whisper the lies we in turn believe are true about ourselves, others, and God, and then something deep in us is *set*. We are not messing up all on our own; we are getting help—a very bad kind of help.

The flow of Life and love is hindered because the enemy's lies hold a place in our hearts. This is not the way God intended us to live, and worse yet, *good* packages can't get through to our heart because wounded packages occupy too much of the space. There is only so much square footage in a man's heart, not to mention kind and loving messages that often get misinterpreted by the old, conditional grid of "If I do this, I get that . . . approval, acceptance, applause, or admiration" or "If I don't do that, I get approval, acceptance, applause, or admiration." As a result, even the good packages are mishandled and feel either conditional or untrue and they then miss their mark of bestowing genuine love on a heart that is unable to recognize it as such. It's sinister and brutal, a bondage to a system of lies that perpetuate more bondage and more lies, keeping a man both down and out.

But the good news is that a conditional grid can be exchanged for an unconditional grid that receives and gives love freely. More accurately, *it can be healed*—and it must be if we are ever going to be men who know who we truly are.

HEALING THE WOUNDS

Declaring my need and hope to be healed moves heaven and earth as Jesus responds. My desire for something more puts my Savior to work undressing me from the dragon skin, removing its captivity over me and setting me free. Remember the prayer of the Warrior King, David: "Search me, O God, and . . . see if there be any hurtful way in me" (Ps. 139:23–24 NASB). It is this cry of the heart that moves the heart of God.

Asking God to help us with anything that is stored up in our hearts, anything that can harm both ourselves and others, means that we accept surgery. We crawl up on the gurney and give God permission to operate: *Jesus, do what you need to.* This has become a regular prayer in my own life. Asking for eyes to see and ears to hear the things God wants me to bring to him often leads me into surgery. I give him the old trusting that he will make it new. If it is anger I am experiencing, then that symptom tells me that God and I have an appointment to talk about something. The same goes for jealousy, shame, or judgment. All are attempts by the enemy to partner with my false self so the woundedness in my life continues and eventually spreads through me into other lives.

Every wounded moment and its message comes with a "consent form" which I signed when I accepted the false message as if it were true. This "form," the contract of my agreement, is what I can bring to God. I confess to him that I signed it, that I believed a lie. Then I repent, turn it in, and turn to him and ask him to heal my broken heart. This is the great exchange: trading an old lying message for a new message that is good and true, one that comes from my Father's heart to mine and allows me to take another step toward freedom. My Father invites me into this transaction as many times as my heart needs.

When wounding moments occur in our lives and the old themes of self-protection, self-promotion, self-provision, and self-defense surge out of our subconscious to the surface, now we have something we can bring to God. We're not *surprising* him, He is aware that there are "hurtful ways in me," and he is at the ready to bring relief.

Often we don't even recognize when we are practicing a harmful pattern; it has become so normal that we just don't see what we don't see. But when we do become aware of a particular wound, we can bring it to God. We may not understand it—we just know that something hurts. And as we present it to Christ and walk with him in it, he brings understanding and healing. He shows us exactly what the wounding package was, who the enemy used to deliver it, when and how it arrived, and how we signed for it, giving it authority to block the flow of Life and love.

There is a great difference between medicating something and having it healed. Men explore many ways of medicating their deep wounds: a bottle, a woman, work, and more. Yet only the Father can bring true healing. He wants to do that for us, and he can—and he will, if we'll bring our hurts to him. It's in this way that pain becomes a gift from God. Pain is an opportunity for us to see the wounding packages we carry with us. If we are willing, we can bring those parts of our story, the history of our life, to God for redeeming and his specialized attention and care.

OVER AND OVER

This incredible healing transaction of seeing a wound and confessing it to the Father allows us to make a second crucial move: *repentance.* Instead of agreeing with a lie, we recognize and renounce it as false. We cross our signature off the "consent form" and unsubscribe from its hold on our hearts and the way we are living. Turning from the old way, we invite God to Father us with *his* way. We ask him to deliver another better package to take the old one's place. The contents of this package are good and true and come from a trustworthy source, the One who made us.

God has the skill and the desire to free us from a small life where the false-self impostor has, for far too long, dominated the scenes and moments of our lives—*if* we will engage our wills, turn to God, and let him have both his will and his way, we will get better.

These healing moments are to be repeated over and over until there is far less *false* on the shelves of our hearts and far more *true.* Doesn't that make sense, especially if the wounding moments are many and our enemy is *opportunistic*? Such re-defining moments mark the turn of the tide, the inauguration of change that every comeback needs and for which every man is destined.

Author and counselor Leanne Payne wrote in her book *Healing Prayer*,

> The healings that we see never cease to astonish us, and illustrate how simply and wonderfully God reveals and then heals the heart of man. . . . In prayer for the healing of the heart from fears, bitterness, etc., we see primal fears as well as the lesser ones dealt with immediately: those fears that the sufferer often has not been aware of, never been able to name—they only know that their lives have been seriously restricted and shaped because of them. . . . In short, the miracles occur as easily and as wonderfully as though they are naturally to be expected. And they are.

RECOVERY

Where wounds arrive in a moment, healing often takes time—time for what's broken in a man to be reset and then time for it to mend and become strong. Think of what it's like when the bandages come off after a surgery; everything is tender, and a few painful months lie ahead. What has been repaired and restored needs to be exercised. It will be a little painful, but that's okay. The wounds of our lives may have happened in a moment, but their subsequent effects and symptoms settled in over time, and so it also is with healing. In time, the healed areas within us become our "new normal," our new way of living. Scripture talks about seeds sown that will eventually bear fruit (Gal. 5:19-26). Both kingdoms know and operate within this as it is God's ordained framework.

The wounding moments and messages of our past become part of the glorious renovation of *us*. God is reconstructing us! He is healing, training, and restoring us into the Beloved Son that we are.

Remember, we collect the dots in order to connect the dots. The dots are the wounding messages shelved in our heart. We collect them by identifying them, and then we connect them by seeing, confessing, and turning from the false-self they have constructed. It's in this manner that we begin the journey of becoming the Beloved Son and lay the foundation of Warrior training.

After a few of these glorious healing moments, a man will begin to see the long, sustained assault he has been under. Sooner or later, most men will want to know why such fury and sinister plots were set against them. That is the time a man is ready to see the spiritual realm and hear all that Jesus wants to teach him on how to live well, love well, and fight well—all the things that Jesus himself did.

THE IN-BETWEEN AND NOT-YET

Living in a war asks of men, and at times even demands, that they become Warriors. As author and teacher John Eldredge has taught many men at his Boot Camps, "Steps toward Life and freedom are opposed. If you want Life, you are going to have to fight for it."

We live in a fallen place. We are caught in the middle of what I call "the comings." There was a first coming that had a cross and set us free. There will be a second coming that has a trumpet, a white horse, and a final battle, and it will take us home. It will be what the French call the *pièce de résistance*: the grand finale, the closing of this long chapter of fallenness and the end of this war we fight. It will usher all things into the beginning of a new heaven and new earth. Then, at last, there will be peace! (Rev. 17, 22).

But for now, we live in the middle of the comings, in the not-yet and the in-between. I wish it were otherwise, but you and I both know better. Our situation is similar to that of the ancient Israelites. God promised them a land flowing with milk and honey. It was given to them by God, and yet they were told they would have to fight many battles not only to possess it but also to keep it. That's how it is with us, too. As much as I try to insulate my heart and my family from the fallenness of this present age, the war finds me and reminds me that while there is a peace coming, it is not here yet.

The Warrior is needed and the Beloved Son threatened because we live in a Larger Story where there are great battles. But though we dwell in the midst of spiritual hostility, victims, casualties, and prisoners we need not be. We know how the war on sin ends: Jesus comes again, riding in to defeat all that is evil and carry us home. Until then we live in enemy-occupied territory (Rev. 17), and we are instructed *not* to live in bondage as prisoners or slaves.

But remember, you and I cannot be the Warrior until we know for certain that we are the Beloved Sons. It is the Beloved Son who is deployed into the fight for love and the battles for Life, taking up the great cause of advancing freedom. Love and life are what the kingdom of Christ is all about, and fighting on its behalf will not be easy, but it will be good. Our enemy will not go down without a fight. He will test whether we know who we truly are. If we don't, then a simple spell—a wounding message, a lie that rests in our hearts and presides in our lives—can render us impotent and ineffective in battle. That is why objective number one is for us is to get our own hearts back. Then we can enter into the fight for the hearts of others.

POWER AND AUTHORITY

Guilt, shame, and fear are some of the greatest weapons in the enemy's arsenal. But the image-bearers of God who become the Beloved Sons are entrusted with something far greater:

> But you shall receive power (ability, efficiency, and might) when the Holy Spirit has come upon you, and you shall be My witnesses in Jerusalem and all Judea and Samaria and to the ends (the very bounds) of the earth. (Acts 1:8)

The resurrected Christ declared, "All authority in heaven and on earth has been given to me" (Matt. 28:18 NIV). Where in the world was it before?

Lost.

Adam and Eve naively gave it away with their compromise. The authority God had given them in the garden when he put them in charge of everything (Gen. 1:28–29) was stolen by the enemy. The first Adam lost it.

But the "second" Adam, Jesus, took it back. And now, like a father giving the car keys back to a son *after* the wreck and repair of the family car, Jesus shares his authority with us again. Dallas Willard writes, "Jesus is actually looking for people he can trust with his power."

Why? Because we are up against wolves in sheep's clothing (Matt. 7:15), a roaring lion (1 Peter 5:8), and evil masquerading as an angel of light (2 Cor. 11:14). If there are two things we are going to need, they are *power* and *authority*. They are the weapons and the birthright of Beloved Sons in training. Learning how to wield them is high on our Father's list of priorities for his image-bearers. It's how the Kingdom operates, and those sons who know how will lead hearts to freedom with power and authority (Luke 10:1-18; Matt. 28:18-20). Put on your armor, men; training for Life has begun.

THE WAYS OF A BELOVED SON

HEALING, IN THIS LIFE, IS NOT THE RESOLUTION OF OUR PAST; IT IS THE USE OF OUR PAST TO DRAW US INTO DEEP RELATIONSHIP WITH GOD AND HIS PURPOSES FOR OUR LIVES.

—DAN ALLENDER

BELOVED, LET US LOVE ONE ANOTHER, FOR LOVE IS (SPRINGS) FROM GOD; AND HE WHO LOVES [HIS FELLOWMEN] IS BEGOTTEN (BORN) OF GOD AND IS COMING [PROGRESSIVELY] TO KNOW *AND* UNDERSTAND GOD [TO PERCEIVE AND RECOGNIZE AND GET A BETTER AND CLEARER KNOWLEDGE OF HIM].

—1 JOHN 4:7

Love is what every man longs for. He wants to be seen, wanted, and invited, to belong. Every man deeply desires to offer his strength, to be courageous, and to matter. Love is what every masculine heart longs both to receive and to give; it is what a man was made for, and it is the standard by which every man hopes to abide. It is how we bear God's image. Life goes wrong for a man when he is harshly judged and his hopes of being loved are not met, or worse, are crushed.

The main ingredients of love are validation, acceptance, worth, belonging, and significance. The lengths a man will go to in order to obtain them vary both gloriously and dangerously. Love factors into both our greatest triumphs and our worst tragedies. Love will settle a heart and even set it free, but love distorted can just as easily arrest and imprison a man. Our greatest wounds of the heart come from the perversions of love: jealousy, betrayal, unfaithfulness, and hatred.

The enemy of our Life, of our Belovedness, used to enjoy love himself. Satan knows that love is the greatest thing and he knows the power of unconditional love to set hearts free. He is therefore hell-bent on twisting love into something it's not, using all his wiles and every means at his disposal to turn life's wounding moments to his advantage. Satan opportunistically uses those moments to plant his lies in our hearts about love; God's, others, and our own in order to construct a false image that we wear and operate from as if it were true. This false image keeps us from receiving freely and giving real love freely, the way we were created to.

PERSONALIZED STRATEGIES

Every man has a false self, a tailor-made creature constructed through the wounding of his heart. Referred to as "the flesh" in the Bible, this impostor, this traitor, arises out of a man's strategies to make life work. It creates inner programs to avoid pain or obtain pleasure; his methods of self-protection, self-promotion, and self-provision—all of these are the man's elaborate, false-self construction to arrange for love for himself. The enemy is delighted to assist, knowing that the false self (flesh) keeps a person from experiencing true love and real Life.

That's got to stop. In the fight to reclaim our whole heart we must stop seeking out secondary sources of validation and worth.

The days of settling for less—what John Eldredge and Brent Curtis have called "taking our hearts to Less-Wild Lovers"—must come to an end. Nothing is of greater consequence or requires more courage than going to God rather than things for our deep heart needs. Before we can enter the great battles for the hearts of our wives, children, friends, or anyone else, we must know how to take our own heart to the primary source of Life and love.

MY CRAZY "FRIEND"

I do it all the time, far more than I care to admit: I assume wrongly. My ability to misperceive someone's actions or intentions, and to conceive inaccurate conclusions and heavy-handed attitudes, amazes me. What is this thing in me that desires grace for myself but judges others so harshly?

It's my false self.

Every man's false self specializes in judging, criticizing, and complaining. In other words, holding court. I've heard it said that if we went about with our false self on the *outside*, so we could see it when others encounter it as it aired its opinions unbridled and uncensored, we would be apologizing constantly for our little "friend":

Sorry about him. He is a little crazy.
I apologize. He doesn't have any social skills.
Excuse his language. He has deep, deep issues.
Don't pay any attention to him. He hasn't had his medication today.

If we could meet our flesh, our false self—if we could witness its constant unruliness and even play back an audio/video of its atrocities—we would be speechless. Appalled. If we truly *saw* it, we would go to extravagant measures to wrestle it back into its padded cell and make sure it stayed there.

Why would we feel that way?

Because the false self is not who we really are. Not if we're in Christ. It ain't you and it ain't me, and it ain't welcome to pose as us anytime, anywhere, and in any way! But keeping it locked down, unavailable for comment, will take some power and authority, some understanding and training.

Stop for a second and digest what you've just read. It's just that critical. On our journey to freedom from the false self, a key guidepost is this: *In order to discover who we truly are, we must discover who we aren't.*

Just as important as knowing who we *aren't* is knowing who this Jesus truly *is*. It just makes sense. If we have Jesus wrong, how will we ever get us right? Think about it, if we've viewed life mostly through the eyes of the false self, then how likely are we to perceive anything and anyone accurately, including ourselves and especially Jesus, the One who came to set us free?

THE FALSE SELF ISN'T TRUE

Like the operator of a rigged carnival game, the false self plays the same mean tricks on us continuously. It dangles a prize before us with just enough promise to lure us, take our money, and then convince us it was our personal inability that made us lose.

Winston Churchill said, "When there is no enemy within, the enemy outside cannot hurt you." Now do you see why Brennan Manning called our inner enemy the "great imposter "and why it must be seen and then dismantled, put to death? As our old, false identity is removed piece by piece, a new construction can simultaneously begin. We play a significant part in that process. God will do the lion's share, but it is still a partnership, an alliance based on a Father-and-son relationship. It was Augustine who said, "Without God, we cannot; without us, God will not."

Jesus said, "I am the way and the truth and and the life. No one comes to the Father but through me" (John 14:6 NIV). That is one of the great offers of the gospel! Jesus will show us the *way*, we can know the *truth*, and on that journey, we will come to *life*! But these are more than just promises to reach for: they are a Person. Jesus can offer us these things because he *is* these things. And by being in friendship with him, a man will be free (John 8:32; Gal. 5:1). We will be clothed with power and righteousness, and we will trade the perishable for the imperishable (Luke 24:49; Col. 3:12; 1 Cor. 15:53).

There must be a catch, then, because most men don't seem to live truly free.

There *is* a catch: we must come to know that the false self—ISN'T TRUE! IT ISN'T US! What *is* true is this: we are, and we are becoming, Beloved Sons. And the enemy of our heart and false self will do everything they can to convince us otherwise. It is in the way, a rival set against God for control. It will fight for the throne determined to rule us. It will act like a mole our adversary uses to manipulate us. Darkness will feed us false information in order to control us—all in order to keep us down, far away from our true heart and the one true Father who made you and me to be sons, not slaves.

TRAINING

By discovering the true identity of Jesus, we will find ours as well. This cannot be overstated. He is the One who knows all of a man's sorrows and hopes. The Scriptures say that Jesus *identifies* with us:

> Since the children are made of flesh and blood, it's logical that the Savior took on flesh and blood in order to rescue them by his death. By embracing death, taking it into himself, he destroyed the Devil's hold on death and freed all who cower through life, scared to death of death. . . . That's why he had to enter into every detail of human life. Then, when he came before God as high priest to get rid of the people's sins, he would have already experienced it all himself—all the pain, all the testing—and would be able to help where help was needed. (Heb. 2:14–15, 17–18 MSG)

We are free men when we join Jesus as Beloved Sons. Christ has made that possible through the cross and the resurrection. We died to sin and we are alive in him! And we become more and more free as we learn from our great King about how to live freely.

Yet in my experience working with hundreds of men, most believing men are not living healed and free. And *all* need critical training on how to do so.

Most men go unfathered and unhealed for much of their life's journey. Yet fathering is absolutely critical for abundant life, and this is where much of our training lies: letting God Father us. Even the best of earthly fathers will falter, largely because our enemy is just that good at breaking into the critical father/son relationship and wounding a boy through it. There's no question whether we've been wounded by our fathers. We have. But before we throw our dads under the bus, let's remember that they like us have been assaulted all their lives. Our ancient enemy is proficient at thwarting what a man was made for. But not forever. As a man experiences the perfect Fathering of God through love and training, he moves beyond the wounds of his boyhood and into the freedom of a Beloved Son.

RECEIVING

It was the birthday of one of my best friends, and I had stopped by his house to give him my gift. David and I talk a few times a week. He is an oriented man, a Beloved Son, and is becoming well-trained. Some days he helps me along in my journey and training; other days I get to "ride shotgun" for him.

I watched as he opened the card with my gift certificate and read the lines I had written from my heart to his: "I'm so glad you were born, and I have a deep appreciation to God for our friendship and for blessing me with a brother in the journey."

"Thank you!" David said when he had finished reading. Then, holding up the card like a fan: "You know what? It is hard for me to receive. It's hard for me to believe I'm worth it."

Receive. To take in; to lay hold of something that is given or awarded. Why is it that we find the bad stuff so much easier to believe and take in? And why does the good stuff get stuck at the door? Like most men, including me, my friend David has subscribed to the following notion: *In giving I can be esteemed and affirmed, while receiving, I will be exposed as undeserving, or worse . . . be left feeling the obligation to repay.*

It's a lie. Jesus showed us how to receive when he let a sinful woman wash his feet with her tears (Luke 7:36–38). Peter showed us how *not* to receive when he pulled his feet back and said, "Nope, Jesus, not gonna let you do it" (John 13:3–9).

When we daily receive God's whispers of affection and acts of love, our hearts are settled. We feel no need to create or manipulate for ourselves; we can simply receive. A man who experiences this will tell others. We all like to share the good stuff we get in life, and that's how it is with experiencing the goodness of God.

However, the enemy of our heart has an agenda to the contrary. It looks and sounds something like this:

Cut off the supply lines of love to a man's heart.
Make him believe he must serve in order to be loved. Obligate him to earn or repay.
Have him question his worth and value and shut down trust in the process.
Make a man turn to himself.
Make him see the conditions we place on relationships, on matters of love.
Make a man turn inward for self-reliance and self-dependence, while also instilling in him the lie that God's love is also merit-based, conditional,
And above all, turn him to service. That is our greatest goal: to get a man to believe that love of God is earned through service rather than given freely.

Satan knows that if he can get his agenda operational in a man, it will fuel and motivate that man, and he can be crushed whenever and wherever the enemy wants.

Given this harsh reality, receiving from the Father again and again is central to a life that can freely give. Being loved by God, enjoying his affection, is what makes a man's heart whole and settled. Loving us is not just something he did through Jesus but something he continues to do. The Father's agenda must get through the enemy lines . . . He is speaking to us still, constantly: "*I see you, I made you, and I love you*!"

When was the last time you *received*, felt his love, saw his love, and knew his love to be true? How did you respond? I'll bet you told someone the story!

A FRAGILE FREEDOM

Sooner or later, a man must find that he cannot do enough, give enough, serve enough, or work hard enough in church or ministry to make God love him more. He can only allow himself to be loved freely. That's what the Father is looking for — not performance but a receptive heart. The one leads to burnout. The other leads to burning bright.

We live outside the garden. One day we will be escorted back in (Rev. 22:1-5) , but until then, we contend with hard challenges and foul, dark forces. So it would be more than wise to understand how to navigate our embattled environment, and it would be liberating to learn from Christ what it means to live fully alive and free.

Freedom is available, but freedom is fragile. It was Dwight Eisenhower who said,

"History does not long entrust the care of freedom to the weak or the timid." Oh, how right he was.

Jesus said it this way: "If the Son liberates you [makes you free men], then you are really *and* unquestionably free" (John 8:36). Paul had the same mindset when he wrote,

> It is absolutely clear that God has called you to a free life. Just make sure that you don't use this freedom as an excuse to do whatever you want to do and destroy your freedom. Rather, use your freedom to serve one another in love; that's how freedom grows. (Gal. 5:13 MSG)

LEARNING THE ART

In the 1999 film *The Matrix*, after taking the red pill and experiencing a rebirth, the leading character, Neo, begins training and experiencing the truth for himself. He learns by seeing and hearing, and he takes on a pivotal role in a world very different from the one that had seemed so real to him. Neo learns theory (theology), but more importantly, Neo acquires experiential knowledge. Once he is free, his objective is learning how to live unplugged from the Matrix, "in the world but not of the world." In experiencing the truth, Neo becomes more of who he was created to be.

In an early scene during his training, Neo asks Morpheus, with a snarky undercurrent of unbelief, "You mean to tell me I'm going to be able to dodge bullets?"

Morpheus smiles. "No, Neo, I'm telling you, when the time comes . . . you won't have to."

At the end of the film, having learned the Art of a Warrior, Neo, now with power and authority, sends a message to his adversary and the system that has a hold over so many hearts:

> I know you're out there. I can feel you now. I know that you're afraid. . . . You're afraid of us. You're afraid of change. I don't know the future. I didn't come here to tell you how this is going to end. I came here to tell you how it's going to begin. I'm going to hang up this phone, and then I'm going to show these people what you don't want them to see. I'm going to show them a world without you. A world without rules and controls, without borders or boundaries.

> A world where anything is possible. Where we go from there is a choice I leave to you.

Neo has moved from defense to offense—and so must we.

IF IT ISN'T GOOD . . .

When my three girls were very young, my anger used to flare whenever one of them hurt herself. A head bonked on the corner of the table, a skinned knee from a fall, a finger pinched in a door, and my reaction was intense. I would raise my voice and talk through my teeth. "What were you doing? Why weren't you paying more attention? You have to be more careful! See what happens when . . ."

There they were, ponytailed and in tears, coming to me with their "owwies," and all I had for them was two hands full of anger. What in the world? That was my normal—and my normal wasn't good. I was angrythat they got hurt but, I guarantee it came across that I was angry *at them.*

Pause for a second and consider: God will arrange far more trainings during our daily lives—at home, on the job, in the car, at the store—than we'll ever encounter in Sunday school or a church pew. We just need eyes to see these moments, engage and enter in.

So there I was, being a dad and parenting my girls badly, when God invited me into a training which would free me from something that wasn't good for others and wasn't good for me.

One of the first principles of training is to ask questions and consult God for guidance. My *go to* questions are:

What is this thing I'm dealing with?
How and when did I learn to flash straight to anger?
Why do I do it now?

When I began to ask those questions, God brought answers. They involved experiences I had growing up, seeds planted which grew the bad fruit in me, a desire to control circumstances and people. The anger was merely a symptom. And my heavenly Father was after something much deeper than symptoms: he was after the root and the cause of the anger. My need to control came from fear, the well from which my anger sprang forth. I needed to treat the well, not the bucket.

God taught me a lesson then that he has continued to teach me many times since: *Michael, if it isn't good, it isn't you.* He has brought me more than awareness and understanding of my problems; he has brought healing. Remember, awareness and healing are not the same. Knowing you have a cancer and treating it are two different things. The cancer isn't you but nonetheless, you can have it. The knowing is critical, but it's the treatment that makes things better. And training in asking God questions is key to both.

GROWING INTO

Training is about learning, practicing and exchanging old ways for new, shedding something that isn't you in order to become something that is you. It takes time to get from where you are to where you can be.

Growing up in a middle-class family, we never got the most expensive stuff, but we four kids didn't want for much. Sears and its wonderful catalog, K-Mart, and J. C. Penney were standard outposts for clothing, appliances, and just about anything else our family needed. My brothers and I knew a lot about S&H Green Stamps, coupons, and deposits on pop bottles.

Often, Mom and Dad bought us boys clothes that were too big for us so we could grow into them. Tough Skin jeans, and especially shoes, were always purchased at least one size too large. I hated that silver contraption the man in the shoe department would pull out for me to stand on! It always declared that my feet were bigger than they really were, and then my dad would add another size just for good measure. I'd walk out of Sears wearing shoes as big as the fins on a Navy frogman.

The mission the heavenly Father has for each of us to grow into is a lot like that. Every man bears the image of Jesus in a way that is unique and tailor-made, but for us to mature in it involves a process of becoming. And that is a walk of faith, a walk with God, which requires us to grow into it. We become more and more like Jesus. That's a big pair of shoes to fill. But he'll see to it that we do.

BECOMING IS THE ART OF A WARRIOR

Much is riding on our growing into our identity as Beloved Sons. Not just our own hearts and lives, but the hearts and lives of others hang in the balance. Will we fight for them? If so, then there is an art to master and a skill to practice. There is a code of conduct, an oath to take, a pledge we must make from our hearts. There is a way of life we are to pursue in the company of a brotherhood, and there is a common mission that unites us.

Across enemy lines are those who have yet to see, hear, and taste how good our Father, King, and Guide truly are. Many hearts, both outside and inside the church, lie trapped in a dead-end performance-driven world of conditional love. They need help. They need to hear the stories of redemption and freedom from those who know the Father, King, and Guide. They need to hear his voice and know that he has arranged for their great escape, their glorious healing, and their marvelous freedom.

When people see a free man, they will either call him crazy or want to be like him. Those are the responses Jesus elicited, and as we grow into his likeness, we'll experience them too. Some people are ready to be rescued and begin their training; others haven't yet realized the prison in which they are held.

We need to know the Art of a Warrior. And that includes understanding more deeply the nature of our enemy.

PART TWO

THE WARRIOR

WHAT WE ARE UP AGAINST

NOW THE SERPENT WAS MORE SUBTLE AND CRAFTY THAN ANY LIVING CREATURE OF THE FIELD WHICH THE LORD GOD HAD MADE.

—*GENESIS 3:1*

WE MUST REMEMBER THAT SATAN HAS HIS MIRACLES TOO.

—*JOHN CALVIN*

One of the first great moments of any man's heart is for that man to see his story in light of a larger one. Every boy longs to be a part of something larger. And every boy knows there is a villain: an alien or a bad guy, some evil that must be faced, battled, and defeated.

In one of his Boot Camps, John Eldredge said, "Boys at that age aren't pretending—they are rehearsing." We know this when we are young, but when we get older, we forget and settle for a story that is small and manageable. That is actually the strategy and work of the villain in our story: "Get them to settle for less, invite a man to occupy the center of the story." But it is no way for a man to live. Men want to matter; men want to be courageous; men want to be strong. As Bart Hanson from Ransomed Heart ministries put it once, "I don't want to simply be dangerous for dangerous' sake. I want to be dangerous for good." Amen and yet, we and God are not the only characters in this story.

There is a character in the Larger Story you and I are in who is determined to make us lose our way and fail to find our rightful place, our role to play. He opposes our living full and free from our masculine hearts because he knows the impact we would have if we did.

In order for us to understand the context our personal stories fit into, we need to understand the nature of the Larger Story and its character. Bunnies and chipmunks suggest quite a different story than do cowboys and Indians, or aliens and Jedis, or rangers from the North and orcs from Isengard. The relationship between the characters in the story and the context of the story are inseparable. And it is here that men suffer from a great blind spot in their masculine journey. It is as if our enemy has pledged,

> *We must deceive them, lie to them about where they are and what Life is really about. We must shift the context of their lives a few degrees so they will never find rest for their hearts nor step into the true roles that are theirs to play. We must blind them to the One who made them and loves them by offering the illusion of control and the life goal of comfort and ease—a life they will settle for and yet can never truly have.*

Getting men to settle for a smaller story is a weakness with which the enemy has had a field day. It's like *kryptonite*. In his essay *This World: Playground or Battlefield*, A. W. Tozer wrote, "The idea that this world is a playground instead of a battleground has now been accepted in practice by the vast majority of Christians. . . . A right view of God and the world to come requires that we have a right view of the world in which we live and of our relationship to it. So much depends upon this that we cannot afford to be careless about it."

If we go skipping through the minefields of life, all the while believing they don't exist, believing that we are in an amusement park rather than navigating through enemy-occupied territory, the results are guaranteed: casualties, victims, and prisoners of war. In the words of Jesus to Peter,

> "Satan has asked excessively that [all of] you be given up to him [out of the power and keeping of God], that he might sift [all of] you like grain." (Luke 22:31)

Satan's intentions haven't changed. That's why, years later, Peter warned first-century believers,

> Be well balanced (temperate, sober of mind), be vigilant *and* cautious at all times; for that enemy of yours, the devil, roams around like a lion roaring [in fierce hunger], seeking someone to seize upon *and* devour. (1 Peter 5:8)

YIKES*! Seriously*? These alarming passages give any heart reason for pause, and they are just the beginning. My friend John said a few years back, "Somebody should have told us we were being hunted!" Somebody did. Jesus warned us:

> In this world you will have trouble. (John 16:33)

> Be careful. . . . (Matt. 6:1, 16:6; Mark 8:15; Luke 21:34)

> Be on your guard; stand firm in the faith; be courageous; be strong. Do everything in love. (1 Cor. 16:13-14 NIV)

G. K. Chesterton wrote, "Jesus promised his disciples three things: that they would be completely fearless, absurdly happy, and in constant trouble."

Most of us know all too well the pain, stress, and hardship of constant trouble. Yet living disoriented lives, lives without the awareness of a Larger Story, has led most men to misinterpret their circumstances and often draw tragic conclusions. If you've subscribed to the lie that life is about comfort and control, that it's all about you, then you have gravitated to the center of the story and are living in way too small a story. The enemy has you cast in a role you were never intended to play. The Father has a much better role for you in a far Larger Story. One that is better and abundantly more than we might ever think or imagine.

EVIL'S STORY

Set within the broad narrative of the Scriptures from Genesis to Revelation are many references to a powerful and destructive character, one whose role and presence are so significant that if he and his fallen ones are underestimated or misunderstood, our story can never make sense. In his 1942 classic, *The Screwtape Letters*, C.S. Lewis wrote, "There are two equal and opposite errors into which our race can fall about the devils. One is to disbelieve in their existence. The other is to believe, and to feel an excessive and unhealthy interest in them. They themselves (the devils) are equally pleased by both errors, and hail a 'materialist' or 'magician' with the same delight."

My experience is not that we are *excessive,* but rather that we are far too ignorant and naïve in regard to our enemy. We must know his role and purpose, his story and history, in order to recover and stand our ground in ours.

The great villain in the Story became God's enemy before he became ours. Though Satan appears in the early chapters of our story, Genesis 3, we have to consult other parts of the Scriptures to learn what transpired preceding our arrival. Like so many dark characters in epic tales, our enemy was a friend before he became a foe; he was glorious before he became hideous.

The story of Lucifer's fall can help us better understand our own story. God creates human image-bearers and sets his extravagant and abundant love upon them. The archangel Lucifer, greatest among the angels, responds like a jealous big brother unwilling to share the stage. Distrusting the heart of God, he decides to take matters into his own hands and formulates a rebellion among the angels. When the dust settles, Lucifer loses his role and is banished to take another. John Milton, 17th century poet, penned it this way in *Paradise Lost*:

> Favored of Heaven so highly, to fall off
> From their Creator, and transgress his will
> For one restraint, lords of the world besides?
> Who first seduced them to that foul revolt?
> The infernal Serpent; he it was, whose guile,
> Stirred up with envy and revenge, deceived
> The mother of mankind, what time his pride
> Had cast him out from Heaven, with all his host
> Of rebel angels, by whose aid aspiring
> To set himself in glory above his peers,
> He trusted to have equaled the Most High,
> If he opposed; and with ambitious aim
> Against the throne and monarchy of God,
> Raised impious war in Heaven and battle proud
> With vain attempt. Him the Almighty Power
> Hurled headlong flaming from the ethereal sky
> With hideous ruin and combustion down
> To bottomless perdition, there to dwell
> In adamantine chains and penal fire,
> Who durst defy the Omnipotent to arms.

Defeated and stripped of his glorious role as archangel, and driven by *envy and a thirst for revenge*, Satan plots another evil: "If I can't have the part I want, I will go after the ones who have it. If I can't hurt the Father, I'll go after and ruin his image-bearers, turn the created against their Creator, the children from their Father, and achieve two for one!"

BELIEVING THE LIE

Satan had to have been within earshot when God, walking with Adam in the cool of the day, warned his son, "Do not eat of this tree." How else could Satan have known to zero in on the one thing that was off-limits? He knew the restriction; now it was just a matter of waiting for an opportune time—and it came.

In that fateful moment, Adam and Eve—and through them, you and I—believed the lie and were convinced there was more to be had than God was offering. They bought the lie that they could become *more* like God. But they were already God-like; that is what *image-bearer* means. There was no "more" to be had. That was the great deception: they already had it all!

Not much has changed since that tragic day. Like a child who wants "down" from his father's arms at the corner of a busy intersection, we misinterpret the Father's love and care. In our fallenness we seem to still ache for a better part, to be the captain of our destiny, the god of our own universe, the center of the story. We want to take up a role we were never intended for, aren't equipped for, nor capable of managing. We live turned against the Father and yet struggling to know that he cares.

And so a *great restoration* is required. The good news—no, the surpassingly great news—is that it is already well underway!

Pastor and author John Piper wrote, "Sin is what we do when we are not satisfied with God." That explains why the enemy of image-bearers still practices the same strategy he used in the garden: *Tell them lies, offer imitations, plant seeds of doubt that God will provide and protect. Separate them from the love and Life of the Father, and the two-for-one still plays on.*

And so we are wounded again and again, and both God's heart and our hearts ache. This is the two-for-one. Life without God doesn't work, and yet we continue to subscribe to the belief that we can live independent of him.

It didn't work then and it won't work now. The fall was a monumental turn for the worse and set the stage for the soreness and misery of life outside the garden.

FROM FALL TO WINTER

"Out of the frying pan and into the fire" sums up the next chapters in the Bible's account of our fall.

> God said, "The Man has become like one of us, capable of knowing everything, ranging from good to evil. What if he now should reach out and take fruit from the Tree-of-Life and eat, and live forever [fallen]? Never—this cannot happen!" (Gen. 3:22 MSG, my insertion)

Both for their provision and protection, Adam and Eve are escorted out of the garden. And not long after the garden gate is shut and the guard is posted, the tragedy cuts deeper. Two sons are born and grow into adulthood, the older brother kills the younger, and the jealousy, envy, resentment, and judgment of Lucifer's way becomes our way.

The fall in the garden has deepened into the winter of our souls. And the winter grows colder. Over time, more and more sadness, more and more brokenness, enter the Larger Story. And more and more the heart of God aches as the invading force of sin devastates the landscape of the Story's early chapters. Downward spirals the narrative to the point where God announces, "We have to start over."

> God saw that human evil was out of control. People thought evil, imagined evil—evil, evil, evil from morning to night. God was sorry that he had made the human race in the first place; it broke his heart. God said, "I'll get rid of my ruined creation, make a clean sweep: people, animals, snakes and bugs, birds—the works. I'm sorry I made them." But Noah was different. God liked what He saw in Noah. (Gen. 6:5–8 MSG)

Noah builds the boat, all of creation gets a do-over, and a rainbow marks the promise "Never again" (Gen. 8:21). It has been stated that the worst pain a heart can endure is the loss of a child. If so, then the flood must have been excruciating for God the Father.

After Noah, the temperature continues to drop, but provisions by God have already begun. Covenant promises are formed and sacrifices are made for the redemption and restoration of all things. We will get to eat of the Tree of Life again (Rev. 22:2), but not yet. It is going to take more work, more time, and the arrival of a Son to make and show us a way. The plan of God is unfolding in two installments, as I mentioned before, one of which has already occurred and the other of which is on the way:

> **Phase I**—The first coming of Jesus. The Father has sent his one and only Son to remedy our fallenness and take away our sin.
>
> **Phase II**—The second coming. When the Son comes back, he will restore *all* of creation.

We now live in the in-between of these two phases (Rom. 8:18–23) in the days just before spring arrives. The day is coming when new life will be extravagantly revealed. But that day isn't here yet. Meanwhile, this world remains under the curse of winter.

LIVING WITH THE CURSE

In the Genesis record, the serpent was cursed (Gen. 3:14) and so was the land (v. 17). Adam and Eve, who once knew the provision and protection of God, now begin an existence of exile, a journey separate from God, shackled to a life in which they and all their ancestors will feel estranged . . . divided from their Creator, from the ground, from each other, and even from their own souls. A sin nature is inserted, the false-self (flesh) consequence. For those who are wonderfully born again (from death to Life), the sin nature gives way to a new nature. But like a stain on our favorite shirt—the flesh is there, more than a little inconvenient, and will take some working out for its presence not to be seen.

There is a promise of the curse being lifted (Rev. 22:3), but for now it is in full play. Remember, we live in the in-between and the not-yet, in the middle chapters between two comings in the great story of redemption and restoration.

I have gotten pretty good at making the best of things in this life; however, in doing so, I often lose my orientation and fall quickly into a smaller life where comfort and control slither their way back into the garden of my heart. My false self seems to love living small, running its harsh commentary and devoted to a story that is all about it. Obviously, a lot of work still needs to be done in me and around me. It's perpetually tempting to try to make my circumstances seem like resort living when in reality we're all living on the enemy's front lines.

This Story we live in is both far worse than we know and far greater that we can possibly imagine. The apostle Paul describes our plight with great hope. What went terribly wrong will be made right. What was lost will be reclaimed, reset, and then turned loose . . . free again! Writing to first-century believers in Rome, Paul acknowledges our present hardship and pain but sets it in the light of a coming, far greater glory.

> For [even the whole] creation (all nature) waits expectantly *and* longs earnestly for God's sons to be made known [waits for the revealing, the disclosing of their sonship].
>
> For the creation (nature) was subjected to frailty (to futility, condemned to frustration), not because of some intentional fault on its part, but by the will of Him Who so subjected it—[yet] with the hope that nature (creation) itself will be set free from its bondage to decay and corruption [and gain an entrance] into the glorious freedom of God's children.
>
> We know that the whole creation [of irrational creatures] has been moaning together in the pains of labor until now. And not

> only the creation, but we ourselves too, who have *and* enjoy the first fruits of the [Holy] Spirit [a foretaste of the blissful things to come] groan inwardly as we wait for the redemption of our bodies [from sensuality and the grave, which will reveal] our adoption (our manifestation as God's sons). For in [this] hope we were saved. (Rom. 8:19–24)

NOW EVIL IS INSIDE OF ME

Charles Spurgeon wrote, "Beware of no man more than of yourself; we carry our worst enemies within us." We have explored the false self in some detail already; now it's time for an even closer look. Let's get out the microscope.

If we misunderstand or underestimate the role of evil in our story, we will consequently mistake ourselves or others as that evil. And the mistakes won't stop there. We will mishandle everything and everyone in the story if we try to piece it together without including both the villain (the Prince of darkness) and the inner parasite known as the flesh (aka the false self). The first is not our master and the second is not us. But you and I have to contend with both of them while in the not yet, the in-between of the two phases of Christ's coming .

My friend Scott, one of the bravest men I know, has stage 4 leukemia. During the diagnosis stage, 90 percent of his blood marrow was tainted. When he finally knew it was leukemia, Scott told me, there was a moment of relief. He finally knew what had been affecting him the previous nine months, stealing his energy, clouding his thoughts, making him not himself. Then the relief of knowing quickly gave way to the rigors of treating his affected and infected parts.

Is Scott the cancer, or does he *contend* with cancer?

Am I the evil, or am I *infected* and *affected* by evil?

How we answer this question is vitally important. Are we simply bad men living out our bad identities? Or, as new creations in Christ, are we *good* men who struggle with an evil invader? Our enemy has had us coming and going with a lie he has planted deep in our hearts regarding who we are. But the truth is this: just as Scott is not the cancer he fights, you and I are not the evil inside us that we hate.

IF IT'S NOT ME, THEN . . . ?

Paul describes our miraculous transformation in Romans 6:11: We were once dead in sin, but now we are alive to God in Christ. Our very nature has changed. We have moved from one nature, *sin and death*, to a new nature, *free and alive*! We are made pure. We are made holy. And *that* is the reason we are now learning how to live like Christ, pure and holy . . . intimately connected to the Father. It's not so we can become something we're not. It's so we can live like whom we truly are.

Paul goes into even greater detail in Romans 7. The same truth he shared with the first-century Christians is just as powerful to set us free from the law of sin in our twenty-first century world:

> It is no longer I who do the deed, but the sin [principle] which is at home in me *and* has possession of me.
>
> For I know that nothing good dwells within me, that is, in my flesh. I can will what is right, but I cannot perform it. [I have the intention and urge to do what is right, but no power to carry it out.] For I fail to practice the good deeds I desire to do, but the evil deeds that I do not desire to do are what I am [ever] doing.
>
> Now if I do what I do not desire to do, it is no longer I doing it [it is not myself that acts], but the sin [principle] which dwells within me [fixed and operating in my soul].
>
> So I find it to be a law (rule of action of my being) that when I want to do what is right *and* good, evil is ever present with me *and* I am subject to its insistent demands. . . .
>
> Who will release *and* deliver me from [the shackles of] this body of death? O thank God! [He will!] through Jesus Christ (the Anointed One) our Lord! So then indeed I, of myself with the mind

> *and* heart, serve the Law of God, but with the flesh the law of sin. (Rom. 7:17–21, 24–25)

Back to *the* question . . . is evil me or is it at work *in me*? That *is* the question. And it is balanced by another reality, which Paul describes in Galatians when he writes about the Spirit of God and his fruit. Just as the false self isn't you, so also the Spirit isn't you, but he lives inside you and is at work restoring you in order for the *true you* to emerge. This is so you will grow and develop and then be on display moving about the kingdom offering Life and love. Paul says in Galatians:

> But I say, walk *and* live [habitually] in the [Holy] Spirit [responsive to *and* controlled *and* guided by the Spirit]; then you will certainly not gratify the cravings *and* desires of the flesh (of human nature without God).
>
> For the desires of the flesh are opposed to the [Holy] Spirit, and the [desires of the] Spirit are opposed to the flesh (godless human nature); for these are antagonistic to each other [continually withstanding and in conflict with each other], so that you are not free *but* are prevented from doing what you desire to do. (Gal. 5:16–17)

It works both ways. The flesh and the Spirit both operate within a system. The true man is on the side of the Spirit; the false self is opposed to the true man. Remember, the false self is *false* and is constructed of lies that reside in us and yet is not us. The false self is a powerful and wicked presence, and without the Spirit of God within us, it would guarantee that we have only one nature, *a sin nature* (Rom. 8:5, 8; Gal. 5:19, 24). As a result, we would do what a sin nature naturally does: sin.

In order to become more than that, we need a work done for us at our core, in our new heart, our deepest level, where the ability to operate from a *new nature* must be put in place (Jer. 24:7; 31:33; 32:39; Ezek. 11:19; 18:31; Matt 5:8; Luke 6:45; 8:15; Psalm 51:10; 2 Peter

1:4; 2 Cor. 1:22). If we are to become like Jesus, then a part of him must be put in us. With that piece installed, our personal revolution has begun. His Spirit partners with our spirit and will grow us into the person God intends us to be—the person we have within us to be.

THE GREAT EXCHANGE

Setting us up to receive the Father's love is why Jesus became like us and ultimately took our sin upon himself. He became sin (2 Cor. 5:21) so that we could become like him—holy, righteous, and pure, gloriously equipped for our part in his story. Take a look at how Paul describes this great exchange in the letter to the first century believers in Rome:

> In his Son, Jesus, he personally took on the human condition, entered the disordered mess of struggling humanity in order to set it right once and for all. . . . It stands to reason, doesn't it, that if the alive-and-present God who raised Jesus from the dead moves into your life, he'll do the same thing in you that he did in Jesus, bringing you alive to himself?
>
> When God lives and breathes in you (and he does, as surely as he did in Jesus), you are delivered from that dead life. With his Spirit living in you, your body will be as alive as Christ's! . . . God knew what he was doing from the very beginning. He decided from the outset to shape the lives of those who love him along the same lines as the life of his Son.
>
> The Son stands first in the line of humanity he restored. We see the original and intended shape of our lives there in him. After God made that decision of what his children should be like, he followed it up by calling people by name. After he called them by name, he set them on a solid basis with himself. And then, after getting them established, he stayed with them to the end, gloriously completing what he had begun. (Rom. 8:3, 11, 29–30 MSG)

It's the greatest exchange of all time: Jesus became like us so we could become like him!

But the opposition hasn't vanished. After losing ground, Satan and his minions patrol the perimeters of our hearts, hoping to summon the flesh, our false self, to make an agreement with his lies. Though we are *new*, he wants us to live *old*, get us to bite into something false as if it were true. If we do, we resort to the old and false, something awful in the way of our true self and the love that is ours to receive and offer.

As author Neil Anderson writes, the fallen world around us creates problems. "As a result of the fall, Satan became the rebel holder of authority on planet earth. Even Jesus referred to Satan as the ruler of this world (John. 12:31; 14:30; 16:11)."

This world is not what it used to be. Paradise is lost, and while this place we live in has echoes of Paradise, it is no comparison to our former residence in Eden and a far cry from the place he has gone to prepare for us.

DELIVER US FROM EVIL

"Making the best of it" isn't God's objective for us. Having *Life to the full* is. We are the restoration project of a loving God, and one day—oh, one marvelous day!—what was lost will be fully redeemed, restored, and refinished. *All things made new* (Rev. 21:1–5).

Until that day, though, we need to take heed because a fallen world is a dangerous world. Many things are neither in their right place nor their right mind. The lamb ought not lie down with the lion just yet. Right now the norm consists of facing conflicts and struggles, overcoming challenges, having courage, crucifying the flesh, walking wisely, being alert, armoring up, standing firm, and walking in a manner worthy of what we've been called to. There is a lot going on.

The Life we are meant for, the one granted to us by God, is both fragile and glorious. It must be understood, learned, and practiced. Charles E. Fuller, founder of Fuller Seminary, once said, "Fellowship with God means warfare with the world." Similarly, Oswald Chambers wrote, "Life without war is impossible either in nature or in grace. . . . I must learn to fight against and overcome the things that come against me, and in that way produce the balance of holiness. Then it becomes a delight to meet opposition."

Our enemies are ancient, ruthless, and diabolical, and they are opposed to everything good in us and in this world. They are not to be feared, but they are to be understood and respected. Jesus mounted a revolution against them on our behalf, and now he commissions us to continue his fight for our hearts and the hearts of others.

Men cannot join Jesus in bringing in the kingdom and advancing freedom, nor caring for the injured and releasing those who are bound by being pacifists. Jesus wasn't one, nor should we be. He is the Prince of Peace; it is a peace that is won. It is a peace on the other side of battle, worth fighting for and fighting to keep.

Neil Anderson also wrote,

> The defeat of Satan is the third part of the gospel and the one most overlooked by the western church. "The Son of God appeared for this purpose to destroy the works of the devil" (1 John 3:8). This part of the gospel is just as critical since "the whole world lies in the power of the evil one" (1 John 5:19). Believers need to know that they are now children of God (John 1:12) who are forgiven and spiritually alive in Christ (Colossians 2:13), and they also need to know that they have authority over the kingdom of darkness because they are seated with Christ in the heavenlies (Ephesians 2:6).

Now that we know a little more about what we are up against as Beloved Sons, we are ready for the next step. Kingdom training is on-the-job training. Through it, we learn from the Father what it means to be a son, from Jesus how to live in the kingdom, and from the Spirit how to stay intimately close—all things a man must learn to love and to be fully alive.

BASIC TRAINING
KNOWING AND RESTING IN WHO YOU ARE

I speak in the name of the entire German people when I assure the world that we all share the honest wish to eliminate the enmity that brings far more costs than any possible benefits. . . . It would be a wonderful thing for all of humanity if both peoples would renounce force against each other forever. The German people are ready to make such a pledge.

—*Adolf Hitler*

On January 30, 1933, Adolph Hitler was appointed chancellor of Germany. Then in March, the first official Nazi concentration camp opened in a small village about ten miles northwest of Munich. Heinrich Himmler, in his capacity as police president of Munich, officially described it as "the first concentration camp for political prisoners." The camp was located on the grounds of an abandoned munitions factory near the northeastern part of the town of Dachau in southern Germany. During its first year, the camp held about 4,800 prisoners.

In August 1934, Hitler appointed himself Führer. Two years later, on July 12, 1936, the Sachsenhausen Camp opened twenty-two miles north of Berlin. By the end of that year, the camp held 1,600 prisoners. It was just one among twenty-two primary camps built after Dachau, including Auschwitz, Buchenwald, and Treblinka. And those were just the most infamous of approximately 20,000 camps built by the Nazis between 1933 and 1945.

Two years after Sachsenhausen began its brutal operations, national sports teams from around the world entered Germany, and on August 1, 1936, the Berlin Olympics opened. Nazi Germany rolled out the red carpet to a record 110,000 spectators and journalists flocking to the opening ceremonies. The Berlin games were covered by radio broadcasts in twenty-eight languages and were the first ever to be televised. For a brief time, Germany was the shining star of the modern age. The Nazis had gotten the respectability they craved by impressing the world with what they wanted it to see—all the while concealing the unthinkable.

But we all know what followed. In December 1941, after doing its best to avoid embroiling itself in the European conflict, the United States entered war against Germany and Japan with both hands.

Several hundred centuries earlier around AD 33, you and I were drafted into a much larger war against a ruthless deceiver, powerful beyond the wildest ambitions of Hitler and the Nazis. The signs of this conflict are all around us. Within the enemy's spiritual death camps (in both physical and spiritual realms) desperate hearts cry to be liberated, while others try to make it home. It's up to us—you and me—Beloved Sons. It's time for us to become oriented and well-trained and enter into the freedom fight.

In this chapter, we'll look at seven basic training principles that can foundationally guide and assist Beloved Sons to grow in the ways of a Warrior. Let's begin by briefly reviewing what being a Warrior is about.

THE ART OF A WARRIOR

Love is the practice and presence of Jesus. He made love an art. He showed that love requires both strength and finesse. The battle is over love and all about love.

With that understanding, circle back with me to the scene in *Braveheart* between young William Wallace and his uncle Argyle. Argyle tells his nephew, "Before you can use this [sword], you have to learn how to use [your brain]." A few scenes earlier, young Wallace's father had told him something similar, "I know you can fight, but it's our wits that make us men."

There is an *Art* to the life of a Warrior.

It involves silence, solitude, patience, and an inner world of rhythm, beauty, and strength.

We will have to fight, but fighting isn't primarily what a Warrior does or is. The Warrior is a *peacekeeper* who loves well and is about freedom and life. He provides, protects, promotes and is ready to fight for life when necessary—and only then. He does these things because he is loved and therefore has something to offer, a Life that can be shared.

In his 1862 classic, *Les Miserables*, Victor Hugo observed that "the supreme happiness in life consists in the conviction that one is loved." Amen to that! A man who knows he is loved by the Father is a Beloved Son. And a Beloved Son possesses one of the greatest treasures of the kingdom: a settled heart. He is free to love those around him fiercely *and* tenderly—even those who are against him. "Love your enemies," Jesus says in Luke 6:35. No doubt they will be affected by the presence of a man who is settled, a man knows who he is and how to both fight and dance.

But how does a man receive and give that kind of love? The healing and restoring answers reside in Jesus' final words to his disciples before he headed toward his own greatest act of love, the cross:

> Live in me. Make your home in me just as I do in you. In the same way that a branch can't bear grapes by itself but only by

> being joined to the vine, you can't bear fruit unless you are joined with me. I am the Vine, you are the branches. When you're joined with me and I with you, the relation intimate and organic, the harvest is sure to be abundant. Separated, you can't produce a thing. (John 15:4–5 MSG)

That "vine life"—the connected Life the Father offers, the Life for which Jesus died that we might live, the Life the Spirit empowers us to have—is a Life with a "core training": a basic training of the heart for a life set apart. Getting free is actually part of a Warrior's training. In becoming a Beloved Son, we learn much that we will need to use again and again. Training might simply be defined as *learning how*. It has its trials and errors, victories and celebrations.

BASIC TRAINING 1: STAYING CONNECTED TO THE KING

The first and most essential principle of our training is this: we must stay intimately connected to the King—we in him and he in us. Whatever else happens or doesn't happen, Warriors stay close to their King. Jesus is where our Life is and where it comes from. Through his own deeply connected relationship with the Father, Jesus showed us how we, in turn, can live our lives in a similar connected relationship with the Father, and why we must. And he removed everything that impeded our intimacy with him and the Father (John 17).

Remember, the context of our story is war. Shortly after their defeat in WWI, Germany quietly began regrouping for European domination. Yet not until September 3, 1939, did Great Britain and France declare war. They turned a blind eye to the growing conflict until it finally came to their doorstep. The U.S. did its best to remain uninvolved until two years later when Japan bombed Pearl Harbor. The next day, December 8, 1941, the U.S. finally threw itself into a war it could no longer avoid.

How did two small countries, Germany and Japan, both about the size of California, come to dominate so much of the world? I'll tell you how . . . because they went unchallenged too long.

We fight for a Kingdom of truth that has set us and others free (John 8:32). The other kingdom, the lesser one, offers lies disguised as truth (v. 44) which will bind and enslave our hearts if we let them, keeping us from the thing we were created for, love. The Prince of Darkness has operated unchecked far too long at the borders and well inside the interior of our hearts doing the unimaginable. But no more. We declare war! *We engage!*

Our first "mission" is to reconnect with God, not just once but again and again, staying connected like branches to the vine. Once so secured, so that we are receiving God's love as a lifestyle, we can join the battle for other people's hearts, offering our strength out of what we ourselves are daily experiencing from God. Then and only then can we offer a transforming intimacy that we know firsthand and live to model and share, just as Jesus did.

In his book *The Barbarian Way*, Erwin McManus wrote,

> What if we were meant to be something greater? The invitation of Jesus is a revolutionary call to fight for the heart of humanity. Our weapons are Faith, Hope and Love. . . . [Answering Jesus' call] will cost everything. It is a life fueled by passion . . . passion for God and passion for people. Our mission is to reconnect humanity to Him. Fueled by His presence as a follower of Christ, there is a raw and untamed faith waiting to be unleashed.

It is so important for us to maintain connection with the Vine. Otherwise, we wither and die as a branch. Only by maintaining our personal, life-sustaining intimacy with Jesus can we help others reconnect.

BASIC TRAINING 2: FIGHTING FOR FREEDOM

Setting captive hearts free is no mere abstraction. It's as real as the friend who struggles with alcoholism, the wife who bears the wounds of childhood sexual abuse, or the guy two seats over in church who is contemplating suicide. They're why we fight: because they're in pain, bound and brutalized by an enemy they can't see in a war they don't comprehend.

And a Warrior well knows, "That used to be me."

Our enemy often wants to know if we *know* who we truly are. That's because his greatest weapons against the human heart are falsehoods and lies designed to convince men and women that they are not the Beloved. Our greatest fight is to advance God's kingdom against the lies that imprison us and others. Our false self acts as an assassin, waiting for orders to aid the enemy in its mission to steal, kill, and destroy.

Jesus promises, "You will know the truth, and the truth will set you free" (John 8:32). Paul tells us, "You have been set free from sin" (Rom. 6:18). Peter shouts, "Live as free men" (1 Peter 2:16). And in our own time, Nelson Mandela said, "To be free is not merely to cast off one's chains, but to live in a way that respects and enhances the freedom of others."

What goes on in our physical world is a direct reflection of what is going on in the spiritual world. We fight against accusations, lies, and false beliefs and against the agents of darkness who seek to take us out. Not only do we fight against our false self but the false self in others. And all our fighting, resisting, and overcoming, all our learning and training, is for the sake of freedom—ours *and* others. Love frees!

BASIC TRAINING 3: SEEING WITH THE EYES OF YOUR HEART

Through Christ and in Christ we are free, yet we live with a gravitational pull toward the old ways of the old nature. So after our initial healings from our wounds (during which we confess and repent as often as we need to), we continue to vigilantly engage our will and say no to whatever our enemy throws at us that will impede our freedom. We are trained as our Father's Beloved Sons to see, listen, and discern between the presence and voices of two kingdoms: Life and death. This is what the Father is up to in the hearts and lives of his Beloved Sons. It is what Jesus practiced, and so must we.

Much of the training Jesus takes us through will develop our ability to *see*—to look with spiritual eyes past outward appearances and circumstantial behaviors to the unseen realm at work behind them. Our intuitive skills and discernment abilities must grow. If a man can't see a thing, then he can't possibly discern it; that lack of discernment will cause more harm than good. Jesus faced the challenge of training untrained, naïve men. His disciples didn't see well because no one had taught them how to see. They didn't know what they didn't know and Jesus wanted them to know. Know what? Know experientially who Jesus was, how the kingdom works, and who they themselves (in the midst of it all) really were.

In 2 Corinthians 10:5, Paul admonishes us to "take every thought captive."; however, before a thought can be captured, it has to be detected. It's the things I never see coming that either run over me or run over others.

Of course, no one knows how at first. That's how it is with training. Think of all the firsts in your life. There are too many to count, but most of them have had one thing in common: you didn't know what to do, so many of those moments didn't go so well. That is normal in becoming more like Christ. The things that are not of him or his kingdom ways have to be seen. But if you don't see them, then you don't see them. And that's okay . . . kind of. Keep showing up and you'll learn. *Life* depends on it. You've got an excellent Teacher who is both patient and wise. Where else or to whom would we turn?

BASIC TRAINING 4:
LISTENING AND PATIENCE

It's all training: what to do, what not to do, and learning how to exercise care in drawing conclusions. The false self is quick to run crazy commentary of how we should act, react, judge, or accuse. Every moment consists of a multitude of variables, never just one thing.

The Heart of a Warrior must learn that God is good and is up to good in his life and in the lives of others. The Father's aim is to deploy his Beloved Sons into many different situations where he wants a kingdom presence. Learning how to be that presence takes time. Look at the letters the apostles wrote to the churches. They are the same men who walked the roads with Jesus—and yet they are not. They are *more*. Through time and many redeemed moments each has become more the man God created him to be. More the Beloved Son. More the Warrior. With patience the Father trained them—and with patience, he will train us.

Hearing his "still, small voice" in our hearts is one of the most crucial skills a Warrior must cultivate then practice. Seeing is important, but hearing is imperative. If the Holy Spirit is to counsel, teach, guide, and comfort us, then we must learn how to listen because there is no Life without listening and receiving words, instruction, and validation from God.

Jeffery Satinover, an Orthodox Jew, psychiatrist, and author, wrote, "I have often wondered why the voice of God is so quiet and so still. Perhaps He is trying to train us to listen. Just as by his very quiet the gentleman in a room of shouting oafs eventually compels attention, perhaps God draws us to His voice not by out-shouting our inner babble, but by the whispered truths that reveal His character."

Our inner world is a crowded place, downright rowdy at times. Seldom do we check its voices as to their source. Let's add them up.

We have a true self and a false self living within us. Christ lives in us in the form of the Holy Spirit laying out the truth. And the enemy of our heart is looking for opportune times to drop lies into our mind and heart. Obviously we are never alone! So the question is, can we discern? Do we pay attention to our thoughts? And which voice has the microphone?

Do we know the voice of God?

> I am the good shepherd; I know my sheep and my sheep know me—just as the Father knows me and I know the Father—and I lay down my life for the sheep. I have other sheep that are not of this sheep pen. I must bring them also. They too will listen to my voice, and there shall be one flock and one shepherd. (John 10:14-16 NIV)

Until we are trained, then regardless of our standing as believers, our false self will be the voice that speaks most of the time about most things. Complaining, accusing, labeling, judging, being impatient and frustrated, name calling, overdramatizing, getting angry and vengeful—all are a part of false self's commentary.

Listening stands in sharp contrast to these things. It is one of the kindest, most loving things we can do for the hearts of others and for our own heart. So if you want to develop your ability to hear God, start with your wife and kids. How well do you listen to them? Try and observe your skills for a day. Give your kids your eyes; look at your wife when she is talking. Hone in on their words, shutting out all other noises and distractions.

The apostle James wrote, "Let every man be quick to hear [a ready listener], slow to speak, slow to take offense and to get angry" (James 1:19). The practice of listening positions a man for everything his heart will need to receive. Asking and inviting God to speak . . . and then listening—this is the practice of an oriented man, the practice of a Warrior Heart. It will save you a lot of trouble and disarm the enemy's attempts to lure you into judgment. It will allow for wisdom and understanding, the qualities Christ wants to impart to the men of his Kingdom.

BASIC TRAINING 5: SOLITUDE AND CUNNING

Being still (Ps. 46:10) is a daily practice of a Warrior that is uncommon to most men. *The Message* version of the Bible does a beautiful job of rendering Jesus' instructions about praying in solitude:

> Here's what I want you to do: find a quiet, secluded place so you won't be tempted to role-play before God. Just be there as simply and honestly as you can manage. The focus will shift from you to God, and you will begin to sense his grace. (Matt. 6:6 MSG)

Only by practicing stillness aggressively, pushing all the clamor and busyness of life aside, can a man truly experience God. In the still and quiet, discernment is learned so that in the heart of the battle it can be practiced. If a man can't practice it when things are still, there is no way he will be able to do so when the arrows are flying.

A few years back, I was with a group of good men at a weekend retreat, exploring and discovering the truths of the kingdom. One day was set aside to go whitewater rafting—not my favorite thing, but I was game for what the team had scheduled. We were briefed, then loaded onto our boats of six-man teams with a guide . . . and away we went.

Our guide, a big, burly man in his early sixties, barked at us every chance he got, "You boys paddle like girls! . . . Whose turn is it to bounce overboard on this next stretch? . . . You should probably know, a couple folks died a few years back at this next stretch of rapids"—and so on and so on. When the day was over, my mind was made up: "I hate whitewater rafting!"

Fast-forward a year. Same retreat, same men, and guess what—we're going whitewater rafting again. Not me! I ain't going. *I hate whitewater rafting!*

One of my close friends, Jeff, found out I was staying back, so he asked me what was up. I explained to him last year's debacle. He smiled and said, "Come on, you don't hate whitewater rafting! You hate being guided badly." Sometimes discernment will come from an oriented friend, one *not* caught up in your drama.

My curiosity got the better of me and I boarded the bus. After the briefing, Jeff introduced my team to our guide. She was as wide as she was tall, with arms the girth of my legs. She called me "sweetheart" and called us "her boys." Once in the water, we practiced moving our paddles to her commands, and each time she yelled, "You boys are good!" After we evaded the first hazard the river threw at us, she yelled, "I got the best crew on the river!"

My friend Jeff was right. I didn't hate whitewater rafting (though I'm still not the first one in line). I hated being guided badly.

Jesus is a superb guide—the best! Amid the millrace of life, he knows how to guide and help us accurately discern our circumstances. One way is through listening prayer. In other words, discernment enjoyed through the art of asking questions of God and allowing him to answer.

Follow me here. Jesus was known for asking questions. It was one of the ways he demonstrated love: asking people questions and then giving them his attention by actively listening to their response. He asks that we learn to do the same toward God in prayer. Prayer is a conversation in which we are invited to ask and listen, not just talk. The Warrior in training will see his prayer life become more a discussion and less a monologue. That kind of prayer—asking, seeking, knocking, and listening—becomes our first impulse rather than our last resort.

In prayer, our Father helps us sift through our own thoughts. Inventory your thoughts, take them captive, see and hear . . . pay attention, observe! To find the source of a thought, play it out to its logical conclusion. You can tell where it came from by considering what fruit it will produce. Does it create blessing, encouragement, validation? Is it worthwhile and valuable? If it is loving, then it is from God and the true self. If it is accusatory, if it causes guilt or shame or fear, or if it invites you to judge, hide, criticize, or diminish yourself or another person—then it is not love and it is not for you. Such unruly thoughts come from the enemy of your heart, and they gain a foothold in the false self. They need to be seen, captured, and brought to Christ for him to handle. We are to bring every thought into submission to Christ (2 Cor. 10:5), and in order to do that, a Warrior carefully examines his personal thought life.

He also exercises patience and cunning. Cunning is knowing the difference between merely letting a moment happen and *making* a moment happen. This, too, is a matter of training. Whereas the false self reacts in haste, God teaches us to see, listen, discern, and be ready—because often we are invited to think or say things that are not true, or to judge ourselves or others harshly. In these moments, slowing things down is critical to seeing and hearing, asking God for help, instruction, and direction. Jesus did, and everything he said and did was in harmony with the Father. Jesus knew where people's hearts were. He knew their motives and their hopes and whether they were with him or against him. He lives in us by his Spirit, and he wants to guide, counsel, and teach the man who will let him.

BASIC TRAINING 6: MOVING IN GLORY

The letters of Peter, James, John, and Paul to first-century believers were all written with a common expectation: those who read them would "get better" because they were oriented and equipped to get better. The new believers' old hearts of stone (Jer. 17:9; Ezek. 11:19) had been replaced with new ones (Jer. 24:7; Ezek. 18:31). Now, at the center of their being, they were made *noble and good* (Luke 8:15).

So it is with us as well! Now we too are to learn how to live our lives out of the good heart within us. Our Father invites us to get better, to become *more*—more loving, more kind, more patient, more like Jesus in thought, words and deeds, more who we truly are as Beloved Sons. God gives us the equipment—a good heart and new nature—and then wants to give us the training so we would live from them. We can then offer to the world the unique and personal ways in which we individually bear God's image.

Don't get me wrong—it's no slam dunk. The epistle writers had plenty to say about drifting away from the faith, making poor choices, and compromising the truth of the gospel of grace. They warned against the performance-driven incentives of the Judaizers, the hedonistic practices of the Greeks, and the high achieving through lowly poverty and abstinence of the Gnostics. All these compromisers had their moments in the letters to the new believers of the first-century churches. The apostles shared a message and a way of life that was very different. Their letters to the churches all had similar overtones: *What are you doing? Don't do that! You used to do that because you couldn't help it—it's who you were. But now you* can *help it because it's not who you are anymore. Now you are new. You are ________!* (Fill in the blank: sons, overcomers, holy, co-heirs, accepted, worthy, redeemed, complete, chosen, righteous.) The point is, all of the apostles insist that you and I are *more*.

This seemed especially important to Paul. He goes so far as to say that we have an *ever-increasing glory*!

> All of us, as with unveiled face, [because we] continued to behold [in the Word of God] as in a mirror the glory of the Lord, are constantly being transfigured into His very own image in ever increasing splendor and from one degree of glory to another; [for this comes] from the Lord [Who is] the Spirit. (2 Cor. 3:18)

And why wouldn't we have a glory about us? After all, our Father does. His Glory starts with a capital *G*, and we reflect it with a small-*g* glory of image-bearers who are becoming increasingly like him.

You know the old expressions "A chip off the ol' block" and "The apple doesn't fall far from the tree." That's what the glory of God's children is about. We bear our Father's image! The word *glory* simply means the weightiness, the grandness, the splendor of a thing—and the sons of God (daughters too, for that matter) have that kind of glory. It dwells in our hearts and is meant to be demonstrated in our actions and words, in the way we love one another.

Our *glory* is the true you and me. The glory of who we really are wants to burst out, bear fruit, be offered, and be experienced by others and the world. Our glory is meant to be shared. It expresses itself in the unique, God-given gifts entrusted to each man for the good of others. God invites us to offer it freely. He never *uses* us for the sake of his glory; a Father who loves his children never "uses" them. Rather, he shares his Life with us, bestows his love on us, and takes up residence in our hearts, making us alive in him. Our glory is thus energized and directed by the impulses of his own lavishly giving heart.

That is why our heart is core. John Eldredge writes in *Waking the Dead*,

> The heart is central. That a man needs to be reminded of this only shows how far we have fallen from the life we were meant to live—or how powerful the spell has been. The subject of the heart is addressed in the Bible more than any other topic—more than "works" or "serve," more than "believe" or "obey," more than "money" and even more than "worship." Maybe God knows something we've forgotten.

BASIC TRAINING 7: LOVE

You have a good heart and a glory to your life.

If you know Christ, say it! Out loud . . .

"I HAVE A GOOD HEART AND A GLORY TO MY LIFE."

So when another person in your life operates from their false self toward you, don't take it personally, and whatever you do, don't let your own false self get provoked into reacting, criticizing, or judging that person. Others are going through rescue and redemption too. They are going through healing and training too. Just be the Beloved. Warriors live and love from a good heart, offering their glory.

Jesus said to his apprentices, "You're blessed when you get your inside world—your mind and heart—put right. Then you can see God in the outside world" (Matt. 5:8 MSG). We who possess a good heart and a glory that continually increases through training are being equipped to step into that for which we were made: a Life of love. That is why we battle: so that others may know the deep, unconditional love of God. There is nothing greater. That love gives Life. It is relief for the weary, medicine to the aching heart.

Because it matters so much when men love, the enemy targets their hearts in an attempt to ensure that they won't. A. W. Tozer wrote, "The Christian need not expect to escape opposition. As long as Satan stands to resist the sons of God, as long as the world and the flesh remain, the believing man will meet opposition. Sometimes it will be sharp and obvious, but mostly it will be just the hidden and unsuspected friction set up by circumstances. No one need be anxious about this, however, for God has figured it in and made allowance for it."

Prior to undergoing his crucifixion, Jesus expanded on the second great commandment with these instructions to his friends:

> I've told you these things for a purpose: that my joy might be your joy, and your joy wholly mature. This is my command: Love one another the way I loved you. This is the very best way to love. Put your life on the line for your friends. You are my friends when you do the things I command you. I'm no longer calling you servants because servants don't understand what their master is thinking and planning. No, I've named you friends because I've let you in on everything I've heard from the Father. (John 15:11–15 MSG)

Love is what we were made for, and in love God restores us. Our job as men is first to receive and experience God and then offer him to others—because he is love.

Love is the family business of the kingdom. It will take some training, and everything we have and everything we are as men, to protect love and see it done. Love will not happen without a fight. If we fight for it, the outcome is certain. He became like us so we could become like him.

For most of our lives, as with all those lives around us, we have experienced love so conditionally that the vital move toward unconditional love will take time. A man can't just buckle down and make it happen in a moment. *Love is something that happens* to *a man and then settles the heart within him.*

What does that love look like? Jesus.

Jesus!

Christ loves this way. And he invites us to follow his lead in *the* great romance set amidst the great battles in this fallen place. More training is available to Beloved Sons and Warriors to accomplish all that God has in store for them. It takes time to learn and practice the art of these basic skills. This is just the foundation, just the beginning.

ADVANCED TRAINING
EXPERIENCING THE GOOD THAT GOD IS UP TO

AND WHEN THE DEVIL HAD ENDED EVERY [THE COMPLETE CYCLE OF] TEMPTATION, HE [TEMPORARILY] LEFT HIM [THAT IS, STOOD OFF FROM HIM] UNTIL ANOTHER MORE OPPORTUNE AND FAVORABLE TIME.

—LUKE 4:13

WHEN I WAS A CHILD, I TALKED LIKE A CHILD; I THOUGHT LIKE A CHILD, I REASONED LIKE A CHILD. WHEN I BECAME A MAN, I PUT CHILDISH WAYS BEHIND ME.

—1 CORINTHIANS 13:11 (NIV)

In the 1998 film *The Mask of Zorro*, the elder Zorro (Anthony Hopkins), as he begins training his inexpert young protégé (Antonio Banderas), sums up what lies ahead: "This is going to take a lot of work." Training is hard, yet it is vital to our living well in the kingdom, and therefore it is so, so good.

> The student is not above the teacher, but everyone who is fully trained will be like their teacher. (Luke 6:40 NIV)

Training is essential for the apprentice of Jesus. (1Cor. 9:25; Eph. 6:4; Heb. 5:14; 1 Tim. 4:8; 2 Tim. 3:16; James 1:5).

I wonder how many training moments I have misclassified as inconvenient, punishment, bad luck, my fault or someone else's, but I am convinced that Jesus wants to redeem all such moments. Learning how to get the best out of them takes time. One day you don't know how; the next, you do. All the days leading up to when the old gives way to the new matter. It is over time that training pays off.

There was a time when I didn't understand that much of what God is up to in my training journey. I thought it was about policing me, waiting for me to step out of line so he could dispense the proper punishment. This false belief had great power in my life. It was a false gospel that made sin central and punishment primary. Those two ingredients do not make for intimacy and didn't make for a very good version of me.

Under that old belief system, when hardships or inconveniences arose in my life, I was certain God was using them to punish me or get even. I see it all as training now.

> God is educating you; that's why you must never drop out. He's treating you as dear children. This trouble you're in isn't punishment; it's *training*, the normal experience of children. Only irresponsible parents leave children to fend for themselves. Would you prefer an irresponsible God? We respect our own parents for training and not spoiling us, so why not embrace God's training so we can truly *live*? (Heb. 12:7–9 MSG)

This is great news! If you understand the heart of the Father and what he is really up to in your own heart, then you also understand what he is preparing and readying you for: *more!* It is why the art of *living curiously* is so helpful to the Warrior in training. Asking God questions in prayer puts him in the rightful place of Teacher and us in the safest place, student. If God is going to be more and do more in your life, then it's critical that he have greater access to your heart. Living oblivious to the heart and the Larger Story and how it works is a recipe for being a casualty, not a Warrior.

In order to renovate your heart, Jesus will have you revisit your belief system. What you see, hear and conclude . . . what you *believe* in any and every situation matters. It has authority in your life! Some of our old attitudes and beliefs will need only gentle massaging; others will require surgery, perhaps a series of surgeries. As Zorro put it, *it's going to take a lot of work*. But that's okay. Just wait until you see the results!

UNCOMPROMISING MEN

The Warrior cannot and does not force his way, nor can he make someone change. He only offers who he is and what he knows—a dangerous prospect, because you never know how another image bearer will respond. You never know who is for you or who will be against a man with a settled heart. Jesus didn't win them all, and neither will you.

This is part of a Warrior's advanced training: simply offering who you are in a loving way. Not sweet, but loving. Love knows how to confront, defend, protect and requires courage and strength, yet a gentle strength. Frances de Sales, the Bishop of Geneva in the early 1600's, wrote, "Nothing is so strong as gentleness—nothing so gentle and loving as real strength."

The question for an oriented man is, *How will you live, knowing what you know, among others who don't?*

The answer: Patiently. Kindly. Generously. Lovingly.

And *uncompromisingly*.

This is what Jesus modeled, and this is the life he invites us to share.

> But whoever drinks the water I give them will never thirst. Indeed, the water I give them will become in them a spring of water welling up to eternal life. (John 4:14 NIV)

> As I have loved you, so you must love one another. (John 13:34 NIV)

> Remain in me, as I also remain in you. No branch can bear fruit by itself; it must remain in the vine. Neither can you bear fruit unless you remain in me. (John 15:4 NIV)

Why uncompromisingly? Well, ask yourself, how evil *is* evil? What kind of control does it exert over those who do its bidding, whether on the internet, the street corner, or in the office?

Long before every home had a computer, evil's prince had his own "worldwide web" (Luke 4:6; John 14:30), well-placed to catch anyone who was, or is, in the wrong place at the wrong time. Far from committing random acts of violence, our enemy customizes his hits on our heart: tailor-made schemes that function like lures dragged in front of our eyes. Each one is, in its own way, an invitation to bite Eden's apple once again—to compromise by falling for the oldest lie in the book: *You can be like God. Here, take a bite. Make a life for yourself.*

> Don't let anyone under pressure to give in to evil say, "God is trying to trip me up." God is impervious to evil, and puts evil in no one's way. The temptation to give in to evil comes from us and only us. We have no one to blame but the leering, seducing flare-up of our own lust. Lust gets pregnant, and has a baby: sin! Sin grows up to adulthood, and becomes a real killer. So, my very dear friends, don't get thrown off course. (James 1:13–16 MSG)

ADVANCING!

Advanced training is very much about learning to see your false self, particularly when it is provoked—when it is being summoned by temptation; when you are being lured into compromising your true self.

As God heals your wounds, your enemy will rally to inflict new ones or attempt to reintroduce old ones. But when you hear what is going on and see it playing out, you can engage in offense and defense. Swinging the sword of the spirit and raising the shield of faith becomes your new normal (Eph. 6:16–17). Before the false self takes over, the true man rises up.

How often do you take this stance? The answer is whenever temptation comes. And I'm not talking about immoral behaviors. That is starting way too far down stream. I am talking about compromised thoughts, where the real battle is and the Warrior's fighting must begin. The forces of darkness outside a man are attempting to strike a deal with the darkness in a man by enticing the false self. You may not currently be dealing with a sexual perversion, substance addiction, or deep depression, but that doesn't mean your enemy isn't planning one for you.

This is all-out, bloody battle, and there's no giving it a "G" rating. This creature that lives within you wants to sin. John Eldredge calls it "the poser"; John Lynch refers to it as "the mask"; Paul calls it "the flesh." The good news is, its lead role can be stripped from it and rightly reassigned to your true self, but its presence and power should never be underestimated. Underestimating it is the central contributing factor to the ongoing tragedy of almost every man. So do not drop your guard. Because the kingdom of darkness would love to retrain you.

There is only one way to treat the poser: hear it, see it, and then kill it. We are to put the false self, poser, flesh to death—or, as the Scriptures say, crucify the flesh—again and again as often as it rears its ugly head! (See Rom. 6:6; 8:13; Gal. 2:20; 5:24.) Treat your young heart kindly. Treat your true man with compassion. Treat your wounds gently, but don't treat the false self at all.

Every lie I am offered to believe about myself, God, or others is both a temptation to compromise and an invitation to overcome. Every choice, thought, and move matters. We have worked too hard healing up and training up in partnership with God and becoming the true man, to turn around and forfeit our privileges and responsibilities as Beloved Sons. Compromise will only lead back to bondage, prison, and worse, *torture*. And the enemy won't stop there; he will also use us to wound and eventually torture others. They don't just want you; they want your marriage, your kids, and anyone else they can *use* to get you to do their bidding.

A great advanced training question to prayerfully ask is, "Why does my enemy believe that will work? Why, Lord, do they think I will take the bait and bite at that?"

It's not just one moment of compromise that our enemy is after. It is the ones to whom it will lead. The breach in our heart's security system makes way for the enemy to secure a *stronghold*—that is, control over a man (Luke 11:20–26; 2 Cor. 10:4; Eph. 4:27). When a breach occurs and a man is manipulated and then controlled by darkness, it's not good news. Yet it's epidemic in our culture and our churches; not just "unsaved" men but saved men who are lost, disoriented, and have compromised their true selves. Compromised men do compromising things. It isn't who they truly are, but their false self will take the wheel, drive around and make a mess out of everything.

So once you've retaken ground, do not give it back. Warriors understand and practice good defense. Jesus warned in the gospel of Luke,

> Be on your guard. Don't let the sharp edge of your expectation get dulled by parties and drinking and shopping. Otherwise, that Day is going to take you by complete surprise, spring on you suddenly like a trap, for it's going to come on everyone, everywhere, at once. So, whatever you do, don't go to sleep at the switch. Pray constantly that you will have the strength and wits to make it through everything that's coming and end up on your feet before the Son of Man. (Luke 21:34–36 MSG)

A Warrior isn't immune from battle. Instead, he accepts that he is in one and he has learned how to fight. Moving forward, fight your battles well and fight your battles once. Do not give your enemy reentry to your heart. No *new* woundings for the Beloved Son! And make no *new* judgments, vows, or agreements.

WHO AM I NOW?

"Who am I to you *now* God?" That was an initial question for healing and becoming the Beloved Son, and so that *is* an advanced, prayerful question for the Warrior.

Unlike what we so often experience on this earth, who we are is not based on some award or achievement. Rather, God unveils with ever-increasing glory. He reveals who we have always had it in us to be. While we were knit together in Mom's womb, he says, "I knew you" (Ps. 139:13; Jer. 1:5). There is treasure inside us. The false self has blocked our view of it with all the toxic baggage it has thrown in the way, but God is determined to move that stuff out of the way and free us to be our true selves. God desires to transfigure us; he wants to introduce us first to ourselves, then to a world that desperately needs true sons to arrive on the scene and bring his strength, love, and light.

Paul the apostle puts it like this:

> When God is personally present, a living Spirit, that old, constricting legislation is recognized as obsolete. We're free of it! All of us! Nothing between us and God, our faces shining with the brightness of his face. And so we are transfigured much like the Messiah, our lives gradually becoming brighter and more beautiful as God enters our lives and we become like him. (2 Cor. 3:17–18 MSG)

Because we are becoming more like our Father, we are becoming more like our true selves as well. God has many tools, gifts, and methods at his disposal to unveil our true identity.

One gift that he gives is a new name.

Names carry a weight and an identity. They matter to God and can declare his intimate fondness for us when they are delivered. We are invited to either wear our name or grow into it.

The enemy too has names he wants to impose on us to diminish or shame us (idiot, stupid, lazy, ugly . . .) but when God gives us a name, it reveals something wonderful about whom he calls us to be. That is why, in the Bible, names are changed. Names validate and names bestow. *Names* are written in the Lamb's Book of Life. God seems to delight in setting up the moments when our new names are not only given to us but when they will begin to truly fit.

We must be willing to abandon whom we think we were and invite God to show us whom we truly are. What name might God be trying to give you?

NEW NAMES

Over the past several years, God has at different times and in many ways shown me who I am and how he sees me. In 2006 a film came out called *Amazing Grace: The William Wilburforce Story*. As I sat in the theater, the story undid me. Tears welled up in my eyes. I was a beautiful mess.

I've learned to take such moments to God. Sitting in my seat as the end credits rolled and the music played, I asked God, "What is this about? Why am I such a mess?"

The answer came in the next thought: "You are my abolitionist."

Like a veteran being awarded a medal, I felt undeserving, yet at the same time I wanted those words to be true. God had just given me one of my new names. The work and identity of an abolitionist is what's in my deep heart, and God determined it was time to bring it to the surface. I was already growing into the shoes he had given me. It was good to feel the moment when they first began to fit.

God gave new names to prominent people in the Bible. Abram became Abraham, Jacob became Israel, Simon became Peter, and Saul became Paul. Jesus himself has many names: the Christ, the Good Shepherd, the Way, the Truth, and the Life. Messiah. He is known as the Light, the Lamb, the Lion, the Bridegroom and as the Teacher, Savior, and Master. He is Faithful and True, the King of Kings.

Obviously, names are a big deal to God. They have a way of deeply identifying who someone is and inviting that person to relate to the Creator in a specific way.

My dad called me, Mick, Bud, Poncho, and Loob. Each of those names has a story, and each defines me to someone who loves me. My wife, Robin, calls me Lovey, Sweetheart, and Cutie. Almost every morning I get a "Hey, Handsome!"

It always feels good to be seen and known, called out and called up.

The names God gives us are more than mere compliments. They are *identities*—titles that define us, that say something important about us and are intended to inspire something deep within us. The bestowing of identity doesn't happen just once to a man. There are too many roles and assignments in his life for him to be known or contained by one name only or defined by a single moment. Son, husband, father, and friend are just a few of the roles a man plays. *But what kind of a son, husband, father, or friend?* The answer in each case may become part of a man's name, his new identity.

During his journey, a man will find that the Father has many names for him, just as we have many names for him. In our Advanced Training, Beloved Sons discover who we are to the Father. Invite Him to show you. Ask God, "Who am I to you *now*?"

Then pay attention. Listen.

The answer may come unexpectedly or it may come in installments, but it never comes unplanned. When he does speak, I highly exhort you to write down what you hear.

WRITING IT DOWN

On my office shelf are twenty-five journals dating back to the year 1989. That's when I began writing down my life events and conversations with God. In the early years, similar to my prayer life, my journal entries were like grocery lists. Come to think of it, that is exactly what they were: "God, here is my list: 1, 2, 3 . . . I sure would appreciate your help." Mostly I wrote down the things I wanted or needed. Not much in the way of personal stuff, or how I felt, or what I was seeing God do in my life. Just to-dos for God, with a few of my headlines from the day thrown in.

My, how those journals have evolved! And that's how it should be. We are supposed to evolve and get better, growing increasingly into our true self. These days, when journaling as well as praying, I don't do all the talking. My entries are much more conversational. I write and share my heart, and then I listen as God shares his, sometimes he speaks through thoughts, sometimes through imagery.

Often I wage small battles with distractions: "Look, a bird! . . . That's a funny cloud. . . . What time is it?" I still have my lists of needs and hopes, but over the years, through practice, I have cultivated a deeper dialog.

My friend Kelly said, "Paintings are the pictures of what your eyes see; journaling is the picture of what your heart sees." I have also come to hear and see God speaking and moving in my life through many different things. Central are the Scriptures. He partners with my friends and speaks to me *through* them as well as through places, songs, and books. Stories and films have been frequent meeting places for God's heart and mine. So have sunrises and sunsets and beautiful landscapes. Everyday objects and occurrences can become God's voice. Writing about all of it has been invaluable.

Most often I hear best when I get still, quieting my heart and giving my full attention to God, or at least trying to. This is a fundamental practice of a Beloved Son and essential to a Warrior's well-being. If Jesus regularly got away to be with the Father, then clearly it would do our own hearts some good as well.

I have found that the pace of the pen and the heart move well together. They seem to operate in third gear while the rest of my life is determined to lock into fifth. That fifth gear life is one of the great enemies of intimacy. Most men try to fit God into their lives rather than fit their lives into God. It doesn't work. Think about it. Which is the more romantic, a drive-through meal or a candlelight dinner? Which setting is better for conversation, a traffic light or a sunset? What relationship do you know of that thrives more through multitasking than quality time? Journaling is a means by which a Warrior downshifts from interstate speed into scenic third gear through quiet and solitude, pen and paper, listening and reflecting.

BOOMERANGS OF JUDGMENT

Imagine going to rock concert where, instead of bouncing giant beach balls up and around through the stadium, everyone brought a backpack of boomerangs and, at the count of "one, two, three!"—*let 'em fly!*

That's how it is with judging others. Whenever we judge another person, we are throwing a boomerang into the universe. Sooner or later, it's bound to return and smack us in the head.

Jesus is very clear about this:

> Don't pick on people, jump on their failures, criticize their faults—unless, of course, you want the same treatment. That critical spirit has a way of boomeranging. (Matt. 7:1–2 MSG)

> Judge not [neither pronouncing judgment nor subjecting to censure], and you will not be judged; do not condemn *and* pronounce guilty, and you will not be condemned *and* pronounced guilty; acquit *and* forgive *and* release (give up resentment, let it drop), and you will be acquitted *and* forgiven *and* released. (Luke 6:37)

Our judgments of others are some of the most significant and lethal ways the enemy uses us to deliver pain to hearts, including our own. It gives him permission to deliver at an "opportune time" our verdict right back to us, but when we experience the love of God and exchange our false self for Belovedness, then the training we receive from the Father guides us away from judging others. Instead, it teaches us how to love others with the same kind of unconditional love we receive. The less of the false self we carry, the less the enemy has to work with in tempting us to judge rather than love. The false self loves to judge; the true self loves to love.

JUDGMENTS AND AUTHORITY

In his book *Repenting of Religion*, pastor and author Greg Boyd writes,

> We love God—we affirm the unsurpassable worth of God by obediently ascribing unsurpassable worth to those to whom He ascribes unsurpassable worth. We love those whom God loves, and we love them the way God loves them. . . . We are not satisfied being God-like in our capacity to love; we also want to become God-like in our capacity to judge, which is how the serpent tempts us. . . . But in a spirit toward the latter, we lose our capacity for the former, for unlike God, we cannot judge and love at the same time.

In other words—no judging! When you find yourself judging someone, then just stop; that's all. Be kind and gentle with yourself, ask God for forgiveness, and move on. You may need to ask those you held court on for forgiveness as well; more on that later. To not judge is to make no new agreements with the enemy, because what you believe has authority in your life; harsh, critical and condemning pronouncements (whether spoken or just unchecked thoughts) about others *will* come back to bite you.

Jesus was led into the wilderness for a brutal forty days of tempting and training (Luke 4:1–13). Instead of compromising and taking a shortcut, Jesus declared, in essence, "No. I'm going to take back authority in this world another way." That way led through a brutal beating, a nasty crown, and an awful cross, but afterward, the resurrected Christ told his disciples,

> God authorized and commanded me to commission you: Go out and train everyone you meet, far and near, in this way of life, marking them by baptism in the threefold name: Father, Son, and Holy Spirit. Then instruct them in the practice of all I have commanded you. I'll be with you as you do this, day after day after day, right up to the end of the age. (Matt. 28:18–20 MSG)

The NIV renders verse 18 this way: "All *authority* in heaven and on earth has been given to me."

Remember where it was before? Lost! Adam gave it away, but Jesus bought it back. Then later, in the book of Acts, the risen Christ instructs his friends, the heirs apparent:

> You will receive *power* when the Holy Spirit comes on you; and you will be my witnesses in Jerusalem, and in all Judea and Samaria, and to the ends of the earth. Acts 1:8 (NIV)

Having reclaimed the power and authority that the first Adam gave away, the Savior of the world and all mankind does something absolutely incredible; he gives back to us what had been lost. Why? Because we are going to need it—not just for our personal comeback and benefit, but for the advancing of the kingdom and for the hearts of others.

Refusing to judge others is one of the forms that authority takes. It works like this: just as the physical universe has laws that govern everything from gravity to the interaction of molecules to the behavior of DNA, so the spiritual universe also has its laws. It's within the context of those rules that authority plays out, and one key principle is the law of *sowing* and *reaping*. Plant a seed; reap its fruit. Sow judgment; reap the same, but we have authority as Warriors to create a better dynamic. Sow love; reap love. Sow forgiveness;reap forgiveness. Sow Life; reap *Life*!

Our adversary wants to enlist the assistance of our false self in reinforcing what he is doing to others—accusing them, heaping shame on them, but we have the authority to stand against him by choosing mercy over judgment, blessing over cursing. And in so doing, we unleash the power of Life, not death, in other people's hearts—and in our own.

So don't be lured into being *used* by the enemy. See the lure of judging others for what it is. Consider why the enemy thinks he can use that tactic with you or someone close to you, then wield your authority to oppose it.

FORGIVENESS

The ease and speed with which we communicate today can cause us to be cross-grained with others quicker than you can say "splinter" and "log." Whether it's by email, texting, or actual conversation (or the lack of it), wounding packages are bound to arrive at the door of our heart. It may be a person who delivers it, but the bomb inside comes from the enemy. Along with it, though, comes a kingdom opportunity to employ the most powerful, loving counterattack weapon known to man: forgiveness.

> And forgive us our debts, as we also have forgiven (left, remitted, and let go of the debts, and have given up resentment against) our debtors. (Matt. 6:12)

> So also My heavenly Father will deal with every one of you if you do not freely forgive your brother from your heart *his offenses.* (Matt. 18:35)

Forgiving those who hurt us is the greatest way we imitate our King. It was, and is, his ultimate expression of love, so, not surprisingly, it's core to our training.

Forgive them, Father, for they know not what they do (Luke 23:34)—only a settled heart, a man on mission, a Beloved Son/Warrior could utter those words in those circumstances. He wants us to learn them and practice them as well.

I know, this training module is a tough one. Oh, how I know. I recommend you start with you . . . receive God's forgiveness for yourself. Nowhere in the scriptures are we instructed to "forgive ourselves" but, many times we are invited to receive. This forgiveness thing is a big deal to God. The Warrior will be very familiar with both receiving and offering forgiveness. Jesus taught,

> This is how I want you to conduct yourself in these matters. If you enter your place of worship and, about to make an offering, you suddenly remember a grudge a friend has against you, abandon your offering, leave immediately, go to this friend and make things right. Then and only then, come back and work things out with God. (Matt. 5:23-24 MSG)

There is only one way we get good at this. We practice. I find the words "I'm sorry, will you forgive me?" are coming easier and I am in need of them less often. Yet the art of a sincere apology, one without explanation or justification, takes time. It is one of the greatest weapons we possess in extinguishing the fiery darts of the devil. Few men know how, and God definitely wants to change us in this regard.

Edwin Hubbell Chapin, American preacher and poet of the eighteenth century, wrote, "Never does the human soul appear so strong as when it foregoes revenge and dares to forgive an injury."

You can pursue being right, or you can pursue understanding. The one leads to judgment, wounding, and isolation. The other is far more loving and leads to love.

TRAVEL IN PAIRS

One of the great principles of advance training is *never to go it alone.*

When I was growing up, our family spent many summer days on the lake. The rule was "swim with a buddy." During my school days, on class field trips, we each had a buddy. Having a wingman is always a very good idea.

Jesus himself sent his disciples out in pairs, and it wasn't just for companionship. There is evil out there that does not sleep, and we need another person to watch our back. It's a good rule and an important safety precaution. Solomon wrote,

> It's better to have a partner than go it alone. Share the work, share the wealth. And if one falls down, the other helps, but if there's no one to help, tough! (Eccl. 4:9–10 MSG)

One February a few years back, my friend Scott and I had the privilege of going on a mission to see some friends and allies in southwest New York who wanted to see this message of Life, heart, and freedom established in their community. It didn't take long before God was whispering to both of us, "Narnia."

The trip and our message came into focus as people shared their stories. Many had been through a long, hard winter, and I'm not talking about the weather. Many hearts had endured hurt, pain, and sorrow for years, and the assault on their hope had brought loss of heart. Hope wasn't entirely gone. It was buried. There was just enough of it left for people to feel miserable.

"The good life is out there, but not for you. If you do more, sin less, and get yourself together, then maybe, *maybe*, things will improve—but probably not." That was the enemy's message with which a lot of folks had made an agreement, and now they were suffering under it. Many people succumb to it: the Narnia hundred-year winter with its dismal forecast of hope in the spring—but not for them. It's life under a spell, Narnia under the authority of the White Witch, wearing a man down until he doubts his own heart, or worse, the heart of God.

Having an oriented friend, a wingman, along can be invaluable in helping you sift through what you are seeing, hearing, and discerning. There amid the snow and ice, both physical and spiritual, Scott and I were able to confront the spell, the lie, head-on and deliver truth and Life to people's hearts. As Scott and I shared the realities of the Larger Story, the weightiness of being image bearers, and the good God was up to in our lives, hearts were awakened by the dozens. Men and women began to wipe the gunk from their spiritual eyes and see and hope again. Spring was truly coming!

Scott and I have been on missions together for several years. He often comes with me to the places where I am invited to share. I can't tell you how many times he has encouraged me with, "Best I've ever heard you speak." And, oh yes, he has also mentioned a time or three, "You didn't have it flowin' tonight. Felt you struggling with the words in that one part. What happened?" This is what is meant by "Faithful are the wounds of a friend" (Prov. 27:6) and "As iron sharpens iron . . ." (v. 17). It is what one oriented man can bring to another. God loves me well by partnering with Scott in our friendship, and he loves Scott well by partnering with me. The mutual validation and the training we receive through our friendship is something Scott and I both cherish and desperately need.

PHONE A FRIEND

Remember the show *Who Wants to Be a Millionaire*? Alone in the chair, the contestant is struggling, searching for a high-stakes answer that isn't coming. What to do? Phone a friend!

It was a month before one of the men's conferences my team and I offer. I was driving down the interstate in my town when out of nowhere, like the green, poison gas from an old *Batman* TV episode, a toxic thought flooded into the cab of the truck and a panic began in my mind: *the men's weekend is going to fail. I don't know what I am doing. I never should have tried to offer this.* These threats are often disguised in first person "I." It was if I were being choked. I couldn't breathe, and my heart began to race.

My next thought was to get help, *call Tom*. So I did.

"Hey, what's up, Michael?"

"Tom, I'm dying here," I answered through the green gas. "I'm feeling sick about the men's weekend."

"Whoa, Michael, where are you? What is this all about?"

I explained. And then with a chuckle, Tom said, "Michael, it isn't true."

Relief. Just like that. It was as if he had brought the big "Bat-vacuum" into the truck cab, sucked out the gas, and restored the oxygen. You need someone outside the drama to speak to someone inside the drama. Like a good corner man, that person sees things in the fight that the competitor doesn't. He knows whom his friend truly is and can speak the words his friend needs to hear (Eccl. 4:19).

DEPLOYED HUMILITY

Being a Beloved Son has incredible privileges, but it does not entitle us to the nicest or the best. Look at the Messiah's *birth* circumstances. See how Herod hunted him. Look at his *death*. Think of how many people misunderstood the Messiah throughout his life and how many still do. And yet Jesus' humility is simply astonishing! Scriptures tell us that he did not see equality with God as something to be grasped, instead he took on the likeness of man, and humbled himself, to the point of death, even death on a cross! (Phil. 2:6-8). Several times, he asked those he healed to just keep it between themselves and Jesus. Quiet and yet strong was the way of our King.

In this war-torn landscape, we must drop any sense of entitlement and lose all expectations of ease and comfort. Ease and comfort make for a certain kind of man, but he's not the type you and I need to be. He's not the man of epic stories.

From the manger to the cross, Jesus led a rugged life.

> Jesus told him, Foxes have lurking holes and the birds of the air have roosts *and* nests, but the Son of Man has no place to lay His head. (Luke 9:58)

> Jesus was curt: "Are you ready to rough it? We're not staying in the best inns, you know." (MSG)

In Luke 10:16, Jesus tells his disciples, "If folks reject you, my disciples, then they are also rejecting me and the Father who sent me." We will experience rejection as well as acceptance, and Jesus doesn't want us to take rejection personally, nor, for that matter, should we let acceptance go to our head. Don't let either become a part of the false self's ways. Buckle up. This training module usually takes time to internalize, and the enemy will test you in it often.

Jesus knew who he was, and when coming into knowing who you are, you have less to prove, fear, and hide. Jesus knew who his Father was and received love and instruction while on mission. The result of all this? It didn't puff him up, rather it allowed him to sacrificially and powerfully love. It was St. Augustine who said, "There is something in humility which strangely exalts the heart."

THE HEAVENLY FATHER WOUNDS TOO

There is a kind of wounding that C.S. Lewis referred to as "a broken bone in the universe" being reset. It is painful, but it is but for good. Surgeons cut—to excise cancer. Dentists drill—to remove decay. Physical therapists inflict pain—to break up scar tissue so mobility can return.

Not every trial in life is from the kingdom of darkness. Fallenness takes a natural toll. Bodies wind down, and stress gets the upper hand all too often. Remember, we live in between comings. Learning how to love our enemies, training in how to trust, researching the kingdom and its ways—this walk of a Warrior keeps us constantly on our toes. Looking at Jesus' life shows us the road we ourselves must travel. Gethsemane and Golgotha were mile markers the Father, not the enemy, had dug and posted.

The Father's discipline goes hand-in-hand with his love for you and me:

> Have you forgotten how good parents treat children, and that God regards you as *his* children? My dear child, don't shrug off God's

> discipline, but don't be crushed by it either. It's the child he loves that he disciplines; the child he embraces, he also corrects. God is educating you; that's why you must never drop out. He's treating you as dear children. This trouble you're in isn't punishment; it's *training*. (Heb. 12:5–7 MSG)

All this happens in relationship with the Father. Guaranteed! A scalpel cuts. It wounds, but these cuts and wounds are with great care and intent in order to make things better.

One day I was moving about the house, making some rounds and delivering some hugs to the girls. It is usually a bit of a ruckus and fun; I would call it a hug just short of a tackle. Over the past few years I've learned that my middle daughter, Hannah, does not want to participate. This had hurt my feelings and unbeknownst to me, I had collected some resentments and judgments toward her. Here is how I knew I had: since I usually get three out of four (I often include Robin), I had finished my rounds and gone back to work on my computer. I hadn't been there ten seconds when some arms came around me from behind and I was the one being almost tackled. I looked over my shoulder and saw it was Hannah. In that moment, I bristled and went rigid. I couldn't receive. Not good. Time to check in.

I cannot tell you how many times the Father has invited me to the gurney to do a work in me, perform a surgery to remove something that isn't good. The Father wants us to see him involved in every moment of every day—even the difficult ones. How will we step into those moments? How will we treat the people he sends whether they are loved ones or strangers who provoke our false self so we can see it for what it is, for what has quietly collected over time? Will we see the invitation of the Father to let it go, the freedom being offered, and the opportunity to become more of a whole man? Our Father's best gifts don't always come wrapped the way we'd like. Sometimes he reveals, invites, and *then* wounds, but he wounds in order to heal, and his way of wounding brings wholeness, freedom, and Life.

CAN WE TALK?

It was mid-morning at a Zoweh men's conference, and my leadership team and I were circled up. I was sharing, inviting, exhorting our team to "stay the course, keep at it, not rest or do anything halfhearted." For some it was a pep talk, but not for all. A few found my words and style wounding and then they found each other (funny how it often works like that). I didn't realize it at the time, and certainly it was not my intention, but it was the outcome. They heard that they weren't doing enough and being enough.

Later, during the free time after lunch, our team retreated to our housing for rest and recalibration. I sat down with them at the table. "Ready for the afternoon?" I asked.

A couple close friends were not smiling. "Can we talk with you a minute?"

Uh-oh. There it was: an invitation to training. I sat down with them and listened.

"Michael, your 'pep' talk with us this morning felt more condescending than inspiring. Telling us not to rest or do anything halfhearted—do you realize how that came across? We've been in this with you from the get-go, living it out just as earnestly as you. Yet it felt like you were lecturing at us, with us down here and you up there, telling us to act. How was that about grace or humility?"

Those weren't their exact words, but as I remember, they're pretty close.

Ouch! Faithful wounds inflicted by faithful friends whom I myself had wounded. I have hurt many of God's messengers in my lifetime. I'm glad to say those days are becoming fewer and fewer, but that is because of frank, painful, and loving conversations like the one I've described.

My friends took a chance that day. And so did I. No doubt my false self was ready to jump in and clear the room or maybe run out of the room. It has a habit of showing up, chattering away, accusing, defending, reacting, but it didn't win. I had a choice. In a millisecond, there was a choice to either defend myself or understand. I chose to listen to my friends. I knew they loved me and had my best interests at heart. As a result, they were able to help me become more the man I really am. And they themselves stepped higher into their manhood by asking the courageous question from time to time, "Can we talk?".

That is what Advanced Training is all about: seeing the good that God is up to in your life and taking back lost ground. Winning the fight against the unholy trinity of the world, the flesh, and the Devil. Training is accomplished through relationships. Together, we help each other's hearts to Life in the kingdom under the love of the King.

The enemy of our heart wants to use us, but the God of our heart wants to partner with us. When we are aligned, connected, and in step with the Spirit, he helps, we win, and the Kingdom advances.

WARNINGS AND PROMISES

Teaching you would be simple if I negated your free will or overwhelmed you with My Power. However, I love you too much to withdraw the godlike privilege I bestowed on you as My image-bearer.

—*Sarah Young*, Jesus Calling

If you're going through hell, keep going.

—*Winston Churchill*

Have you ever watched any of the *World's Dumbest* shows? It's not a show for which we want to qualify! If YouTube and reality TV have taught us anything, it is that what seemed like a good idea at the time can end up landing someone in the hospital.

"Experience: that most brutal of teachers," C.S. Lewis is said to have written. "But you learn—my God do you learn." In a more humorous vein, Mark Twain reportedly noted that "a man who carries a cat by the tail learns something he can learn in no other way."

Most of boyhood is a hands-on learning experience of how to do and how not to do. Watching someone else do something, like watching my dad hammering a nail or painting a chair, was never fun, but it was part of my learning curriculum. Whenever he turned that hammer over to me and said, "You give it a whack," I grinned from ear to ear. Try it with any boy or girl under the age of eleven and you'll see. Crack and whisk an egg with a young heart looking on, then casually drop the invitation "You want to try?" and watch what happens next.

Sometimes the learning proposition that is life is grand and beautiful. Other times, the hammer hits the thumb or eggs splatter on the floor. The apostle Paul wrote,

> The world is unprincipled. It's dog-eat-dog out there! The world doesn't fight fair. But we don't live or fight our battles that way—never have and never will. The tools of our trade aren't for marketing or manipulation, but they are for demolishing that entire massively corrupt culture. We use our powerful God-tools for [1] smashing warped philosophies, [2] tearing down barriers erected against the truth of God, [3] fitting every loose thought and emotion and impulse into the structure of life shaped by Christ. Our tools are ready at hand for clearing the ground of every obstruction and building lives of obedience into maturity. (2 Cor. 10:3–6 MSG)

Did you see the "1,2,3"? Read it again. Far too many men believe their mission is to fight for other peoples' lives. I believe Paul is talking about the "1, 2, 3" as mission of a man's comeback. Walking with God to smash my own warped philosophies helps me to tear down the truth barriers in my heart, and to restructure my life in alignment with that of Christ's. The School of Hard Knocks has a high tuition. I hear stories every day of the mistakes people make and their hopes of recovering. Some mistakes are innocent enough, casual mishaps or the messy debris of an unfocused moment. Other mistakes can take months, even a lifetime, to repair. We've all heard the lines and maybe even said them ourselves:

"I only did it once."
"Never again."
"I wish someone had told me."
"I should've listened to my . . ."

These are not promising ways to begin a story.

OVERWHELMED

> Look carefully then how you walk! Live purposefully *and* worthily *and* accurately, not as the unwise *and* witless, but as wise (sensible, intelligent people), making the very most of the time [buying up each opportunity], because the days are evil. (Eph. 5:15–16)

I'm glad Paul's exhortation in Ephesians 5 has expired—right? It was appropriate for back then, but today, now—"evil days"? Maybe if I were deployed to Afghanistan or on patrol in some major city at 3:00 a.m. I might—*might*—live as if *the days were evil*, but while rolling down the highway thinking about and planning for a men's retreat? Come on!

The belief, the agreement, that the kingdom of darkness doesn't really exist, or that it was in force back then but isn't today, has put countless men and women in captivity. And those spiritual prison bars have physical ramifications. If we *don't* feel overwhelmed, at least from time to time, then we are living in way too small a story.

Think back on your life. What moments of bad judgment or split-second miscalculations have led to wounds of your heart or those you love? I have a history of casualties due to impulsivity, misunderstanding, or simply being at the wrong place spiritually at the wrong time physically. It's what can happen when a Warrior helps others sort through their stories, helps in uncovering the lies, and escorts a heart to healing. The rescue, redemption, and restoration of any man, and the validation, acceptance, worth, and belonging he continues to seek in his story, is an incredible experience in which to play a part. This is why a man's first mission and training is to get his heart back, journeying with Jesus through his past in order to partner with Jesus for the future—first the man's own future, then that of others. It's an overwhelming proposition, inviting us to settle into God . . . *always*.

Jesus will often cross the path of a Warrior with that of a captive in order to see an overwhelmed heart healed and set free. The world needs Beloved Sons walking the planet, well-trained and ready to fight for the hurting by loving them rather than feeling annoyed by them. There are many such souls tossed about in the sea of life, exhausted, clinging to whatever is available to help them stay afloat. A Warrior can come alongside them and pull them to safety. He can assure them that things will be okay. And he can encourage them to partner with Christ against the creatures that caused the wreckage in the first place and invite their hearts to experience all that God has for them.

IGNORANCE

Our enemy's schemes work best when we're ignorant of them. That's why he does his best to stay undetected. He hopes to remain underground and work covertly. The number one rule in his playbook is, "Convince a man his problems all originate from himself and we'll keep him in the dark forever." Under those conditions, ignorant of their existence and influence, Satan's legions are at their best making our lives the worst. As long as we are naïve, ignorant, and in the dark, our false self will continue to blame and judge others, ourselves, and God.

All of us once were in the dark, and darkness *is* what all of us are up against. It is where the enemy wants to keep men, even those of us who have been rescued out of darkness. Our enemy wants to bring the darkness back, but the Warrior knows and enjoys the experience of forgiveness at the cross. And there is more to the cross than forgiveness alone; there is power and there is freedom. The kingdom of darkness knows this. The Warrior comes to know it as well. It is "by the cross" that a Warrior has authority. Paul has this to say:

> This [note with its regulations, decrees, and demands] He set aside and cleared completely out of our way by nailing it to [His] cross. [God] disarmed the principalities and powers that were ranged against us and made a bold display and public example of them, in triumphing over them in Him and in it [the cross]. (Col. 2:14–15)

Our enemy hopes we never learn how to *use* the cross. Yes, *use*. The masculine heart was made for moments of strength and courage, times when a man stares oppression in the eye and says, "Enough of this crap." The cross of Christ empowers him to do so. *The cross disarms the enemy and frees us.* And free men can make a huge impact simply by living freely. Doing so should invite others to also pursue healing and walk free themselves.

If we're ignorant of the enemy and his activities, then we won't fight what we don't see. And if we're ignorant of the power of the cross, we won't know the freedom and authority we have to battle for the hearts of others. Always remember: our enemy wants to know if we know our authority through the cross and how to use it. He hates the cry of "Freedom!" because through the cross of Christ, we have what it takes to declare freedom, protect it, and advance it.

MANY WARNINGS

The more I explored the cautions in the Scriptures, the more alarmed I became. Even in our daily lives, it's difficult to make it through the day to day without encountering a warning of some kind.

Drug Warnings. In order to pick up a prescription at the drugstore, you have to sign a statement declaring that you understand the risks and dangers of using that particular drug. Most of us pay little or no mind, but next time you're in the waiting room of your doctor's office, pick up a brochure and browse through a medication pamphlet. The fine print contains serious potential side effects:

> WARNING: *If you lose feeling in your extremities or experience severe bleeding or massive internal explosions, or if your ear falls off, stop taking immediately and consult your physician.*

My physician? You mean the guy who prescribed the medication in the first place?

Severe Weather Warnings. One night our family spent thirty minutes in our downstairs closet. The National Weather Service interrupted our TV show with its all-too-familiar *eehh . . . eehh . . . eehh* followed by the guy who sounds like he is actually in the middle of the storm: "The National Weather Service has issued a tornado warning for the following counties. . . . people in the path of this storm should seek shelter immediately." Later that night, we found out that a tornado touched down two miles from our house. Everyone was warned. Many were fortunate. A few were not.

Surgeon General Warnings. The surgeon general is the nation's leading spokesperson on matters of public health. We have gotten so used to the warnings that we hardly give them any attention at all. For instance, nearly 70 percent of Americans are overweight; the surgeon general states that obesity is the number one contributing factor to the number one killer of Americans, heart disease. Odd how the same killer in the physical realm, *heart disease*, is also the number one killer in the spiritual realm. Hmmm.

Often we get in trouble not because we're unaware of danger, but because we don't heed the warnings. Many men know the warnings in the Scriptures, what to do and what not to do; they just choose to ignore them. The idea of educating folks to the risks and letting common sense take over doesn't seem to work. It isn't enough. Something larger is going on that seems to outweigh common sense and control hearts. It affects everyone including men who have devoted their lives to ministry, memorized Scriptures, fervently served, and observed, as well as officiated the sacraments and traditions. These men are high-priority targets: take out the generals (the pastors, bishops, and priests) and the troops will suffer. It's time to take back ground, fight back, pull for one another, befriend our ministry leaders and let them befriend us. As the ancient Greek storyteller, Aesop, wrote, "United, we stand. Divided, we fall."

We are not safe.

The physical realm is not right because of the things in the spiritual realm that are not right—yet.

A Warrior knows this. He keeps it in the front of his mind and practices life accordingly. He is to be less and less "surprised." One of the classic mistakes a Warrior can make is to retreat into passivity by underestimating either the fragility of freedom, the power of darkness, or both. There is another classic mistake in which a Warrior will play right into the enemy's hands. If it's not underestimating them, it's the mistake of overestimating *ourselves*.

PRIDE AND SELF-RIGHTEOUSNESS

It doesn't take long. Get good at something and the temptation to be recognized for it comes knocking. Be committed to something and the lure to make everyone else care as much as you do is almost inescapable. When I am wounded or wronged, I feel a strong urge to assemble a posse of sympathizers. At the root of all these things lies pride.

Pride is always a risk when we receive training from our Father. We learn how the kingdom works and discover the important place we have in it. Through the experiences God allows us, we come to see Life more clearly, understand it more deeply, and walk in the responsibilities that come with knowing what we know. Yet ironically, it is right here in this place of growth and training, privilege and responsibility, that pride can take root. We begin to seek our value and worth *from* what we do rather than bringing our value and worth *to* what we do. We become confident that we're the ones who see the clearest, know what's best, and have "got it right." And others need to listen up.

If you ever find yourself harboring that attitude, lose it fast. Religious pride and self-righteousness will cause compassion and caring to give way to comparison and judgment. The shift is both subtle and sinister. It happens without our noticing it—but not without warning. It's why Jesus cautioned his followers:

Don't advertise your good works in public.
Don't take a place at the head of the table.
Don't pray for show.

The Scriptures warn against climbing up onto the platforms of the world in order to receive the applause and awards of men. Yet it happens again and again in ministry as much as in any other walk of life. The Warrior needs to be on his guard against it because we are not infallible. The more truly wise we are, the more humbly we will walk. Our source of Life, meaning, and wisdom is Jesus, and the only validation we seek as Beloved Sons should be that of our Father.

STAYING OUT OF TROUBLE—AND GETTING INTO IT

Jesus went many rounds with the religious leaders of his day, the Pharisees. They were highly trained in the Jewish religion, deeply knowledgeable, and politically ambitious. In their culture, and certainly in their own hearts and minds, they were the *seriously committed*—the highest servants of God with the highest salaries among the people.

The role came with a uniform, position, and privileges that led to intense altercations with Jesus. Picture today's congressmen, senators, and CEO's and you are getting close. Every society has them: lords and nobles, chiefs and tribesmen, royalty and aristocracy . . . all capitalizing on their culture for personal profit or gain. It's an age-old practice: elevating one's self by oppressing and using others.

In the film *Braveheart*, William Wallace has this to say to the Scottish nobles of his time:

> *You think the people of this country exist to provide you with position. I think your position exists to provide those people with freedom.*

It got Wallace in a lot of trouble. The same message got Jesus into hot water as well. Rebels of their day are the reformers of history, and they were never very popular with those in control. Churches are in no way exempt. Ministry has always had its Pharisees—men and women with a little knowledge, a little ambition, and a little power. You can feel it sometimes when you are around an organization's leadership. They have come to believe that somehow they earned their position through their achievement for God. He is now fortunate to have them on his team. Of course, they would never say it out loud (I never did.) It is cemented deep in the false self, and it comes out disguised as humility and servanthood, but judgments, justifications, pride, and rebellion lie at its core.

Be warned: earning God's love has become a profession. If the enemy can't convince you that you are nothing, he will then slowly and meticulously try to convince you that you're *something*, but based on your merit rather than God's unconditional love. The shift is subtle, but however it occurs, Satan wants you to believe that whatever you get, you've earned it. The good *or* the bad—you've earned it!

The big difference between Jesus' telling you that you're something and the enemy's saying it is that Jesus loves you and is particularly fond of you, while the other hates you and wants to see you buried in a coffin of service, rules, and performance. The results are vastly different depending on to whom we listen.

How does such deception happen? Slowly, gradually, much more like erosion than a lightning strike. Lightning happens in a moment and is easy to see; erosion is the collection of one subtle agreement after another, like wave after wave coming in against the dunes, eating them away little by little, changing their character and eventually advancing on the homefronts that lie behind the dunes.

TWO GUARDRAILS

Like guardrails on a highway, there are two boundaries a Warrior avoids crossing: caring too little and caring too much. Irresponsibility and over-responsibility may appear as opposites, but both are equally capable of leading Beloved Sons back into bondage. Good men, redeemed men, who cross over either of the guardrails become trophies for our enemy to mount on his wall.

Over-responsibility trades intimacy with God for activity in the name of serving God. It happens all the time in churches, but it's not what Christ ever had in mind for his church—a works-based system, an institution—rather than a vibrant organism. When a man trades intimacy for service, when he mistakes friendship *with* the King for only service *to* the King, he compromises relationship, the freedom and Life that Jesus purchased for him.

Irresponsibility is no better. We're designed by God for action; the kingdom doesn't advance through passivity. But the things we *do* need to flow out of our relationship with our King, and no religious system can substitute for that intimacy.

Warriors recognize the two guardrails in their own lives and avoid crossing them. Between those guardrails is the narrow road where a Warrior enjoys freedom for himself and fights for it effectively for others.

THE INSIDE OF THE CUP

The *religious* life versus the *free* life . . . you can hardly turn around in the gospels without bumping into an altercation between Jesus and the Pharisees. In Luke 18 Jesus tells a story of two men praying, one a Pharisee and the other a tax collector. The Pharisee is on display with his prayers, hoping to be seen by many. The tax man is quiet and humble, hoping to be seen by just One. At the end of his story, Jesus says,

> This tax man, not the other, went home made right with God. If you walk around with your nose in the air, you're going to end up flat on your face, but if you're content to be simply yourself, you will become more than yourself. (Luke 18:14 MSG)

A few chapters earlier, Jesus accepts an invitation to dinner by one of the Pharisees. Upon entering the religious leader's home, Jesus doesn't "wash up" for dinner and the host is aghast. Jesus says,

> Now you Pharisees cleanse the outside of the cup and of the plate, but inside you yourselves are full of greed *and* robbery *and* extortion and malice and wickedness. You senseless (foolish, stupid) ones [acting without reflection or intelligence]! Did not He Who made the outside make the inside also? (Luke 11:39–40)

Ouch! Yet to deliver those lines lovingly—now, that was something only Jesus could pull off. And it was by no means the only time. Jesus gave many other warnings to and about the Pharisees.

> Jesus said to them, Be careful and on your guard against the leaven (ferment) of the Pharisees and Sadducees. . . . How is it that you fail to understand that I was not talking to you about bread? But beware of the leaven (ferment) of the Pharisees and Sadducees. Then they discerned that He did not tell them to beware of the leaven of bread, but of the teaching of the Pharisees and Sadducees. (Matt 16:6, 11–12)

On too many occasions, I can still see and feel the enemy luring me to simply stop walking in this message and look down my nose at those I judge who do not . . . as if I know their hearts and where they are in their journey with God. I've learned it's a fine line between observation and criticism, of staying on the road versus going over the guardrail.

A FATHER'S WARNINGS

My dad often used to say to my brothers and me, "Nothing good ever happens past midnight." I've modified that a bit as a father of three girls and dialed it back to 10:00 p.m. A good father is always ready to lay down a few "encouragements" to his kids about the dangerous environments that lurk beyond the safe borders of home. It is part of how the masculine heart reflects the heart of God to protect and provide.

The book of Proverbs is really King Solomon sitting his son down with a home school curriculum aimed at the heart of a Hebrew child. The textbook's title would be *How to Live Well: A Father's Guide to What to Do and What Not to Do*. Solomon himself got his education from his earthly father, David, and his heavenly Father, Yahweh.

> These are the wise sayings of Solomon, David's son, Israel's king—written down so we'll know how to live well and right, to understand what life means and where it's going; a manual for living, for learning what's right and just and fair; to teach the inexperienced the ropes and give our young people a grasp on reality. There's something here also for seasoned men and women, still a thing or two for the experienced to learn. (Prov. 1:1–6 MSG)

There's more; it gets better!

> My son, if you accept my words and store up my commands within you, turning your ear to wisdom and applying your heart to understanding—indeed, if you call out for insight and cry aloud for understanding. . . . For wisdom will enter your heart, and knowledge will be pleasant to your soul. Discretion will protect you, and understanding will guard you. Wisdom will save you

> from the ways of wicked men, from men whose words are perverse. (Prov. 2:1–3, 10–12 NIV)

Wow, who wouldn't sign up for that class! Sounds like a transfer from the School of Hard Knocks to the University of Freedom. The best part might be the source of the teaching—a trusted heart who has been down the road of life and knows it well. A good father imparts to his son wisdom and encouragement for life's dangerous paths which is a very good thing. Something rises up within me. *When do we start?*

But it's not mandatory. This wisdom still comes as an invitation, a proposition in which my will, my enrollment, allows the relationship and training to begin.

Just as Proverbs is full of warnings and promises from an earthly father to his son, so the whole of Scripture is full of guidance from a heavenly Father who deeply desires his sons to live well, love well, and make it safely home.

MANY PROMISES

All of us are familiar with the concept of a promise. Unfortunately, we are also all too familiar with the experience of a broken promise.

"I'll be there, I promise."

"You have my word."

"I promise to love and to cherish till death do us part."

Jesus makes his promises to us heart-to-heart, and he keeps them all. Take this one, for instance:

> I have told you these things, so that in Me you may have [perfect] peace *and* confidence. In the world you have tribulation *and* trials and distress *and* frustration; but be of good cheer [take courage; be confident, certain, undaunted]! For I have overcome the world. [I have deprived it of power to harm you and have conquered it for you.] (John 16:33)

Note that Jesus didn't promise us *easy*; he promised us *full* (John 10:10). "Full" seems to include moments of trials and distress. We have the upper hand, but do we know how to wield it? The enemy will test us to find out. If we don't know our position as Beloved Sons and how to see Christ's power and authority at work in us to love as Warriors, then the enemy will proceed unchecked and ruthless. Jesus didn't let him do so, and neither should we.

A FINAL WARNING

In the middle of Jesus' exchange with the Pharisees recorded in Matthew 12, the Pharisees accuse him of driving out demons by the power of Satan. "Now you're really, *reeeally*, reaching," he responds. "Let me explain something to you, how this all works." And over the next several verses, he does just that. Which brings us to verses 43–45, rendered here in *The Message*:

> When a defiling evil spirit is expelled from someone, it drifts along through the desert looking for an oasis, for some unsuspecting soul it can bedevil. When it doesn't find anyone, it says, "I'll go back to my old haunt." On return it finds the person spotlessly clean, but vacant. It then runs out and rounds up seven other spirits more evil than itself and they all move in, whooping it up. That person ends up far worse than if he'd never gotten cleaned up in the first place.

This explains a lot! It explains why people *relapse*, doesn't it—why some believers experience victory in a certain area of their life for a time, then fall back into their old ways. An addiction or behavior that long tormented them, that had mastery over them, is temporarily lifted. The enemy leaves under the power and authority of Christ for a while, but the victory is short-lived. The enemy returns . . . with seven friends!

Hmmm . . . they have friends? Yikes!

Conversely, I love what *The Message* says in 1 John 4:4:

> My dear children, you come from God and belong to God. You have already won a big victory over those false teachers, for the Spirit in you is far stronger than anything in the world.

We have a Friend too, bigger and more powerful than all of the enemy's buddies put together. The Spirit of Jesus dwells within us, closer than our own heartbeat. So stand your ground. Once you've gotten back an area of your life, stay alert and guard it with care. They are coming back to see if you are a Warrior who knows and can practice the art of "greater is he who is in me than he who is in the world." Spoil their counterattack and you may not have to fight that particular dark force for long. Enjoy your freedom; guard your heart.

FIGHT YOUR BATTLES ONCE

When we seek Life and love from any other source than their author, Christ, we give permission for the agents of darkness to re-enter our life. And once again they will screw it up, causing as much collateral damage as possible. So fight your battles once.

And if you do fall, don't stay down. Go back to the Father who loves you so deeply. Share with him what happened, and invite him to show you why you did what you did.

The other day, I said something snippy to Robin in the kitchen. As soon as it came out of my mouth and landed on her harshly, she turned, and I knew I had hurt her. My immediate impulse was to say something funny in an attempt to make her laugh. Instead, I apologized and asked her to forgive me. She did, though her furrowed brow told me it might take her a few more minutes, and I went away with some important intel.

What was that "funny impulse" about? When I asked God, he replied, "You wanted to feel better and not feel what you did."

Oh my! *Thank you, God. I didn't know.*

As I continued to pray and ponder, God revealed a nasty device I had used often in my life: rather than tending to the heart I had wounded, I tended to my own.

That is not how I want to live. Nor will I—not when I see the choice before me. It's in this manner that a man can take back ground even when he falls.

C.S. Lewis wrote,

> Every time you make a choice you are turning the central part of you, the part of you that chooses, into something a little different than it was before. And taking your life as a whole, with all your innumerable choices, all your life long you are slowly turning this central thing into a heavenly creature or a hellish creature: either into a creature that is in harmony with God, and with other creatures, and with itself, or else into one that is in a state of war and hatred with God, and with its fellow creatures, and with itself. . . .
>
> Each of us at each moment is progressing to the one state or the other.

The world desperately needs—*desperately needs*—more oriented, uncompromising men, Beloved Sons who know how to fight and know how to dance, sons who are strong in the face of trials, fierce in the presence of their enemies, and compassionate with the hearts they have been commissioned to love. Warrior men who, when it is time, can take up the shield of faith and the sword of the spirit and fight each battle once and for all.

ONE LAST PROMISE

When someone tells you, "Don't be afraid," what does that imply? That there is something to be afraid of! Heads up! Danger! Hazardous life moment ahead!

When I tell my child, "Don't look over there. Keep your eyes on me. Stick with me. Hold my hand. Stay close," I have good reason.

> Have not I commanded you? Be strong, vigorous, and very courageous. Be not afraid, neither be dismayed, for the Lord your God is with you wherever you go. (Josh. 1:9)

> A thief is only there to steal and kill and destroy. I came so they can have real and eternal life, more and better life than they ever dreamed of. (John 10:10 MSG)

> Go out and train everyone you meet, far and near, in this way of life, marking them by baptism in the threefold name: Father, Son, and Holy Spirit. Then instruct them in the practice of all I have commanded you. I'll be with you as you do this, day after day after day, right up to the end of the age. (Matt. 28:19–20 MSG)

Don't be obsessed with getting more material things. Be relaxed with what you have. Since God assured us, "I'll never let you down, never walk off and leave you," we can boldly quote,

> God is there, ready to help; I'm fearless no matter what. Who or what can get to me? (Heb. 13:5–6 MSG)

There is good reason God repeatedly tells us, "Don't be afraid." There is also good reason he invites us continually to trust him. This Story isn't nearly as safe as we have been led to believe. If you don't sometimes experience what it means to be overwhelmed, then you will rely on your own strength and believe you can control all the variables. That's a small life without God. It's not the life for which you and I were meant.

Jesus knows the way. He is the truth and he holds the light. He promises to stay with us. Staying close to him is always priority—one—for a Beloved Son. It is the platform on which a Warrior practices his art, loving fiercely and fighting courageously for the hearts of others. That is what our King did and what he still does when he takes up residence in a man. "In this world you will have trouble," Jesus warns us—but then reassures us, "Take heart. I have overcome the world" (John 16:33).

LOVING A WOMAN

Women are made to be loved, not understood.

—*Oscar Wilde*

Be not ashamed women. . . .
You are the gates of the body, and you are the gates of the soul.

—*Walt Whitman*

Being a woman is a terribly difficult task since it consists principally in dealing with men.

—*Joseph Conrad*

It was just a few minutes before the session was to begin at a Women's Deepening Weekend, one of Zoweh's women's initiatives. I was a guest speaker on hand to share my talk, "The Core Desires of a Man's Heart." Shuffling my notes while the music played, I distinctly heard Jesus whisper to my heart, "Apologize." I instantly knew what he was inviting me to do.

The music ended—my cue to step to the podium. Looking out into the crowd of women, sorrow and remorse filled my heart. After a few seconds of silence, I began: "Before I share in this session about the hearts of men, I first want to say—I am sorry. I am so sorry. I want to apologize for what we men have done to you and the part we have played in the wounding and breaking of your hearts."

The words seemed to softly echo in the room, landing gently and finding their place not only in the hearts of the women but also in my own heart. In that moment, I was representing and confessing on behalf of "my kind." But there was more. I realized this was also *my* apology.

Like the vast majority of men, I learned early and believed deeply the lie that many boys have been told. It is the lie about what girls are for, the lie that they are meant for my use, my gratification, here to validate me and tell me I am a man.

What begins early as an assault on the masculine heart later has ramifications, becoming an assault on the feminine heart. The killing of sexual innocence is a high priority for our enemy, and boys all too often play right into his hands. It is a matter of too soon and of desires gone wrong.

GETTING HELP

It was the summer of 2001 when I first read a book entitled *Wild at Heart*. That same winter I went to a weekend conference hosted by the author, John Eldredge. I came home so excited!

During the first days back, I read portions of my conference journal and excerpts from *Wild at Heart* to my wife, Robin. I told her about the upcoming feminine counterpart weekend that Eldredge and Ransomed Heart Ministries were offering to women later that year. Lovingly I told her, "Sweetheart, you need to go and get your heart back!"

I distinctly remember hearing our mantle clock ticking as I looked into a face that, without a word being said, was clearly communicating, "What did you just say?" After several seconds ticked loudly by, Robin decompressed her lips and curtly replied, "My heart is just fine, thank you!"

Hmmm, that didn't go so well. It was in that moment that Eldredge's closing words swooped back into my consciousness: "Now, whatever you do, *don't* go home and tell your wife you are 'new and improved,' and now this is what *she* needs to do." Nailed by hindsight once again.

Later that day, Robin swung by and visited me in the doghouse to tell me, "Yes, I think I would like to go." I thought she was saying yes to the weekend adventure of a lifetime and the deep spiritual waters that awaited her. I found out later that she was saying yes to Colorado and a four-day break from three little girls and me.

But when she returned home, Robin told me through teary eyes, "The most significant thing for me during the weekend was that, at a deep heart level, I began to understand and experience God as my Father—a most loving Father who adores me! This Father knows me, sees me, wants to be with me—who *delights* in me just as I am, right where I'm at, in this moment, in my brokenness, in my mess. I am his BELOVED DAUGHTER!"

I remember thinking, "See, I knew that weekend away was a good idea!" As she shared more over the next few days, I began to understand something. Even though we both bear God's image and live in the same Story, the way we bear that image, and therefore the desires we hold deep in our hearts, are as different as pink and blue. Not only do we hold different core desires, we are also subject to unique and specific assaults on those desires.

There is a reason God made man strong and placed him in the role of provider and protector. It is not for the man's well-being; it is for the well-being of others, starting with our wife and then our children, in that order.

I must confess that I consulted with a few in writing this chapter. I spent several hours interviewing my wife and listening to some of her closest friends weigh in on the heart of a woman. They provided the voices of experience needed to shape what follows. I hope it will provide an effective counterattack for the critical losses sustained by the women we love—and arm us with new and better ways to fight for them and to love and relate to their hearts.

HIS-AND-HER WOUNDS

The spiritual assaults on men and women are not gender-equal. Because God made us male and female, the enemy has devised customized his-and-her wounds. The first ones come early in childhood, they accumulate, and the enemy will see to it that one day *his* and *hers* will collide. All it takes is for either his false self or hers to pull the other down. The couple who began their union with the promise "for better or worse," over time begins to dwindle. Separate small stories emerge, the kind in which they may live under the same roof but they live far apart from the other. Tolerance is a far cry from love.

Evil keeps individual files. You think the IRS keeps files? There's no comparison. Equipped with an intricate knowledge of our histories and personalities, the kingdom of darkness knows exactly how to pit one wounded heart against another for maximum effect—especially in the God-ordained covenant union of marriage. Satan wants to twist that harmony into discord: Robin *versus* Michael rather than a Robin *and* Michael. He knows he can get a double return for his efforts. If it's true, according to Genesis 2:24, that a husband and wife become one, then the enemy need only yank the chain of one and he will get the other as well.

A PARTICULAR KIND OF HATRED

If the masculine heart is opposed, the feminine heart is all-out assaulted. Satan comes at a woman's glory with a jealous and vengeful hatred. And it makes sense. The archangel Lucifer was the strongest and most beautiful of all created beings. He was the reigning general of the angel armies—until he went astray.

Why did he go astray? *Jealousy*. Lucifer did not want to share the glory of God with God's new creations, man and woman. He was unwilling to hand over his crown to Eve, the beautiful image-bearer of God. The mutiny was Lucifer's idea. And the book of Revelation (12:7) tells us that in a new role and playing a new part in the story, the ol' dragon, hurled to earth, continues his old campaign of hatred, making war against the Sons of God (Rev. 12:17). The prince of this dark world is a liar who wants to *steal* the crown back, *kill* the image-bearers, and *destroy* love.

Achieving the world's standard of womanliness is exhausting for women—always striving and yet never measuring up. If you know the glory of your wife's or daughter's heart—what they love to do, what they are passionate about, what makes them come alive, what each one uniquely brings to the kingdom—then you know what the enemy is up to in their lives. The question is, do you know those things? You must know each of their stories, their journeys of heart, but most men don't. What happened to them?

Men's wounds and those of our mates mixed together make for the perfect storm. Women cannot turn to us for healing just like we cannot turn to them. We cannot heal one another. Love each other, yes; heal, no. That is God's department. God will often partner with a man by giving him a message of truth to deliver to a wounded feminine heart, but the man never heals her, nor can she ever be his source of healing. Just as neither image-bearer, man nor woman, can be the primary source of life for one another, there must be someone else they turn to for Life. Our hearts are far too needy to put that kind of pressure and demand on one another.

You must know the daughters of Eve hold a special place in the Story. They are in our story and lives for God to teach us how to love. As men, we can play an important part of their healing journey, or we can aid the enemy in wounding them. When God lovingly allows us to see the wounds women bear—the lies, brokenness, and false self they carry within themselves—what then? How are we to help the feminine heart be free?

NOT READY

I was a kid of the seventies. TV shows like *Charlie's Angels, Wonder Woman, Dukes of Hazzard, Three's Company,* and *Dallas* were all the rage. Those were the days when four channels expanded to forty. None of my friends watched these shows for the ingenious writing, intriguing characters, or superb subplots. Sheesh, I remember watching *Gilligan's Island* reruns, and not because they were funny. Remember Mary Ann and Ginger? You know what I'm talking about.

Boys get the cart before the horse. Men have believed the lie that having a lover would make us a Warrior. Worse, we have believed they would settle our hearts and make us a Beloved Son. But a girl won't settle a man's heart, no matter how many he goes through, whether in person or on a screen. She can't answer his deepest questions, nor will having sex with her prove he's a man.

Few things are scarier than a man attempting something he is neither ready nor equipped to do. We watch with one eye open and one eye closed, waiting for the sounds of wreckage and pain. And so it is with boys going after girls. The culture delivers its message loud and clear: "As soon as you can and as many as you can." Most boys subscribe early to the belief that if they can get a girl to like them, they are somebody. And girls buy into the same program. So the tracks are laid early for horrific train wrecks of pornography, affairs and divorce. We have been set up. We are not ready to love a woman.

Reading a book or throwing a few weeks of marriage counseling at our ignorance before saying, "I do" won't cut it. The enemy just laughs. They've been planning and laying their explosive charges since our boyhood. One day they'll push down the plunger and watch with glee as it blows up, then all comes crashing down. Usually approximately ten years after the honeymoon, sometimes twenty, is when the kingdom of darkness gets its biggest bang for the buck and inflicts the most collateral damage. Cheat or be cheated on, one spouse traded for another, a second marriage for a third, a relocation complete with all the boxes and bags of wounds and agreements, and the attempt to build a new house on the sand—the enemy loves it.

There is a reason why 50 percent of all first marriages fail and why 67 percent of second marriages and 73 percent of third ones land in the graveyard. We men carry our beliefs down the aisle with us. And the lies about what girls are for render us untrained and unprepared to truly love a woman. Something has gotta give. Someone has gotta *learn to give.*

JUST A CONSUMER

Let's be honest—the *image* of the feminine image-bearer has its pull. It's another of God's great ideas. From the moment Adam was introduced to his naked Eve, to the first time a boy's eyes open wide to the curves of a woman's body, the result was, is, and always will be the same: it's all over. Smitten is how it starts. Then curiosity gives way to exploration, and innocence is often exchanged for addiction. In adolescence, we learn the practice of *using* one another; it's the enemy's chief tactic for sending future marriages to the graveyard. Why such opposition? Because our enemy knows there are few things more powerful and life-giving than two people, a husband and wife, walking with God together. Our enemy also knows there is nothing more destructive than when they don't.

When we buy the lie that women are here to gratify us and prove our manhood, we adopt the mentality of a consumer, not a provider. We throw them in the basket, purchase them at the checkout, use them to get us through the day, and then eventually, once we've gotten all we want out of them, toss them in the trash. There's nothing loving about using, but that's what we're taught early in the masculine journey: use her and consume her. And that's how it will be—until our beliefs about women are fully renovated. That's the good part: our Father knows how to help us exchange the consumer lie for his heart toward his daughters.

In the grocery store one afternoon, I came upon a display featuring dozens of flowers, beautifully arranged and ready to find a home. Robin loves flowers, and it had been a while since I had bought any for her. With excitement, I found a bunch that would let her know how special she is to me, but as I turned toward the checkout, I heard a voice in my head: "You know you're only doing this to try to get sex. How selfish!"

My shoulders dropped as the green gas of shame seeped into my heart. All the way home I felt slimy and condemned. By the time I stepped through the door, I was already checking myself into the doghouse. And then the light flicked on and clarity came. I *used* to give Robin flowers and a card to "improve my chances", but that was the old me. It wasn't me anymore, and it was no longer true.

The enemy was using old lies to ruin a new moment. It was time to fight back. "Nope, I'm not going to yield and take this guilt whipping any longer." My excitement returned. Of *course* I could give Robin flowers with no strings attached—because that was my true heart toward her! Along with the bouquet, I started learning how to give my strength to her, ward off the enemy's taunts and resurrect the first hints of unconditional love from the grave.

THE FEMININE HEART

The feminine heart, the deepest and truest thing about a woman, was designed to be loved, pursued, delighted in, enjoyed, protected, and fought for. Like us, women long to be loved—to be the Beloved Daughters, to know that God sees them and loves what he sees. Every feminine heart on the planet desperately needs to experience God's love and possess it as her own. If a woman does, it will change *everything*.

Like men, women struggle with not knowing who they really are. They too fail to see the context of the Larger Story and their significant role in it. Women bear the image of God in that they are deeply relational, love fiercely (think "Mama Bear"), are nurturing and comforting, and offer mercy and creativity. Women are life-giving. They have a unique strength to offer the world through the beauty that is theirs to unveil. These things are true of God, and they are true of his feminine image-bearers.

It starts early. Every daughter desires to be known and loved by her daddy, to be the object of his affection, the apple of his eye, to be seen and validated by the most important man in her life. Every woman longs for this, and like our heart, hers is asking the questions, *Do you see me and do you love what you see?*

HER CORE DESIRES

If you understand how a woman is designed, the way she bears the image of God, then you can easily see her heart's desires. And if you can see her desires, then you know the questions she is asking and the answers she longs for.

Wherever my wife Robin speaks, she shares about the number one core desire of the feminine heart: *It longs to be seen and known.* Like men, women also are deeply heart-wired to be the Beloved. Every little girl's heart is asking the question, *Do you see me and do you love what you see?* What happens with that question as the girl moves from six years old to sixteen . . . and twenty-one . . . forty . . . seventy? It remains with her, that's what. As with us men, it is always the central question.

In their book *Captivating*, John and Stasi Eldredge share three additional core desires of a woman's heart:

- Women bear God's image in that they are designed and desire to offer beauty.
- The feminine heart longs for romance.
- Women want to play an essential role in a Larger Story.

A few years back, Robin and I watched the movie *Avatar*. It is a film of many themes and a variety of ingredients, the obvious ones being big, blue, cat-like aliens and explosions. Lots of explosions. More than once I thought, "This isn't going well. She doesn't like it."

Walking out of the theater, I asked the usual question: "What did you think?"

"I loved it."

"Really?" I was shocked. "What did you love?"

"I loved how the main characters fell in love, and especially the scene where Jake says to Neyteri, 'I see you,' and she says, 'I *see* you.' It's not just 'I'm seeing you in front of me.' It's 'I see *into* you, and I love what I see.' And when she tells him that she sees his strong heart—I loved it!"

I thought, "Whoa, she is revealing a part of her feminine heart." For far too long I have missed seeing it. It is right in front of us men like a big screen with blue aliens and explosions, and we still miss it. I saw the epic battle; she saw the romantic love story. God gave us eyes to see and ears to hear! We need to learn to use them to see and hear one another.

Every little girl comes into this world asking questions just like every boy does: "Do you see me? Do you like what you see? Do you want to be with me? Do you delight in me?"

The primary person she longs to hear *Yes*! from is her daddy. A good dad fighting for the heart of his little girl will not fight in vain. I have pictures of each of my three girls and me when they were young wearing camo, donning basketball jerseys, outfitted with ball caps, holding golf clubs, and sporting fishing poles. I'm not entirely sure they wanted to do those things, but I am absolutely sure they wanted to be with their dad.

It all comes down to where—or better, to *whom*—girls take their questions. Mid-eighteenth-century writer Charles-Augustin Sainte-Beuve wrote, "Tell me who loves, who admires you, and I will tell you who you are." That is both dangerous and glorious. To whom do we primarily go to for love? Ultimately, women and men alike need to take their questions to the Father, looking to him to discover the things that are truest about themselves.

A DESIGN AND A DESIRE TO OFFER BEAUTY

Beauty is core to a woman; it is *who* they are and *what* they long to offer. It is one of the most glorious ways they bear the image of God in a broken and often ugly world. "True beauty in a woman is reflected in her soul," Audrey Hepburn often quoted from a favorite poem, "It is the caring that she lovingly gives and the passion that she shows. The beauty of a woman grows with the passing years."

Beauty, as it is defined by the world, is a source of much pain for women. They never seem to measure up or be enough. Robin shared with me,

> Every time I turn around, I am bombarded with images of what the world calls "Beauty/Beautiful"—in the checkout line, on magazines, on TV, in movies. They mock us, reminding us on a daily basis that we can never measure up to that standard. As a mom of three teenage daughters, I am particularly aware of their cruelty and how powerful these diminishing messages are. The enemy taunts us with, "Are we enough to hold someone's gaze?" And the voice in our head is most often, "No, I am not enough."

Yet women still long to be beautiful and to offer beauty. And that is a good thing. That longing may be shut down. It may be screaming for attention, but either way, it is there, hoping to be discovered and enjoyed. And in that desire is a reflection of God and how he designed them.

Our God is a beautiful God, and he created a world of incredible beauty. What mortal soul hasn't been left speechless by a flaming sunset or the view from a ridge top into a valley? Gaze upon the oceans, mountains, wildlife, a flower. Words are inappropriate at such moments. How often are we captured, even if for just a second, by a simple bird or butterfly? That's what beauty does: it holds our gaze, inviting us to enjoy it.

God too longs to be discovered and enjoyed, and our masculine hearts were made to respond. It was King David, the first Warrior-Poet, who declared,

> One thing I ask from the Lord,
> this only do I seek:
> that I may dwell in the house of the Lord
> all the days of my life,
> to gaze on the beauty of the Lord
> and to seek him in his temple. (Ps. 27:4 NIV)

In a woman's beauty, and in her desire to offer it and have it received and admired, a man finds a reflection of God's nature that is unique to the feminine heart.

BEAUTY'S ESSENCE

Remember Halloween? The boys dress up as the superhero. How do the girls dress up? As princesses! Young feminine hearts come to the door, gowns and crowns, ruffles and plastic heels, hoping for far more than a piece of candy. Just watch what happens when you give them something good for their heart. Next Halloween, when a little princess comes knocking, open the door, take a knee, and proclaim, "Your majesty! How beautiful you are, inside and out." She will forget why she knocked.

My wife tells this story from her junior high days:

> We didn't have a lot of money growing up, so Halloween costumes were typically homemade by my creative and resourceful mom. This particular year, family friends of ours loaned my sister and me several dresses and outfits we could choose to wear. I immediately

> chose a long, gorgeous, ornate red dress with a crinoline and black lace. When I put that dress on, I felt like a Spanish baroness! *I remember so vividly that feeling!* I felt beautiful, regal. I stood up taller and *hated* running with my friends from house to house! I wanted to *glide* through the neighborhood! I'll never forget my dad told me, "Honey, you look beautiful!" *And I believed him.*

Where does that young heart go ten, twenty, thirty years later? It journeys through the story and the battle for the heart just like all the boys trying to become men. Similarly, the feminine heart loses its way.

Beauty is commonly misunderstood. Culture puts a premium on beauty as an external thing. Just watch a few minutes of any of the "Wives" reality shows. There are many beautiful exteriors, but very unattractive interiors. On the other hand, I know several women who may not win any of the world's beauty pageants or whose external beauty is fading with age, yet they are very beautiful. Their presence *radiates.* They shine when they smile, light up a room with their laughter. Their voice may be beautiful or their touch. They make a beautiful, hospitable table for friends; they make sure you enjoy a bite or a sip of something they have made.

Beauty is a craftswoman arranging flowers, or painting on a canvas, or writing the words to describe what is right, good, and true in the world. Holidays and other special days are made beautiful because beautiful women have it in them to make those occasions so. True beauty longs to be shared.

BEAUTY'S FIERCENESS

In the 1995 film *A Little Princess*, the main character, Sara Crewe, believes her father's words over all other voices. When her father leaves to fight for his country in WWI, Sara is enrolled in a prestigious boarding school.

When news arrives that her father has gone missing in battle, the jealous and rigid headmistress demotes Sara from a boarder to a servant girl, but the impact of her father on Sara's life and heart remains even though she now wears an apron rather than a uniform. The other girls want to be with her. They *need* to be with her because Sara gives warmth, encouragement, and hope at every turn. In a climactic scene in the attic of the boarding school, with tones of disdain and hatred, the headmistress scolds and threatens Sara.

> HEADMISTRESS: It's a cruel nasty world out there and it's our duty to make the best out of it—to be productive and useful! Do you understand what I'm saying?
>
> SARA: Yes, ma'am.
>
> HEADMISTRESS: Good.
>
> SARA: But I don't believe it.
>
> HEADMISTRESS: Don't tell me you still fancy yourself a princess. Look around you! Or better yet, look in the mirror.
>
> SARA: I am a princess. All girls are. Even if they live in tiny old attics. Even if they dress in rags, even if they aren't pretty, or smart, or young. They're still princesses. All of us. Didn't your father ever tell you that? Didn't he?

Beauty can be fierce at times. Sara's father bestowed on her belovedness. She embraced it and treasured it in her heart. And one day, it became the weapon she wielded against the lies of the enemy.

Stasi Eldredge wrote in the book *Captivating*, "Beauty is what the world longs to experience from a woman. We [women] know that. Somewhere down deep, we know it to be true. Most of our shame comes from this knowing and feeling that we have failed here. So listen to this: beauty is an *essence* that dwells in every woman. It was given to her by God."

Beauty is extravagant and generous *for* others. It is not used in order to get, but it is offered to be enjoyed, no strings attached. Beauty can point hearts toward its Founder, the beautiful God who holds creation together and unfolds sunrise after sunset day after day. The Beautiful One paints extravagance on a new canvas every single day for those with eyes to see. And he orchestrates an alluring new song for those who have ears to hear.

When a man fails to see and invite a woman's true beauty, adhering instead to the world's prescription of what beauty is and does, he just adds to the confusion and deep pain of the feminine heart. Our ignorance contributes to their lostness. There is a better story to be written here. Beauty has a right to fiercely insist that it is what it is, and nothing less. And as Warriors, we are called to recognize the true beauty of our princesses, and to fight for it, defend it, and invite it with love, tenderness, and valor.

ROMANCE

In 2012, according to U.S. Consumer Market statistics, romance fiction held the largest share of books sales, $1.4 billion. Just to compare, sales for all religious and inspirational books totaled $720 million. Romance authors are capitalizing on a massive market premised on two questions in every young girl's heart: "Do you see me, and do you love what you see?"

When the girls grow up, their questions graduate. We see it in the heart of a woman—the longing to be seen and pursued for who she is, not what she can do or how she can make a man feel.

Why this desire for romance in the feminine heart?

Because God loves romance! He is the author of it. *He* wants to be wanted.

Look at the Scriptures. How many scholars, theologians, or Bible teachers do you know who would have included the romance stories of Ruth, Esther, Hosea, or the Song of Songs? They're scandalous! Had they been written and published separately, few copies would ever have found their way into church libraries or Christian schools. The bold imagery in the Bible of the *bride and bridegroom . . . lovers* . . . there's nothing G-rated about it. Yet it's the way God depicts the relationship he wants with his people. Consider this scene from the book of Ezekiel:

> I came by again and saw you, saw that you were ready for love and a lover. I took care of you, dressed you and protected you. I promised you my love and entered the covenant of marriage with you. I, God, the Master, gave my word. You became mine. I gave you a good bath, washing off all that old blood, and anointed you with aromatic oils. I dressed you in a colorful gown and put leather sandals on your feet. I gave you linen blouses and a fashionable wardrobe of expensive clothing. I adorned you with jewelry: I placed bracelets on your wrists, fitted you out with a necklace, emerald rings, sapphire earrings, and a diamond tiara. You were provided with everything precious and beautiful: with exquisite clothes and elegant food, garnished with honey and oil. You were absolutely stunning. You were a queen! You became world-famous, a legendary beauty brought to perfection by my adornments. Decree of God, the Master. (Ezek. 16:8–14 MSG)

This isn't the only steamy romantic love letter in the Great Book. There is actually quite a collection—because God is the great romancer! Our story climaxes with the wedding feast of the Lamb and the honeymoon that will follow for all eternity.

ROMANCE WINS

When I say that women long for romance, it might be helpful for us to take a look at a few examples that illustrate what I mean. Men take notes—these are the scenes that *undo* the women at our conferences. It never fails . . . every single time one of these clips is shown there is a collective sigh and all the ladies start whispering, "I *love* this!" Then, after the clips come smiles and tears!

> *The Last of the Mohicans—the waterfall scene*
> Hawkeye to Cora: "Stay alive! No matter what, I will find you. No matter how long it takes, no matter how far—I will find you!"
>
> *Pride and Prejudice—the sunrise scene*
> Mr. Darcy to Elizabeth: "Surely you must know. It was all for you. You have bewitched me, body and soul, and I love you, and I never wish to be parted from you from this day on."
>
> *Shall We Dance—the escalator scene*
> John to his wife, Beverly: "To dance, you need a partner, and my partner is right here. Beverly, will you dance with me?"
>
> *Revelation 19:7—the honeymoon*
> Let us rejoice and shout for joy [exulting and triumphant]! Let us celebrate *and* ascribe to Him glory *and* honor, for the marriage of the Lamb [at last] has come, and His bride has prepared herself.

This is how God chooses to tell the end of his story? The way he tells of his loving pursuit and the consummation of our lives together with him forever!

AN ESSENTIAL ROLE

A woman also desires to be caught up in something larger than herself. She wants *to play an essential role in the Larger Story*—not just a small supporting role in some man's story, but a more significant role in a larger one. A woman wants to be needed, to be important and have something of value, something that matters, to offer those she loves and the world around her. Women don't really want to *be* the adventure, but they do want to be a part of one, to be caught up in one. The longing in the heart of a woman to share life together with a man as part of a great adventure—this too comes straight from the heart of God.

When I invited Robin to step in and share more of her heart at our conferences, she was reluctant. She believed that what I was asking was too large and too much. She thought she didn't have anything to offer. "I'm not a speaker and I'm not articulate," she said, statements that reflected the wounding messages of her past.

It was the fact that I invited her, and that she was needed, that finally tipped the scale for her to take a step of faith.

Over the years, I have learned two *unhelpful* ways I have handled Robin's heart: first, running ahead and leaving her behind, and second, staying behind and pushing her by over-instructing, over-advising, and just plain running her over. The Father is training me. She isn't to be invited to help me, but rather, to offer her glory in her role. I can encourage her to share what she knows and has experienced, but I can't make her.

Speaking is still not something she aspires to do, but she has admitted that sharing this message of Life is a passion of her heart. I have heard her say many times, "I want every girl, every woman, to be free—to know who she really is, how her loving heavenly Father sees her, and how her heart matters to him. To know her beauty, her Belovedness, the glory of her life, and to be free to offer it to the world."

Most women have no idea how they fit into this Larger Story. Like most men, they have no idea that there is so much more going on: how two kingdoms are at war over their hearts, how greatly their hearts matter, and how much they have to offer and are needed! Most women, like most men, are disoriented. And the results are disastrous. The enemy seeks to diminish and distort what a woman is, luring her from Belovedness, beauty, romance, and her essential role that is uniquely hers to play. Like men, their life with God and with others is opposed.

THE WOUNDS OF THE FEMININE HEART

When you know the core desires of a woman's heart, then you also know the enemy's plans against her.

Do you see me? She wants to be seen and known,
to be the Beloved.
The enemy seeks to have her go unseen, unknown,
and dismissed.

Do you delight in me? She is designed to offer beauty.
Satan wants her to feel overlooked, ugly, and "not enough."

Do you love what you see? She longs for romance.
Darkness desires that she be rejected, abandoned,
and replaced.

Do you want to be with me? She desires to play an essential role in
a Larger Story.
The Devil seeks to diminish her role or disqualify her from any
role at all, and to ensure that she remains uninvited, discounted,
or deemed "too much."

Did you hear the messages the headmistress attempted to deliver to Sara Crewe? "Our job is to make the best of it, to be productive and useful." Like those, what follows is a list of common lies women believe and live under from the wounding moments in their lives:

I don't have anything to offer.
I am stupid.
I am fat.
I am ugly.
I am unlovable.
I don't fit in.
Nobody wants me.

Why even bother? It won't be right; it won't be good.
I am alone.

There are themes to every woman's wounds. They are gender-specific, but the goal is the same as for men: to produce guilt, shame, fear, abandonment, and isolation. At the core of her ache lies the fear that she will journey through life unseen, unvalued, unloved, and alone.

Because a daddy is so critical to a daughter's story, the enemy strives to ensure that a woman's deepest wounds are inflicted on her early in life by her father. A father is to bestow identity, provide security, and protect the core desires of his daughter's heart. These are difficult tasks if a dad doesn't understand how his little girl is made and what the enemy's plans are against her.

Mother-wounds also occur because Dad is afraid of Mom or oblivious to the wounded heirlooms she is passing along. A man may need to step in and protect his daughter from her mother, but many fathers don't. And so, at a young age, the messages sink in:

You are not worth fighting for.
You are being silly.
If you were stronger, tougher . . .
Just make the best of it. I do, and you should too.

Young girls learn early to stop living from their core desires. They stop living from their hearts. They learn to cope, to compensate, but neither *productivity* nor *neediness* will heal their hearts. They win ribbons at the fair and awards for locker room reputations, but those are like putting a Band-Aid on a broken bone.

VALENTINE'S DAY, MOTHER'S DAY, AND MARRIAGE CONFERENCES

A couple times every year, the pulpits of America become platforms for men to get a good talking-to. "You're just not cutting it" is the message. And heaven forbid that a man should step into a full-blown marriage conference. Session after session dwells on what he isn't doing right or well.

For men, the program mostly boils down to the familiar religious agenda: *Do more, try harder, and quit being so selfish.* A favorite weapon with which to whack a man is found in Ephesians 5:25: "Husbands, love your wives, just as Christ loved the church and gave himself up for her" (NIV).

We must understand that the passage is for Beloved Sons, for Warrior men, oriented men who know who they are, where they are, and the good the Father is up to in their lives. This is what Christ knew and experienced. Until a man has that same orientation, which comes from Belovedness, he will choose himself over his wife, his life over hers and his needs over hers—every time.

If we are ever going to truly love a woman the way Christ loves the church, then we will need our whole heart, and we will need to go on mission to understand hers.

HOPEFUL AND HELPFUL

I am not a big fan of lists. However, I *am* a big fan of things that can help me be a part of rescuing and restoring hearts. Here are some wise recommendations from women on how men can help set feminine hearts free and restore their hope:

Pursue healing for your own heart first. This principle is similar to the in-flight safety instruction about first putting on your own oxygen mask in an emergency before you assist other passengers. Pursuing healing for your own heart is like putting on the mask. Why? Because you will need all of your strength and all of your courage in order to see a woman set free. As you allow God to bring healing to your heart as a man, and as you continue to walk intimately with him, you will be more able to go after your wife's heart or your daughter's heart and not be taken out in the battle. You must be free to fight for her without demanding or needing anything from her.

Be curious about your wife's heart. Ask questions. Become a student of who she is. You cannot fight for her if you don't know where the battles are or how her glory is held captive. So know her story. Start with simple observations: What are the color of her eyes? What makes her laugh? What are her favorite things—foods, books, films, flowers, pictures? What are her best memories? Worst memories? In the answers and in her stories lie the clues to where she has been wounded, how her little-girl heart was assaulted. Ask Jesus to show you. Ask Jesus to show *her*.

Invite her. Invite her into your story. Invite her to allow you deeper into *her* story. Invite her into the Larger Story in which she plays a role that is uniquely hers as well as the role both of you play as a couple. Ask *more* questions: "What do you think about . . . ?" "How do you feel about . . . ?" Ask gently, kindly, and patiently. She may not dive in at first, wondering, "What does he want?" or "Why is he asking?" or "Where is my husband, and who is this caring impostor who has replaced him?" Honestly, when was the last time you asked your wife or daughter a question just to get to know her?

Invite her to read what you are reading or share with you what she is reading. I invite Robin and the girls on walks in the woods behind our house, on errands around town, into the stuff of my day-to-day world. They don't always say *yes*, but then that's not the point. The invitation is the point—*I want to be with you.*

Invite her to see beauty—moons, sunsets, sunrises, clouds and storms. Show her what you love; show her your favorite spots and your favorite things. Don't take it personally if she can't or won't jump in. Just invite. Give it time.

Allow her to be wherever she is. This may be one of the most courageous and difficult things you do. It might be misinterpreted by her as passivity on your part when, truly, you are simply and intentionally giving her space. She might think you are trying to fix her when you are attempting to help. These misunderstandings are almost always connected to her wounds, her false self, and the work of the enemy. See it as good intel. The enemy will always tip his secrets and overplay his hand if a man is paying attention. Trust that God is at work in her story like he is in yours and that he is up to good. Don't forget; he is still writing!

He's got her. John Eldredge once said at a Ransomed Heart Boot Camp, "Her wound is your mission." The mission is not for you to accomplish, but it is for you to *engage*. As a dad of teenage daughters, I panic if I feel them slipping away, and so I react and go heavy on them, demanding that they do as I say if I see them wandering dangerously close to the guardrails. I think back on all the times Jesus has said to Robin and me, at very significant points in each of our girls' journeys, "I've got her."

Fight for her. Learn how to shut down the spiritual attacks that come against your marriage, your children, your relationships. Pray *the Daily Prayer* from Ransomed Heart Ministries or Zoweh's websites. Pray it together if she's comfortable with the idea. Robin and I do so, and I have grown to love this point of contact. It's a lifeline and another place for our hearts to connect.

Accept her invitations. Whether it is to engage in conversations of the heart, the Larger Story, or life, step into any moment in which she invites you. Enter her world.

Just two minutes ago, Robin asked me if I wanted to bring some of the manuscript and share with her on a drive she has to make across town. Wild? Not so much. God is offering me more and more of the moments I have been praying for as well as all the moments I have likely missed.

Be ready when she asks, "How was it?" "How did it go?" "How was your day?" "How do you think we should handle our seventeen-year-old?" Take a deep breath, ask Jesus what you should say, then share your heart. Share the journey. As you lovingly pursue her heart without an agenda to change or "fix" her, *God will come.* Give her grace and space. He is at work revealing and restoring. Again from Stasi Eldredge and the book *Captivating*:

> Now—can you see how the desires of a man's heart and the desires of a woman's heart were at least meant to fit beautifully together? A woman in the presence of a good man, a real man, loves being a woman. His strength allows her feminine heart to flourish. His pursuit draws out her beauty. And a man in the presence of a real woman loves being a man. Her beauty arouses him to play the man; it draws out his strength. She inspires him to be a hero.

The tower or dungeon where the enemy is holding your fair maiden may look a lot like your home, her professional career, her volunteering at church, or the shackles she wears in being a mom. You'd be surprised where women build their jail cells. Just as we can hide behind our roles rather than bringing our hearts to our roles, so can they.

The enemy and a woman's false self will not give up ground without a fight, but just because things don't seem to be going well doesn't mean they aren't going according to plan. Remember, her false self will attempt to provoke yours. Do not be easily duped or lured. Be a student of your own heart and false self as well as your wife's heart and her false self. Discernment is key. Seldom are things what they first appear. You can do this! You can love your wife or your daughter "as Christ loved the church." She is waiting... you are the man for the job!

My oldest daughter, Ashley, recently placed this quote in front of me: "Imagine a man so focused on God that the only reason he looked up to see you is because he heard God say, 'That's her.'"

She then said, "Dad, this is what I want."

Men, it's what they *all* want.

FOLLOWING THE KING

Be careful to leave your sons well instructed rather than rich, for the hopes of the instructed are better than the wealth of the ignorant.

—*Epictetus*

The true test of civilization is not the census, nor the size of cities, nor the crops—no, but the kind of man the country turns out.

—*Ralph Waldo Emerson*

Follow me.

—*Jesus*

In the 2009 film *Invictus*, South Africa is host to the 1995 Rugby World Cup where Nelson Mandela has a vision for his country. Morgan Freeman plays newly-elected South African President Mandela at the transition into his presidency of the "Rainbow Nation." Matt Damon plays François Pienaar, the captain of the South African Rugby team. During this hostile time in the country's history, the two men meet for afternoon tea at the request of Mandela.

MANDELA: How do you inspire your team to do their best?

PIENAAR: By example. I've always thought to lead by example, sir.

MANDELA: Yes, that is right. That is exactly right. But how do we get people to be better than they think they can be? Now, that is very difficult, I find.

PIENAAR: Yes sir, it is.

MANDELA: How do we do that? By example? To an extent, but there is more to it than that. . . . (Pause as he searches for the right word.) *Inspiration,* perhaps? How do we inspire ourselves to greatness when nothing less will do? How do we inspire everyone around us? Sometimes, I think, it is by using the work of others. On Robben Island, when things were very hard, I found inspiration in a poem.

PIENAAR: A poem?

MANDELA: A Victorian poem. Just words. But they helped me to stand when all I wanted was to lie down.

Later in the film, the day before South Africa is to play in the Rugby World Cup finals, Pienaar arranges for the team to visit the prison on Robben Island. The camera pans across the prison that held Nelson Mandela for much of his twenty-seven years of incarceration. The voice of Morgan Freeman narrates the great poem as the scene moves through his former cell, to the yard, and then to the prison:

Out of the night that covers me,
    Black as the pit from pole to pole,
I thank whatever gods may be
    For my unconquerable soul.

In the fell clutch of circumstance
    I have not winced nor cried aloud.
Under the bludgeonings of chance
    My head is bloody, but unbowed.

Beyond this place of wrath and tears
    Looms but the Horror of the shade,
And yet the menace of the years
    Finds and shall find me unafraid.

It matters not how strait the gate,
    How charged with punishments the scroll,
I am the master of my fate,
    I am the captain of my soul.

—William Ernest Henley, "Invictus" (published 1888)

Where there is no inspiration, there is no direction. Where there is no direction, you find bored men. And a bored man is a dangerous man, a man without wheel or rudder. Mind you, a bored man isn't a man who doesn't have things to do. He is a man who just doesn't want to do them. A life with God and all its adventures and battles has somehow fallen to domestication. Boredom is what got King David in trouble with Bathsheba. At a time when his men were out fighting and kings were with their men, David was at home instead, bored. Unable to sleep, he wandered to the rooftop, which is likely the place where he looked at the stars, sunsets, and sunrises and penned many a psalm, but not this time. This time he found something different—or something found him. Our enemy smells "bored" like a shark smells blood.

A. W. Tozer wrote, "Every man must choose his world." Every man *will* choose his world, and then he must live in his choice. The worst scenario is when it seems he has no choice. The pull of the false self is so strong because the true self lies limp, covered up in boredom or fear through a sequence of unfortunate events and men compromise.

It wasn't the rooftop that set up David's fall; it was staying home. Not a good day for the king and an even a worse day for his kingdom.

Solomon wrote, "Where there is no vision, the people perish" (Prov. 29:18 KJV). Maybe Solomon had his dad in mind when he wrote it. Lack of vision renders uninspired, bored men. And where they are, there will soon be casualties: a wife, children (all suffering because of a man's loss of heart), and eventually, the loss of his kingdom (the places and people God has given him to reign and rule). It is what William Wallace meant when he delivered the great line to the "nobles" of Scotland (the bad kings) in the film *Braveheart*; "There's a difference between us. You think the people of this country exist to provide you with position. I think your position exists to provide those people with freedom. And I go to make sure that they have it."

DANGEROUS FOR GOOD

Remember, every Warrior requires two things greater than himself to keep him on the path of becoming himself. He needs a cause worth living and dying for, and he needs a king to love and a king who loves him back—one who loves first and loves the most, and to whom the man can turn for counsel, guidance, and training. Great kings lead by example, inspiring and imparting to their men power and authority when they are ready to wield it. The foundation of the relationship between a king and his men is trust, love, admiration, and respect.

When a man has these two interlocking things, a cause and a king, he is ready to be turned loose, deployed back into the Story *dangerous for good.*

The King of small-k kings heals, settles, and trains Beloved Sons. And in the same way a mission finds us, the King and the cause find the man. They come provoking, inviting, intriguing, even disrupting a man. They come with answers to a man's questions: do you see me? am I worthy? am I strong? can I come through?

The Father's answers are yes, yes, yes and *yes*. A man longs to hear them, and when he does, his heart is both settled and inspired. The relief this can bring is tremendous. Since every man has a unique and personal path to hearing the Father's answers, the answer *yes* may be the same but will be delivered at tailored times for each man. This relieves us from being in charge of one another (you're not the boss of me, nor I you). What we *can* do for our brothers is lovingly point one another to the King, encourage one another with his cause, and walk as friends on the journey.

Friendship bears a great fruit: accountability. Without friendship, accountability becomes just a chore or a job. Few men receive Life from a chore, but from a friend—that is a different story. Many "accountability" arrangements fail for lack of real friendship; there's no time invested or trust earned in one another's life. The result is just two men policing each other. And who wants to be policed?

The Warrior doesn't go to others to have his heart policed or the questions of his deep masculine heart answered. The weighty answers come from his Father, his King, and by the Spirit that dwells strong within him. This is an enormous and fundamental shift for a man, changing to whom he goes with questions about his worth and ability. As long as he seeks validating answers from others (a woman, his kids, or other men), a man is vulnerable to the enemy's using anyone, but if his source for validation and affirmation is God, then the answers he receives are final, transformational, and settling for the man's heart.

A settled heart is a declaration that a man is ready to re-enter the Story. His Warrior Heart will then be tried and strengthened through battle. We see this principle at work all through the chapters in the book of Acts. The disciples *are* settled, trained, and initiated. Then they are deployed, stepping into the fray to ensure that the freedom campaign, the cause of their King, advances. It doesn't take long before the first casualty is recorded, a beautiful heart named Stephen. He knows the truth, tells the truth, and just like his King, he is killed by those who hate the truth.

But the truth can't be killed. Where there is persecution, hearts are convicted of the truth. When truth convicts hearts, change occurs. And when change occurs, persecution comes. The friends of Jesus experienced who he truly was and were changed. Equipped with their convictions, they were then deployed into the uttermost parts of the earth (Acts 1:8) with their King's promise, power and presence, telling them "I am with you always." The effect of it all reminds me of a quote I recently heard, "Be the kind of man that when your feet hit the floor in the morning, the Devil says, 'Oh crap, he's up.'"

ANYTHING BUT IRRELEVANT

Jesus was a real person with a real personality, and that personality had tremendous impact on people. You don't leave your fishing business, or push away from your lucrative government tax job, to follow a man who is irrelevant. You don't tear the roof off a house in order to lower your crippled friend to a man of no consequence, nor tell your whole neighborhood (including all your ex-spouses) about someone who doesn't matter. And for certain, for absolute certain, you don't crucify a man who is irrelevant.

The effect of Jesus on a heart was either catastrophic or cataclysmic. After you met him, either you couldn't stand him or you couldn't stand to be apart from him. To this day, he calls his followers to be one or the other, hot or cold, but never lukewarm and thus irrelevant.

I've heard it said that Jesus had one of three effects on a person: he was either inviting, or intriguing, or disruptive. Jesus came to set the record straight, to alter everything. He came to show and tell that being holy is cool. He came to give himself. And yet, until we discover him for himself, we don't, *we can't*, truly understand what we have found when we have found him.

Following Jesus is not like following a legend. He has set it up to be much better than that. Following Jesus is a journey to becoming more and more like him. It's a literal proposition and invitation in which the idea is way more than just having your sins forgiven. Glorious as forgiveness is, to be sure, it's not the main selling point of Christianity. *The key selling point is that we get to be like Jesus.* In order to be like him, we first need our sins forgiven. We need to ask Jesus to remove all that is in the way. John Eldredge summed it up when he wrote in his book *Beautiful Outlaw*,

> You are meant to have this Jesus, more than you have each new day, more than you have your next breath. You are meant to share life with him—not just a glimpse now and then at church, nor just a rare sighting. And you are meant to live his life. The purpose of his life, death and resurrection was to ransom you from your sin, deliver you from the clutches of evil, restore you to God—so that his personality and his life could heal and fill your personality, your humanity, and your life. This is the reason he came. Anything else is religion.

HOLY AND COOL

I've given quite a bit of thought and prayer to the idea of Jesus being "cool." Am I being irreverent in describing him that way? I've had to discern whether it was the Holy Spirit discouraging me or the religious spirit accusing me. I hung onto the question for a day and mentioned it to a few of my friends. Is "cool" in some way diminishing to our King? Nobody flinched. So I asked Jesus what he thought and I heard, "I know what you mean, I know your heart. I like 'cool,' and now I'll show you why *you* like it so much, Michael."

A few days later I was sharing this story with my friend David. He said, "The Jesus I knew growing up wasn't cool. The Jesus I am getting to know and experience now is more than cool. He is *sooo good*!"

The image of Jesus most men inherited in their youth, the one grafted into their hearts, needs redeeming. If Jesus isn't both holy *and* cool (good), then that's a huge problem, especially if we are invited to be like him. Admiring someone or appreciating something they did is one thing, but being told you need to be like someone you're not sure you even like, or worse, whom you don't know—that is a problem!

Back in 1980, long before Facebook walls existed, you could tell who I followed as a young teen by looking at the walls of my room. Posters of Larry Bird, Joe Montana, the Doobie Brothers, and Farrah Fawcett set the tone. They were cool. You know who wasn't on my wall? Jesus.

I was the kid who grew up going to church. The picture I had in my mind of Jesus was Mr. Rogers with a beard. A poster of Mr. Rogers wasn't making the wall. One of my friends might walk in and see it. Granted, I watched my fair share of Mr. Rogers' Neighborhood, but aspirations to be like him never crossed my mind, just as it never crossed my mind to tell my friends what I heard in Sunday school or that I wanted to be like Jesus.

Most of us, whether growing up in the church or otherwise, got a pretty large dose of Jesus' holiness. He was holy, holy, holy, and he died for us. What most of us never got was how really cool he was . . . how *good.* Out of all the exposure to church I got growing up—Sunday mornings, Sunday school, Sunday nights, youth group, church work days, mission trips, the whole kit and caboodle—what I remember was a lot of talk about sin and warnings that I'd better get my act together and serve Jesus or else. I remember a lot of references to God having a two-by-four. I don't recall anyone ever talking about *intimacy* with him.

Those church leaders were just passing along what they believed about him based on what they were told by their predecessors, who had received what got handed down by the generations before them. Their degrees and credentials didn't help with freedom, but they did seem to promote service. The thing is, you can serve someone and not love them, but it is just about impossible to truly love someone and not serve them—and it doesn't feel like service. Why? Because you are in love with them.

That's the kind of Jesus I've come to know—the real one whom I can't help but love because I've tasted the reality of his love for me. The Jesus who is really, really cool because he's really, really *good* loves me and I am certain he is crazy about you. How good and cool is that!

FOLLOW ME

I've always liked fishing. Oceans, lakes, ponds, rivers, and streams, the sounds and smells, the beauty of the water—all are a magnet for those with the right charge in their hearts. When I was a boy, I would grab my trusty Zebco 33 and my dad's old Plano tackle box and hit the ponds around our house. I looked like a knight in a joust as I rode my bike through the neighborhood and down the well-worn trails to my favorite holes. Whether by myself, with my Dad, or accompanied by friends, I always thought fishing was a good idea.

I have a few friends who love to leave early in the morning from our area and head to the North Carolina mountains to fly fish. Getting in a river or stream at sunrise, or staying on the water until sunset, is life-giving.

I'm not an avid fly fisherman—I don't give it the time and attention it takes to cultivate the art and skill, but I fish with some men who have done so. It is cool to watch them. They are so good!

To grow in skill, to master a craft of any kind, takes time and attention. "Follow me," says Jesus in Matthew 4:19, "and I will make you fishers of men." Much is required to master the craft of fishing for men and battling for their hearts, but the soul that invests time and attention to walking with God will see a glorious work done.

Experiencing who our King really is and what he is like is critical to learning from him. As with any apprenticeship, stay near our Teacher as it will help us get better at what we do as we become more like him. He'll make sure that happens (Phil. 1:6). And we'll gain so much more than expertise.

Shouldn't it be that way? Do you think the disciples had any idea what kind of road they were stepping onto when Jesus invited them to "follow me"? I'll bet you that not five minutes into the trip one of them asked him *the* question: "Uh, Jesus . . . where exactly are we going?" Can't you just picture Jesus turning with a smile and a wink saying, "You'll see."

At the core of a Warrior's Heart is the practice of being a follower. It was Sun Tzu who in the sixth century wrote in *The Art of War*, "Regard your soldiers as your children, and they will follow you into the deepest valleys; look on them as your own beloved sons, and they will stand by you even unto death."

Jesus knew the answer to the question "Where are we going?" and he took about three years getting his followers ready for it. The Original Beloved Son was making other Beloved Sons and then entrusting his power and authority to them, his friends. Then he deployed them into battle, living and carrying his kingdom message right up until their martyr's deaths. Jesus showed them how to fish, empowered them to do so, and now he does the same for us.

A ROLE MODEL

Jesus came not just to tell us how to live but to show us. He came to model what a life with God looks like, what the Father-Son relationship can be. It's a great way to teach: show the newly adopted image-bearers their Father's heart toward them. Jesus *showed* his apprentices how to love long before he told them to love one another.

When Jesus teaches, there are moments when he says, "Do it like this; don't do it like that." Sometimes he shares parables, but mostly he is in dialog, quietly modeling, inviting men to "do it like me." That's how he is with us. Jesus showed the way so that we could live The Way, taking our places as Beloved Sons and then, like our Teacher, entering into our Warrior roles in the Larger Story to fight for the hearts of others.

Jesus was, *is*, a Warrior—one who knows how to fight and dance. This is the Prince of Peace, our role model whom we are invited to know and enjoy as our friend—and love as our King!

> Your God is present among you, a strong Warrior there to save you. Happy to have you back, he'll calm you with his love and delight you with his songs. (Zeph. 3:17 MSG)

> The Lord is my strength and my song; he has become my salvation. He is my God, and I will praise him, my father's God, and I will exalt him. The Lord is a Warrior; the Lord is his name. (Exod. 15:2–3 NIV)

> The Lord is with me like a mighty Warrior; so my persecutors will stumble and not prevail. (Jer. 20:11 NIV)

> So Pilate asked Him, are you the King of the Jews? And He answered him, [It is just as] you say. [I Am.] (Luke 23:3)

He could have called down 80,000 angels (Matt. 26:53), but he didn't. He won us another way, not by might but by spirit. And we thought Satan was tricky in the garden! Jesus' ransoming us was the most courageous thing that ever was done. And it wasn't a trick, however off-guard it caught the kingdom of darkness. The Lion of Judah became the great Lamb of God and made the fierce sacrifice, the greatest of great prisoner exchanges. His plan all along was "Take me instead, my life for theirs"—all to win us back.

If we understood his courage, knew Jesus for who he truly is, we wouldn't have just a poster of him on our wall; I daresay we would have the house wallpapered with him. We would have his picture on our phones, "selfies" with him on our Facebook pages, framed moments with him on our mantles and desks, and a headshot or two of us together in our wallet.

But the most important thing we can do is carry him in our hearts, for there is where his Spirit takes up residence:

> [He has also appropriated and acknowledged us as His by] putting His seal upon us and giving us His [Holy] Spirit in our hearts as the security deposit *and* guarantee of the fulfillment of His promise. (2 Cor. 1:22)

His new home is our new Home. Maybe that is his idea of interior design; maybe that's what he carries in his wallet, pictures of us with him. That sounds just like something Jesus would do: remodel us to be like him on the inside, then turn us loose to show the world what walking with God, what Life with him, really looks like.

HE IS LOVE

So what does our King look like, and what are we to look like? In a word, *love*. Jesus' friend John penned it well when he wrote, "God is love" (1 John 4:7-8). That is as true of the Son as it is of the Father. So in 1 Corinthians 13, when Paul writes about the "greatest thing" being love, he is writing about Jesus. It reads like a resume, Jesus' resume, with some of Paul's recommendations thrown in for good measure. Try this: wherever the word love appears in the chapter, substitute the name of Jesus. Here's how that looks using *The Message*:

> Jesus never gives up. Jesus cares more for others than for [him] self. Jesus doesn't want what [he] doesn't have (*that's because he is whole*). Jesus doesn't strut, doesn't have a swelled head, doesn't force [himself] on others, isn't always "me first," doesn't fly off the handle, doesn't keep score of the sins of others, doesn't revel when others grovel, takes pleasure in the flowering of truth, puts up with anything, trusts God always, always looks for the best, never looks back, but keeps going to the end. Jesus never dies. . . .
>
> We don't yet see things clearly. We're squinting in a fog, peering through a mist, but it won't be long before the weather clears and the sun shines bright! We'll see it all then, see it all as

> clearly as God sees us, knowing him directly just as he knows us! Yet for right now, until that completeness, we have three things to do to lead us toward that consummation: trust steadily in God, hope unswervingly [and express the life of] Jesus extravagantly. And the best of the three is Jesus. (1 Cor. 13:4–8, 12–13). (The words in italics are mine.)

Love is our cause and love is our King. I know it sounds a bit easy, but easy is the last thing it is. As a matter of fact, without substantial help the journey and the mission are downright impossible.

Most days, my aspiration *to live and love well* is challenged, if not downright violently opposed by the enemy who would rather I not love well. Love is life and the kingdom of darkness is all about death . . . fallen days surrounded by fallen souls and far too many believers living more in tune with their false self than singing their true song. This is why the Warrior is so desperately needed. This is what being a Warrior is all about, showing up and loving well. *Loving* is life giving, it is fierce and tender, honest and kind. Just above forgiveness, love is our greatest weapon in this spiritual battle. When we don't love or aren't loved, it is *forgiveness* that treats and heals the wounds. Forgiveness is the next most loving thing we can circle back and wield, but *above all else, put on love.*

RE-

The prefix *re-* means that something that occurred in the past occurs again. Though our past is behind us, I promise you, it is also with us still. So now that we are starting to see all the spiritual battles we once lost, it's time for us to *re*-enter the battle and *re*-claim for good what we lost.

Do you realize you can fight a battle today that you lost twenty years ago? This is no small endeavor, but neither you nor I were made for smallness. That is what healing is all about: going back to reclaim what was lost or stolen and resurrect what the enemy killed.

A Warrior knows he must protect his own heart in order to protect others. He's not much good to anyone else if he's sprawled out somewhere, reeling from his mistakes and bleeding from his wounds. The Warrior trains with others in mind so they will be free. G. K. Chesterton once wrote, "The true soldier fights not because he hates what is in front of him, but because he loves what is behind him."

Do you know what is behind you? Do you understand *your* story and the great *re*deeming, *re*claiming, *re*storing work that Jesus is up to on your behalf in the Larger Story?

Our original job description included the assignment to *reign*. When Jesus comes back for the second time, his plan is to share his authority, invite us to reign and rule with him—again:

> They shall see His face, and His name shall be on their foreheads. And there shall be no more night; they have no need for lamplight or sunlight, for the Lord God will illuminate them *and* be their light, and they shall reign [as kings] forever and ever (through the eternities of the eternities). (Rev. 22:4–5)

When a man comes to know the Larger Story and how it works, he will understand why having the Heart of a Warrior is critical. He will abandon a life of using others and receive the Larger Life, which lives *for* others. Until the day when we finally see Jesus face to face, we follow him heart to heart and, in the process, receive the training he provides. Joining him is seeing others' glory re-claimed and re-stored.

CIVILIANS VS. SOLDIERS

William Wallace wants to live in peace, be a farmer, raise crops and have a family. Maximus counts the days until he can return to Spain and rejoin his family. Frodo would much rather have remained in the Shire and wishes the ring had never come to him. Simon wasn't looking for the Messiah; he was looking for fish.

And Saul had been living dutifully, a regular "sheriff" of Judea trying to put an end to this Jesus character and his rebellious followers. Yet in one of the greatest and most ironic trades of all time, the Pharisees' number one man becomes Christ's number one man. Saul changes teams as well as his name, his identity, and his role. And that's how it is to be for each of us too in our own stories.

Life isn't what we thought it would be. It's better. The Larger Story and its Author comes after us, and with them an evolving mission. It's one we couldn't have guessed given a million chances, let alone conjured up for ourselves. It is as if we get drafted and must trade in the civilian life for the life of a soldier. That's how Paul describes it. Like a battle-seasoned veteran seeking to inspire a young up and coming Warrior, Paul writes to Timothy,

> Take [with me] your share of the hardships *and* suffering [which you are called to endure] as a good (first-class) soldier of Christ Jesus. No soldier when in service gets entangled in the enterprises of [civilian] life; his aim is to satisfy *and* please the one who enlisted him. (2 Tim. 2:3–4)

It is a very different kind of life, one that boasts of the last being first, and of turning cheeks, and of loving one's enemies and of more concern for what we believe in our heart, not just what we do. When a man takes on a cause and a King, taking them into his heart, that is when the man can truly engage in Life—and gets far more in return than he could possibly imagine. It is the time when that man begins to co-write his true song with God, the time when he coauthors with God the content he will contribute to Life's story.

In the famous St. Crispin's Day speech from the Shakespeare play *Henry V*, King Henry utters these memorable words:

This story shall the good man teach his son;
And Crispin Crispian shall ne'er go by,
From this day to the ending of the world,
But we in it shall be remembered—
We few, we happy few, we band of brothers;
For he to-day that sheds his blood with me
Shall be my brother; be he ne'er so vile,
This day shall gentle his condition;
And gentlemen in England now a-bed
Shall think themselves accurs'd they were not here,
And hold their manhoods cheap whiles any speaks
That fought with us upon Saint Crispin's day.

Teddy Roosevelt said, "The credit belongs to the man who is actually in the arena . . . who at the worst, if he fails, at least fails while daring greatly, so that his place shall never be with those cold and timid souls who neither know victory nor defeat."

And it is Jesus, our great and glorious King, the One we follow and whose image we bear, who will one day say *Well done. Well done!*

POSTSCRIPT

The defeat of evil in this world depends upon human beings actually stepping forward to use the Kingdom power and authority that is given to them.

—*Dallas Willard*

I have told you these things, so that in me you may have peace. In this world you will have trouble. But take heart! I have overcome the world.

—*John 16:33 (NIV)*

It's all for nothing if you don't have freedom.

—*William Wallace in Braveheart*

I must tell you. You need to know: *you can do this!*

You truly can.

You can find your Life—because it is what God wants for you.

It will take two, three, maybe even four years for your heart to become settled. That is not entirely up to you. It's also very much up to God to determine your individual journey of healing and your custom apprenticeship with him in training. You will find your courage, but it will not be absent of fear or without momentary battles with hopelessness and dread. Fear is what summons a man's courage and invites him to partner with God for the *more*, more of the Father's love so a man can learn how to fight off what isn't true.

> There is no fear in love [dread does not exist], but full-grown (complete, perfect) love turns fear out of doors *and* expels every trace of terror! For fear brings with it the thought of punishment, and [so] he who is afraid has not reached the full maturity of love [is not yet grown into love's complete perfection]. (1 John 4:18)

Being tempted, or invited, to be afraid is different from being *overwhelmed. Overwhelmed* is an invitation to walk with God. Fear is a temptation to walk alone.

So be encouraged. You, Beloved Son, you are on a path of training, a journey of learning how to love.

You truly have Nothing to Hide.

Nothing to Prove.

Nothing to Fear.

IT'S ALL CONNECTED

The older I get, the more I seem susceptible to getting hurt. Like any fifty-plus-year-old, I live with more than a few daily aches and pains. My most recent was a strained Achilles.

Now, I can almost hear you: "Man . . . that ain't nothing!" Bear with me a second. My point is, as you're probably well aware, *it's all connected.*

My initial visit to the orthopedist was what got me the next nine trips to the physical therapist. (By the way, *physical therapy*— PT—is just a code for the more accurate term, *pain therapy.*) During my first PT appointment, I underwent a series of assessments primarily for joint and muscle strength. Most of the tests involved my answering the question, "Does this hurt?"

After several yesses, another question broke into the lineup: "Have you had any other injuries in the past few months?" I hadn't thought of that, but yes, eight months earlier I had torn a hamstring in the same leg. At the time, the bruise looked as if someone had hit me with a bowling ball on the inside of my thigh.

For the next nine weeks, my therapist hardly touched my Achilles. Instead, we spent the majority of our time rehabbing my hip, hamstring, and core. "Waking them up" was what my therapist called it. "They have shut down due to the earlier injury and have never been turned back on," she said. "We will have to remedy that."

I learned a great lesson that day: it's all connected. One injury leads to another and to another and another . . . unless it's treated.

HOW THINGS WORK

All the pieces—characters, landscapes, and circumstances—in God's Larger Story are connected. It is easy to miss the immensity of it all, fail to see the forest for the trees.

We live in the intersection of two realms. They are not far-apart galaxies or separate subatomic planes. The spiritual and physical realms are both right at hand, and we live smack-dab in the middle of them where their traffic crosses. However, one realm is greater than the other, and one has the right-of-way.

The spiritual realm is not "out there." It is right here, right now, and it is the greater realm in which we must see, hear, and engage. The spiritual realm is where we are encouraged to get our bearings, receiving our orientation and the elevation at which we are invited to live. We are constantly subject to its presence; it is where we began, where we have our roots. We are spirit men on a physical journey hoping to one day get back home. We will live forever. We are built for eternity.

In the realm that matters most, the spiritual realm, there exist two kingdoms, and again, one kingdom is greater than the other. One is the kingdom of light; the other is the kingdom of darkness. One is the kingdom of the Son; the other is the kingdom of this dark world.

Kingdoms work by authority and rule. They have citizens—or in this case, one has citizens while the other has prisoners. The latter kingdom is ruled by lies and the Father of Lies, the prince of this dark world (Luke 11:15; John 8:44; 12:31). The other kingdom is ruled by the Son, the Prince of Peace, the King of kings. His kingdom is eternal, and he reigns and rules by love, which is the most freeing and validating force in the entire universe. One kingdom results in fear, guilt, and shame—the other, Life, joy, and happiness!

These two kingdoms are at war over something precious. Of course, I am talking about the heart. One kingdom fights for hearts to freely give them their true selves; the other schemes to steal it away. Both know that whoever gets the heart, gets the person. So the kingdoms battle. They war over the allegiance and affection of every person's heart. Life and death are both their weapons and their mission. The casualties are many, but so could be the heroes.

You and I are invited to become part of something larger than ourselves, larger than your church or mine. God is inviting us to much more. We were made for *more,* but until you see it, until you hear it, until you understand how it works, this Larger Story that our story is in, how can you play your part well?

KEEP SHOWING UP

The immediate objective of any battle seems obvious: *don't get hit*; however, most men do with little effort on the part of the enemy. A whispered suggestion, a misdirected desire, an intimidating order, some lame imitation of Life dangled enticingly in front of us, and *bang*, we're hit! Though free through Christ, a man nevertheless may become reckless, unwise, or worse. He knows better, yet chooses poorly, giving the enemy power and authority in his life once again. He's saved, sure. But free? No.

The flesh quickly resumes charge of the man, and the enemy is in charge of the flesh. George MacDonald wrote, "Foolish is the man, and there are many such men, who would set the world right by waging war on the evils around him, while he neglects that integral part of the world where lies his business, his first business—namely, his own character and conduct."

If it isn't *good* yet, God isn't done yet. "He who began a good work in you will complete it" (Phil. 1:6 NKJV). It won't be easy, but it will be good. My advice (as I look at the man in the mirror) is to just keep showing up. If you'll show up and ask your King each morning, "Jesus, what are we doing today?" then the good work will become more and more evident to you. I've come to love his answers, the way he invites me to step into most days: "I'll show you. Follow me." Remember, the mission finds you.

Jesus has commissioned us to live a certain way (Matt. 28:18–20). Peter tells us to be prepared (I Peter 3:15). And Paul exhorts us,

> If you're serious about living this new resurrection life with Christ, *act* like it. Pursue the things over which Christ presides. Don't shuffle along, eyes to the ground, absorbed with the things right in front of you. Look up, and be alert to what is going on around Christ—that's where the action is. See things from *his* perspective. Your old life is dead. Your new life, which is your *real* life—even though invisible to spectators—is with Christ in God. *He* is your life. When Christ (your real life, remember) shows up again on this earth, you'll show up, too—the real you, the glorious you. (Col. 3:1–4 MSG)

FEW MEN TRULY LIVE

The reason late twelfth-century Scotland was so easily oppressed by England's ruthless king, Edward the First (a.k.a. Longshanks), was because Scotland was a house divided. Easy pickings for a ruthless bully—easy until a real man shows up. In the movie *Braveheart*, with more and more of Scotland being taken back under the leadership of William Wallace, young Robert the Bruce is inspired. Wallace comes to a meeting of the nobles to ask once again for their engagement. He calls young Robert to unite the clans. They shake on it and go to war, but a massive betrayal leads to Wallace's capture and the haunting line just before his torturous death:

Every man dies, but few men truly live.

With the rebellion all but stamped out, what is left of Scotland's demoralized men, together with their newly appointed king, Robert the Bruce, meet on the battlefield to "pay homage," to surrender to Longshank's army. This is the reward for Robert's betrayal.

But in that moment, something stirs in the young king's heart, the first ingredients of a *comeback*. "You bled with Wallace," he cries. "Now bleed with me!" Wallace's loyal friend, Hamish, responds by hurling William's giant Claymore sword in support, and seconds later, the men cry out and charge to win their freedom.

Does it all sound familiar? Can you think of another inspiring Warrior who gave his life so others can have theirs? The Scots fought for and won what was rightfully theirs. Like them, we are to fight for what is and has been made rightfully ours through Christ: our freedom and our true self.

It is for freedom that Christ has set us free. (Gal. 5:1)

Before you can become the Warrior, you must become the Beloved Son. It can all sound a bit more glamorous than it is. The themes of freedom inspire us, but the work often discourages us. The questions I have for you now are,

How free do you want to be?
What kind of man do you want to be?

Do you have a King?
Will you fight for a cause?
What are you willing to leave behind?

> For whoever is bent on saving his [temporal] life [his comfort and security here] shall lose it [eternal life]; and whoever loses his life [his comfort and security here] for My sake shall find it [life everlasting]. (Matt. 16:25)

An oriented man is a man who knows who he is, where he is, and the good that God is up to in his life. His life is lived in Christ, with Christ, and like Christ, with nothing to prove, nothing to hide, and nothing to fear. He is a man who intimately knows the King whose image he bears, whose voice he hears, and whose instructions guide and shape his character and his life. They are the closest of friends. The allegiance and affections of that man's heart will direct his every decision.

An oriented man knows that his heart is fragile and he is never immune from the attacks of the enemy, but he is trained to know what those attacks are, why they are, and how to guard against them.

It starts with your heart, Beloved Son—and it doesn't ever, ever end.

IF

Every story has its turns, moments where joy or despair lie around the corner. We do not get to choose what awaits us; however, we do get to choose whether we will take another step. Becoming a man, a good man, is a dangerous and glorious proposition. It's one step at a time. It's incredibly hard. It requires calculated risk and bold faith. It is fiercely opposed. And it is mightily needed. That is why there are so few good men, but more are coming. More Beloved Sons are being healed and becoming orientated. More Warriors are receiving their King's training.

If you have turned the pages to this point, if you have allowed me to walk with you as you have grabbed the hand of God and walked with him, then you are well on your way and can practice The Way—and you must keep going.

If you stay the course.

If you take another step.

If you continue in what a Beloved Son knows and what a Warrior Heart practices, you will see this through to "well done."

I leave you with this. In 1896, Rudyard Kipling at age thirty-one wrote the poem "If." It was written as a tribute to two men who had a great impact on Kipling: Leander Starr Jameson and Cecil Rhodes, whose qualities the poem acknowledges. Kipling writes to his young son, John, who a few years later would step into World War I. In the spirit of Solomon's proverbs, "If" is a father's encouragement to his beloved son. Kipling's and Solomon's missions are the same: guiding that son into becoming a man.

If you can keep your head when all about you
Are losing theirs and blaming it on you;
If you can trust yourself when all men doubt you,
But make allowance for their doubting too;
If you can wait and not be tired by waiting,
Or being lied about, don't deal in lies,
Or being hated, don't give way to hating,
And yet don't look too good, nor talk too wise;
If you can dream—and not make dreams your master;
If you can think—and not make thoughts your aim;
If you can meet with triumph and disaster
And treat those two imposters just the same;
If you can bear to hear the truth you've spoken
Twisted by knaves to make a trap for fools,
Or watch the things you gave your life to, broken,
And stoop and build 'em up with worn-out tools;
If you can make one heap of all your winnings

And risk it on one turn of pitch-and-toss,
And lose, and start again at your beginnings
And never breath a word about your loss;
If you can force your heart and nerve and sinew
To serve your turn long after they are gone,
And so hold on when there is nothing in you
Except the Will which says to them: "Hold on";
If you can talk with crowds and keep your virtue,

Or walk with Kings—nor lose the common touch;
If neither foes nor loving friends can hurt you;
If all men count with you, but none too much;
If you can fill the unforgiving minute
With sixty seconds' worth of distance run,
Yours is the Earth and everything that's in it,
And—which is more—you'll be a Man my son!

Here at the end of this book, as at the beginning, my hope remains this:

To one day see the hearts of men so foundationally settled, so well-trained, so well-equipped, and so well-engaged that when evil dares raise its head, Beloved Sons/Warrior men will know what to do and will do it well.

I hope and I pray that one of the men I speak of is you. And I will continue to hope and fervently pray that more and more such men will join you.

Your Warrior Heart is needed. The kingdom is waiting, and so are the many hearts that need a man who knows he is the Beloved Son of a good Father. A man who can hear both the music inviting him to dance and the cries of hearts hoping he will fight. A man who will practice the ancient art of living and loving well.

God speed, Beloved Son.

God speed, fierce and gentle Warrior.

APPENDIX

THE HEART

From *The New Unger's Bible Dictionary*
(Used by permission of Moody Publishers)

The ***heart*** is: (1) the *center* of the bodily life, the reservoir of the entire life-power (Ps. 40:8, 10, 12; Judges 19:5-6, 8-9; 1 Kings 21:7; Acts 14:17), becomes the strengthening of the whole man; (2) the *center* of the rational-spiritual nature of man; thus when a man determines upon anything, it is called to "presume" in his heart to do so (Esther 7:5, marg.); when he is strongly determined, he "stands firm in his heart" (1 Cor. 7:37); what is done gladly, willingly, and of set purpose, is done "obedient from the heart" (Rom. 6:17). The heart is the seat of love (1 Tim. 1:5) and of hatred (Lev.s 19:17). Again, the heart is the center of thought and conception; the heart *knows* (Deut. 29:4; Prov. 14:10), it *understands* (Is. 44:18; Acts 16:14), and it *reflects* (Luke 2:19). The heart is also *the center of the feelings and affections*: of joy (Is. 65:14); of pain (Prov. 25:20; John 16:6); all degrees of ill will (Prov. 23:17; James 3:14); of dissatisfaction from anxiety (Prov. 12:25) to despair (Eccl. 2:20, KJV); all degrees of fear, from reverential trembling (Jer. 5:24) to blank terror (Deut. 28:28; Ps. 143:4); (3) the center of the moral life; so that all moral conditions, from the highest love of

God (Ps. 73:26) even down to the self-deifying pride (Ezek. 28:2, 5-6), darkening (Rom. 1:21), and hardening (Is. 6:10; Is. 63:17; Jer. 16:12; 2 Cor. 3:15) are concentrated in the heart as the innermost life circle of humanity (1 Pet. 3:4). The heart is the laboratory and origin of all that is good and evil in thoughts, words, and deeds (Matt. 12:34; Mark 7:21); the rendezvous of evil lusts and passions (Rom. 1:24); a good or evil treasure (Luke 6:45); the place where God's natural law is written in us (Rom. 2:15), as well as the law of grace (Is. 51:7; Jer. 31:33); the seat of conscience (Heb. 10:22; 1 John 3:19-21); the field for the seed of the divine word (Matt. 13:19; Luke 8:15). It is the dwelling place of Christ in us (Eph. 3:17); of the Holy Spirit (2 Cor.1:22); of God's peace (Col. 3:15); the receptacle of the love of God (Rom. 5:5); the closet of secret communion with God (Eph. 5:19). It is the center of the entire man, the very hearth of life's impulse.

ENDNOTES

Chapter 1: From Beloved Sons to Warriors

Pg. 15 *"Art is not"*: Elbert Hubbard, *Little Journeys to the Homes of Great Teachers* (New York: Wm. H. Wise & Co., 1918), 219.

Pg. 21 *"Every moment"*: Norman Mailer in Richard G. Stern and Robert F. Lucid, "Hip, Hell, and the Navigator," *Conversations with Norman Mailer*, ed. J. Michael Lennon (Jackson, MS: University Press of Mississippi, 1988), 37. First published in *Western Review* No. 23 (Winter 1959).

Pg. 21 *"Another episode"*: David L. Ulin, "Ego with an insecure streak," *Los Angeles Times*, November 11, 2007, http://articles.latimes.com/2007/nov/11/local/me-appreciation11.

Chapter 2: Getting Your Heart Back

Pg. 30 *"Above all the grace"*: Francis of Assisi, quoted in "Saint Francis," *Mystic Poets*, http://onetruename.com/francis.htm

Pg. 34 *"To find God"*: John Eldredge, *Waking the Dead: The Glory of a Heart Fully Alive* (Nashville: Nelson, 2006), 49.

Chapter 3: It's Worse Than We Think

Pg. 36 *"The hill"*: John Bunyan, *Pilgrims's Progress in Modern Language*, (Lafayette, IN: Sovereign Grace, 2000), 21.

Pg. 38 *"Most men"*: John Eldredge, *Fathered by God: Discover What Your Dad Could Never Teach You* (Nashville: Nelson, 2009), Introduction-xii.

Pg. 40 "Having or showing": Dictionary.com, http://dictionary.reference.com/browse/naïve.

Pg. 43 *"When a resolute"*: Oliver Wendell Holmes, *Elsie Venner: A Romance of Destiny* (Boston, 1861), 23.

Chapter 4: Where It Hurts

Pg. 55 *"Every adversity"*: Napoleon Hill and W. Clement Stone, *Success Through a Positive Mental Attitude*, repr. (New York: Simon & Schuster, 2007), 222.

Pg. 60 *"We who live"*: A. W. Tozer, *The Knowledge of the Holy: The Attributes of God: Their Meaning in the Christian Life* (New York: Harper & Row, 1975), 41.

Pg. 63 *"So it becomes"*: A. W. Tozer, *I Talk Back to the Devil: The Fighting Fervor of the Victorious Christian* (Chicago: WingSpread, 2008), 1.

Pg. 63 *"To be nobody"*: E. E. Cummings, "A Poet's Advice to Students," in *A Miscellany* (New York: Argophile Press, 1958), 13.

Chapter 5: Belovedness

Pg. 70 *"The true story"*: Brent Curtis and John Eldredge, *The Sacred Romance: Drawing Closer to the Heart of God* (Nashville: Nelson, 1997), 7.

Pg. 71 *Kierkegaard*: Soren Kierkegaard, *The Essential Kierkegaard*, eds. Howard V. Hong and Edna H. Hong (Princeton: Princeton University Press, 2000), 12

Pg. 74 *"God's desire"*: Linda Boone, *Intimate Life Lessons: Developing the Intimacy with God You Already Have* (Kearney, NE: Morris, 2008), 49.

Pg. 75 *"Though the witch"*: C.S. Lewis, *The Chronicles of Narnia: The Lion, The Witch and The Wardrobe* (London: HarperCollins, 2002), 169.

Pg. 77 *"We are the ones"*: Curtis and Eldredge, *Sacred Romance*, 95.

Pg. 81 *"We aren't meant"*: Eldredge, *Fathered by God*, 11.

Pg. 83 "*We live in a Love Story"*: John Eldredge, *EPIC: The Story God Is Telling* (Nashville: Nelson, 2004), 102.

Pg. 84 *"If you go back"*: Gary Barkalow, *It's Your Call: What Are You Doing Here?* (Colorado Springs: David C. Cook, 2010), 111, 114.

Chapter 6: Being Fathered

Pg. 89 *"To be trusted"*: George MacDonald, *The Marquis of Lossie*, vol. 1 (London, 1877), 35.

Pg. 95 *"Wherever you are"*: John Eldredge, *The Way of the Wild Heart: A Map for the Masculine Journey* (Nashville: Thomas Nelson 2006), 26.

Pg. 102 – 103 *"God made us"*: C.S. Lewis, *Mere Christianity* (New York: HarperCollins, 2009), 50.

Pg. 106 *"Build me a son"*: Douglas MacArthur, "A Father's Prayer," in Courtney Whitney, *MacArthur: His Rendevous with History* (New York: Knopf, 1956), 547.

Chapter 7: Intensive Care

Pg. 109 *"Pain has a way": Paul Young, The Shack: Where Tragedy Confronts Eternity (Newbury Park, CA: Windblown Media, 2011), 96.*

Pg. 110 *"God gives"*: Attributed to Augustine of Hippo by C.S. Lewis, this quote is likely a paraphrase of the following from Augustine's *Homilies on the Psalms*: "It is good for the rich man to . . . recognize that his hands are empty so that God can fill them," from *Augustine of Hippo: Selected Writings*, trans. Mary T. Clark (Mahwah, NJ: Paulist Press, 1988), 244.

Pg. 117 *"The healings"*: Leanne Payne, *Healing Presence: Curing the Soul through Union with Christ* (Ada, MI: Baker), 137.

Pg. 120 *"Jesus is actually"*: Dallas Willard, *The Great Omission* (NewYork: HarperCollins, 1998), 16.

Chapter 8: The Ways of Beloved Sons

Pg. 123 *"Taking our hearts"*: Curtis and Eldredge, *Sacred Romance*, 127.

Pg. 124 *Brennan*: Brennan Manning, *Abba's Child: The Cry of the Heart for Intimate Belonging* (Colorado Springs: NavPress, 2002).

Pg. 124 *"Without God"*: This quote, popularly attributed to Augustine, is uncertain in its origin. It is likely a derivative of a statement in Augustine's "Sermon 169": "He who created you without you will not justify you without you."

Pg. 128 *"History does not long"*: Dwight D. Eisenhower, from his inaugural address, January 20, 1953. Accessed through *The American Presidency Project*, http://www.presidency.ucsb.edu/ws/?pid=9600.

Chapter 9: What We Are Up Against

Pg. 135 *"The idea"*: A. W. Tozer, *This World: Playground or Battlefield* (Chicago: WingSpread, 2009), 4.

Pg. 136 *"Jesus promised"*: This frequently quoted saying has been attributed to both G. K. Chesterton and R. W. Maltby. The exact source is uncertain.

Pg. 137 *"There are two"*: C.S. Lewis, *The Screwtape Letters*, repr. (London: HarperCollins, 2009), preface-ix.

Pg. 138 *Milton*: John Milton, *Paradise Lost*, 1.30–49.

Pg. 139 *"Sin is what you do"*: John Piper, *Future Grace: The Purifying Power of the Promises of God*, rev. ed (Colorado Springs: WaterBrook Multnomah, 2012), ii.

Pg. 143 *"Beware of no man"*: Charles Spurgeon, *John Ploughman's Talk: Or, Plain Advice for Plain People* (Philadelphia, 1896), 72.

Pg. 147 *"As a result"*: Neil Anderson, "Teaching Our Identity in Christ," SermonCentral, *http://www.sermoncentral.com/article.asp?article=a-Neil_T_Anderson_03_26_07&*. Repub. by perm. of Freedom in Christ Ministries.

Pg. 148 *"Fellowship with God"*: Widely attributed to Charles E. Fuller, this quote is difficult to trace but probably originated in one of his sermons in *The Old Fashioned Revival Hour* radio broadcast.

Pg. 148 *"Life without war"*: Oswald Chambers, "The Law of Opposition," *My Utmost for His Highest*, rev. ed., ed. James Reimann (Grand Rapids: Discovery House), Dec. 4.

Pg. 148 *"The defeat"*: Anderson, "Teaching Our Identity."

Chapter 10: Basic Training: Knowing and Resting in Who You Are

Pg. 152 *"The supreme happiness"*: Victor Hugo, *Les Miserables*, from ch. 4, "M. Madeleine in Mourning," trans. Isabel F. Hapgood (1887), accessed through *The Literature Network*, http://www.online-literature.com/victor_hugo/les_miserables/43/.

Pg. 154 *"What if"*: Erwin McManis, *The Barbarian Way: Unleash the Untamed Faith Within* (Nashville: Nelson, 2005), 5.

Pg. 155 *"To be free"*: Nelson Mandela, *Long Walk to Freedom: The Autobiography of Nelson Mandela* (New York: Little, Brown and Co., 2008).

Pg. 157 *"I have often wondered": Jeffery Satinover, from an unpublished article, quoted in Leanne Payne, Listening Prayer: Learning to Hear God's Voice and Keep a Prayer Journal (Grand Rapids: Baker, 1994), 142.*

Pg. 163 *"The heart"*: Eldredge, *Waking the Dead*, 39.

Pg. 164 *"The Christian"*: A. W. Tozer, *The Next Chapter after the Last: For the Child of God, the Best Is Yet to Come* (Chicago: WingSpread, 2010).

Chapter 11: Advanced Training: The Good God Is Up to in Your Life

Pg. 168 *"Nothing is so strong"*: Frances de Sales, quoted from Jean Pierre Camus, *The Spirit of S. Frances de Sales*, trans. Henrietta Louisa Lear (London, 1872), 13.

Pg. 177 *"We love God": Greg Boyd, Repenting of Religion: Turning from Judgment to the Love of God (Ada: Baker, 2005), 68.*

Pg. 180 "*Never does the human soul"*: Edwin Hubbell Chapin, *Living Words* (Boston, 1861), 61.

Pg. 184 "A broken bone": C.S. Lewis, *The Problem of Pain* (New York: HarperCollins, 2001), 46.

Chapter 12: Warnings and Promises

Pg. 188 *"Experience"*: Commonly but unverifiably attributed to C.S. Lewis.

Pg. 188 *"A man who carries"*: Commonly but unverifiably attributed to Mark Twain. The source note in *iz quotes* says, "Earliest attribution [to Twain] was found in 'Impact of Federal Policies on Employment, Poverty, and Other Programs, 1973', p. 447: 'He who swings a cat by the tail, learns things that one can only learn by swinging a cat by the tail.'" For the complete source note, see http://izquotes.com/quote/187899.

Pg. 194 *United we stand"*: Aesop, "The Four Oxen and the Lion," *Fables*, retold by Joseph Jacobs, vol. 17, pt. 1, The Harvard Classics (Bartleby.com, 2001), http://www.bartleby.com/17/1/52.html. First pub. by P.F. Collier & Son, 1909–14, New York.

Pg. 203 *"Every time"*: C.S. Lewis, *Mere Christianity* (London: HarperCollins, 1952), 92.

Chapter 13: Loving A Woman

Pg. 215 *"Tell me"*: Charles Augustin Sainte-Beuve, "A Critic's Account of His Own Critical Method," vol. 22 of *Library of the World's Best Literature, Ancient and Modern*, ed. Charles Dudley Warner (New York, 1897), 12,666.

Pg. 216 *"True beauty"*: From a poem commonly misattributed to Audrey Hepburn. The poem was indeed a favorite of the actress's, but it was in fact written by humorist and writer Sam Levenson, reportedly in a letter to his granddaughter.

Pg. 219 *"Beauty is"*: Stasi Eldredge, *Captivating: Unveiling the Mystery of a Woman's Soul*, rev. ed. (Nashville: Nelson, 2011), 133.

Pg. 228 *"Her wounds"*: Eldredge, *Wild at Heart*, 184, 192.

Pg. 229 *"Now—can you see"*: Eldredge, *Captivating*, 19.

Chapter 14: Following The King

Pg. 232 *"Out of the night"*. William Ernest Henley, "Invictus," *Book of Verses*, pub. 1888, accessed through *The Poetry Foundation*, http://www.poetryfoundation.org/poem/182194.

Pg. 233 *"Every man"*: A. W. Tozer, *The Pursuit of God: The Human Thirst for the Divine* (Chicago: WingSpread, 1982), 58.

Pg. 237 *"You are meant"*: John Eldredge, *Beautiful Outlaw: Experiencing the Playful, Disruptive, Extravagant Personality of Jesus.* (New York: FaithWords, 2011), 140.

Pg. 240 "*Regard your soldiers"*: Sun Tzu, *The Art of War*, trans. Lionel Giles (1910), 10.25, *The Internet Classics Archive*, http://classics.mit.edu/Tzu/artwar.html.

Pg. 244 *"The true soldier"*: The quote is universally attributed to G. K. Chesterton, but its exact source is unverifiable.

Pg. 246 Shakespeare, *Henry V*, act 4, scene 3, lines 59–70, *Shakespeare Online*, http://www.shakespeare-online.com/plays/henryv_4_3.html.

Pg. 246 *Roosevelt*: Theodore Roosevelt, "The Man in the Arena," excerpted from Roosevelt's April 23, 1910, "Citizenship in a Republic" April 23, 1910, speech at the Sorbonne, Paris, France. Accessed through *The Almanac of Theodore Roosevelt*, http://www.theodore-roosevelt.com/trsorbonnespeech.html.

Postscript/Epilogue

Pg. 251 *"Foolish"*: George MacDonald, "George MacDonald Speaks on Practical Faith: Excerpts from *Wisdom to Live By*," accessed through *Leben*, http://www.macdonaldphillips.com/leben.html.

Pg. 254 "*If you can*": Rudyard Kipling, "If," *Rewards and Faeries* (New York: Doubleday, 1910).

Appendix

Pg. 256 Merrill F. Unger, "Heart," *The New Unger Bible Dictionary*, rev. ed., R. K. Harrison ed. (Chicago: Moody Publishers, 2008).

Made in the USA
Middletown, DE
09 August 2022